Lindos lightness of being

John Wilton

ISBN: 978-1-917293-09-9

Copyright © 2024

All rights reserved, including the right to reproduce this book, or portions thereof in any form. No part of this text may be reproduced, transmitted, downloaded, decompiled, reverse engineered, or stored, in any form or introduced into any information storage and retrieval system, in any form or by any means, whether electronic or mechanical without the express written permission of the author.

This is a work of fiction. All names and characters are the product of the author's imagination and any resemblance to actual persons, living or dead, is entirely coincidental.

PublishNation

www.publishnation.co.uk

Acknowledgements:

I would like to say yet another huge thank you to all my friends in beautiful Lindos. My warm thanks go to my good friends Jack Koliais and Janis Woodward Bowles, both of whom encouraged me greatly to get on and write my first Lindos novel, published in 2015. Without their support and encouragement none of these Lindos stories would have been written.

My thanks also go to everyone in Lindos and beyond, including many regular Lindos visitors, who have said and written such nice things about all my previous novels, inspiring me to once more write a story based on the little village.

Endless gratitude goes to my proof-reader Fiona Ensor for her tireless efforts on all my novels in identifying my errors. Any that remain are entirely my responsibility.

Needless to say, this story is total fiction. However, without the magical village of Lindos, and the people in it, all my novels could never have been written. For that reason, as with all my previous Lindos novels, I will always be eternally grateful to the people there, my friends of many years in that magical paradise.

Finally, my eternal gratitude goes to my daughters, Carly and Kathy, for their support and love at all times, especially throughout my writing struggles and tribulations.

Author's website: www.johnwilton.yolasite.com

Previous novels by John (all available on Amazon and Kindle):

The Hope (2014)   *Lindos Retribution* (2015)

Lindos Aletheia (2016)   *Lindian Summers* (2018)

Lindos Affairs (2019)   *Lindian Odyssey* (2020)

Lindos Eros and Hades (2021)   *Karagoulis. Lindos life and times (2022)*

Four Lindos July Days (2023)

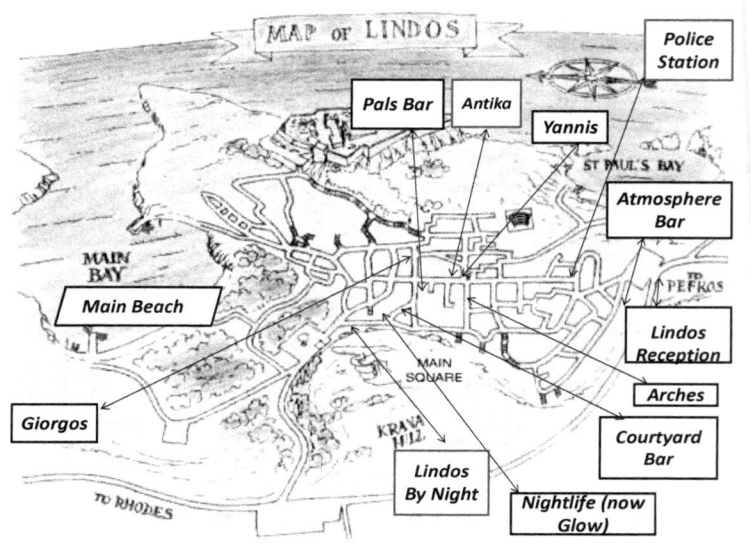

By way of a Preface

"The stupidity of people comes from having an answer to everything. The wisdom of the novel comes from having a question for everything ... A novel does not assert anything; a novel searches and poses questions ... I don't know which of my characters is right. I invent stories, confront one with another, and by this means I ask questions.

It seems to me that all over the world people nowadays prefer to judge rather than to understand, to answer rather than to ask, so that the voice of the novel can hardly be heard over the noisy foolishness of human certainties" **(Milan Kundera)**

This novel is in part homage to the Czech writer Milan Kundera, and is a wholly inadequate attempt at a small appreciation of his work, much of which he completed in often difficult times. With an acknowledgement to Kundera's fine novel 'The Unbearable Lightness of Being', it attempts to explore and examine the tension between freedom and responsibility; the irreconcilable tension between infidelity and love in a new and growing relationship within a web of political intrigue.

By the conclusion of *The Unbearable Lightness of Being*, Kundera held that the theories of both the German philosopher Friedrich Nietzsche and the 6th Century BC Greek philosopher Parmenides are false, (both theories are very briefly outlined here in Chapter One) as both the "light" and "heavy" characters in his novel meet unhappy fates. Furthermore, he demonstrated how unbearable it is that each choice can only be made once with one possible result and that no one can ever know what other choices would have brought.

Upon its initial publication in English and French Kundera's novel enjoyed international popular acclaim.

PART ONE:

UNBEARABLE LIGHTNESS OR ETERNAL RETURN?

1

In the 6th Century BC the Greek philosopher Parmenides saw the world as divided into pairs of opposites; one key one of which was lightness and weight. For Parmenides, in life lightness is positive, weight negative.

Around two-and-a-half thousand years later towards the end of the 19th Century the German philosopher Friedrich Nietzsche, building on Parmenides idea of the dichotomy of lightness and weight, believed everything in life happens an infinite number of times, over and over, causing the "heaviest of burdens." This was his philosophical concept of eternal return, or eternal recurrence. Consequently, a personal life in which everything happens only once loses its "weight" and significance, resulting in "the unbearable lightness of being." A life in which all the events and affairs between individuals within it disappear once and for all and do not return or reappear is like "a shadow without weight" and they mean nothing. So, one night spent sexually together between two individuals which happens once and then disintegrates, disappears once and for all, is without weight. It is meaningless. It means nothing, and simply contributes to, is part of, the "unbearable lightness of being". Even a slightly longer meaningless sexual affair without love between two individuals is part of the "lightness of being". Based on Nietzsche's philosophy the Czech writer Milan Kundera's novel 'The

Unbearable Lightness of Being' centred upon the question of whether a person should live their life with weight and duty or with lightness and freedom.

This was the philosophy of the way in which David Alexander now lived his life. At least, he believed it was until he met Alice Palmer in the little picturesque tourist village of Lindos on the island of Rhodes in the middle of May in the summer of 2019. For quite some time before that one-night sexual encounters, or even slightly longer affairs, were static for him. They were fixed in time, one-offs. As per Nietzsche's philosophy they had no "weight". Everything within them, everything about them, rested essentially on the non-existence of any expectation or desire for transition, transition into anything more permanent; no expectation or desire by him for any development into something more long-lasting. They were part of, the essence of, his "lightness of being". In that way he could forgive himself in advance for everything he did in his sexual life, his actions and encounters. Consequently, in his mind, in that part of his life everything was cynically permitted, even when this philosophy and his actions in his personal life based upon it, conflicted with elements of his professional life.

That belief was to be severely tested and challenged throughout the summer of 2019 after he met Alice Palmer, as well as into the first part of the following summer of 2020. He was faced with a choice. One he never expected or anticipated ever having to make now in his life. Carry on with his life in the same way or pursue and take up the burden of responsibility and 'weight' of fidelity. Abandon his 'lightness of being' life and instead pursue and embrace the weight of responsibility and a meaningful, permanent, long term relationship with Alice Palmer, if of course that was what she wanted. When he was finally faced with that dilemma, that choice in mid-July of 2020, he initially convinced himself that to actually choose the option of the 'weight' of fidelity in his life was not possible due to circumstances he thought beyond his control. The hidden, secret part of his professional life prevented it, as it would only mean danger for both Alice and him.

PART TWO:

A BODY

2

Tuesday 8th September 2020

"Female, Caucasian, not Greek, probably European, German perhaps?"

"What makes you think that, that she's German?"

"Just a guess, Yiannis. Nothing on her indicating where she was from or where she was staying, and no handbag. I'm certain she's not Greek, and not southern European, so, northern European maybe, a tourist probably. But apart from my educated guess there's no clues on her, no documents telling us where she was from. I'd say she's late thirties, maybe early forties. Tall with a slim figure, so I suspect she worked out, kept fit. No distinguishing marks, no tattoos, well dressed, but … erm …"

Inspector Yiannis Papadoulis had become well accustomed to the little evasive games pathologist, Christof Costas, liked to play. He seemed to take great pleasure in dragging out as long as possible relaying his initial findings to the Inspector at the site of any body found on the island. He knew it would wind up Papadoulis. It always did. This was no exception.

The pathologist was kneeling beside the body inspecting what he could as he hesitated. The Inspector loomed over the body, saying, "Yes, yes, Christof, as usual you are making me wait for and ask for the important stuff. Time of death? Any preliminary idea? I presume it was before the sun came up, and it doesn't look as though there's much light along here at night?"

The sun had indeed made its very reliable regular summer early morning appearance in the little tourist village of Lindos well before the Inspector and his Sergeant, Antonis Georgiou, arrived at the scene from their Rhodes Town Police Station. It was already now beating down its hot rays. Costas had arrived at the scene from his home in Rhodes Town half-an-hour before the two policemen at just before nine, to be greeted by a local Lindos police officer and the British tourist couple who'd discovered the body. On their early morning stroll into the village from their holiday flat for some breakfast they came across it in one of the narrow alleyways sloping up towards the Lindos Acropolis, just a little way up it to the right of the Broccolino restaurant. While Papadoulis spoke to the pathologist by the body his Sergeant got the details from the couple and the local police officer.

"Yes, Yiannis, the sun would still have been hiding its rays from our little part of the world here, but it's obviously making up for it now."

The sun's rays were bouncing off the white walled buildings either side of the narrow sloping alleyway with its somewhat uneven path and irregularly spaced out small steps. In places the surface was broken up a little, particularly where the body lay. Even though he was a Rhodian the pathologist's stout figure didn't cope at all well with the heat of the Rhodes sun, even the not quite so hot early morning beginning of September version. A man of medium height in his early fifties he'd been born and bred in Rhodes Town and had qualified in Athens, but he was clearly not immune to the heat piercing the clear blue sky with not the slightest hint of a cloud in it. The small wet patches on his white short sleeved shirt betrayed his unfit physical condition, as well as the slightly larger ones under his armpits. Even the short walk from Lindos Main Square to where the body was discovered had made its mark. His reputation in the Rhodes police force was of someone who enjoyed more than his share of Mythos and Alfa cold Greek beer, something that palpably contributed to his poor physical condition. Nevertheless, most of the officers recognised that he was good at his job, particularly Inspector Papadoulis, who because of that had learned to live with, and accept, Christof Costas' little ways and quirks. They had developed a very good working relationship around that.

The Inspector was born and raised in Rhodes Town and was married to a local woman he'd met when they were training at the Hellenic Police Officers School, although recently their marriage had been experiencing some bumpy times, partly because of his work and the increasingly unsociable hours. They had two teenage children. His whole police career had been spent on the island. He was promoted from Sergeant to Inspector following the killing of his superior officer Inspector Dimitris Karagoulis, during a murder case investigation in 2010.

Yiannis Papadoulis was a quite tall, upright man, relatively slim, and with thick swept back, typically Greek, dark hair. Approaching fifty – he was forty-eight – there were already traces of his hair beginning to slightly grey at the edges. Unlike some of the more unorthodox methods of investigation employed by his murdered previous boss Papadoulis was very much a regulation policeman. Very organised, he played everything methodically by the book. Karagoulis was from Athens and had been forced to transfer to Rhodes in the year 2000 following a fatal mistake he made on an Athens murder case. He was suspended for that and then given an ultimatum of transfer to Rhodes or retire. Financially Karagoulis had no choice but to accept the transfer. During his ten years in the force on the island he became well known for his quirky methods of investigation, often based on his obsession with Greek Mythology, much of which he sometimes employed in trying to solve cases. Initially, as his Sergeant, that irritated Papadoulis, but gradually he grew to accept it, and even like it. So much so that he occasionally dipped into some of it for his off duty leisure time reading. At times the Greek Mythology applied approach of Karagoulis even made Papadoulis smile, and an excellent relaxed working relationship developed between the two men. Papadoulis came to see from working with him that basically Karagoulis was a very good detective. However, following his promotion to Inspector from Sergeant after Karagoulis was killed Yiannis Papadoulis generally wasn't usually one to delve into philosophy or Greek Mythology when it came to trying to solve cases. He preferred to simply deal more methodically with the facts, what he saw, and what he and his officers discovered in their investigations.

"Yes, yes, Christof, before the sun came up, but any chance you could be a little more precise, despite the fact that I realise you'll have a clearer idea once you get the body back to your lab?"

"I'd say she's been dead between six to eight hours. So, time of death possibly between midnight and two a.m."

"Cause of death? No sign of any wounds, knife or bullet, so …?"

"No, none."

He glanced up at the Inspector before adding sarcastically, "Very observant of you, Yiannis. We'll make a good detective of you yet."

A slight grin spread across his lips at his own humour before continuing.

"No, she wasn't stabbed or shot. That's for certain. No immediate obvious signs. At this stage I'd say death was probably from her broken neck. There's some swelling and bruising on her neck, which is usually a sign. Maybe from a fall here? The path is pretty rough and uneven, and so are some of these steps, as well as being very irregularly spaced out. She was wearing high heels. I'm no expert, but they look expensive shoes, certainly not cheap."

He pointed to a woman nearby and added, "My female assistant here knows more about those things than I do of course, and says they are a quite expensive brand. As we know, wearing high heels is not really a good idea on some of the paths and steps in Lindos. Given how dark it would have been along here at that time, it wouldn't have been difficult for her to have misjudged the spacing of one of the steps on her way up them, possibly on her way back to wherever she was staying up here. Tripped maybe, stumbled in her expensive looking very high heels, lost her footing and was unable to stop herself tumbling down the steps, fell and the fall cracked her neck, especially if she'd had a drink or two or more on a night out in Lindos. I'll have a better idea about it once I get her back to the lab, including how much alcohol she has in her blood. Can't really tell you much more than that for now. Just need to get her, and myself, out of this unusually bloody hot September sun."

The Inspector rubbed the back of his sweaty wet neck with the palm of his right hand as he searched just once more for some further information.

"If that's what happened though isn't it odd there doesn't appear to be any other bruising on her body, from the fall I mean, except for the swelling and bruising on her neck. Strangled perhaps?"

"Could be strangled, but at first glance it looks like a clean break to me, and if people have had a bit of a drink sometimes a fall doesn't always produce bruising. Some parts of the body can be pretty relaxed after consuming a fair amount of alcohol. Can soften the blow somewhat. That is if she had had a bit of a drink, of course, but as I said, I'll find out more about that once we get the body back to the lab."

The pathologist tilted his head slightly and opened his eyes a little wider as he looked up towards the Inspector.

"Sounds like you're bored and eager for a murder case to keep you busy, Yiannis?"

"No, Christof, not at all, but a clean break sounds like a professional job doesn't it, and not just from a fall, and there's the bruising on her neck, so ...."

The pathologist glanced up again from crouching over the body as he added, "So, it isn't just a murder case you're after now? You want a professional killing, a hit job?"

"No, but I-"

"Too soon to say, Yiannis. With a broken neck it's quite usual for bruising to occur after death. It may still be strangulation, but there are no other marks on the body as far as I can see. I'd expect to see a lot more bruising and marks on the neck than there is if she was strangled before someone broke her neck. If it is strangulation though, then yes you'll get your professional job."

Costas stood up before adding, "By the way, as I indicated before, there's absolutely nothing with or on the body. No handbag, no phone, no hotel card or key or accommodation information, no identification at all on her. Like her shoes, her dress looks quite expensive, as does the silver chain around her waist. You're going to have to scratch your head on this one, Yiannis. You and your officers are going to have to do some work finding out who she is, even if it is only an accidental death and not some professional killing that you seem so keen to want."

As he finished the pathologist took his handkerchief out of one of his trouser pockets and wiped some sweat from his forehead and the back of his neck.

"Seems like it, Christof. We'll get a photo of her face before you take the body and do some enquiries at some of the apartments further up here to see if anyone recognises her. See if we can find out who she is and where she was staying. Although, if when she fell she was heading up these steps back to an apartment she was renting, one of the ones further up, surely she would have had a key or something on her."

The Inspector scratched the back of his head and frowned a little before adding, "Anyway, I'll see you back at your lab later for what else you can tell me, if anything. Around four?"

"Ok, that should be plenty of time. See you then," the pathologist agreed.

With that he left one of the Inspector's officers to take a photo of the victim's face, as well as leaving his assistant to deal with transporting the body to the Rhodes Town lab while he made his way down the slope towards the Broccolino restaurant and on through the narrow white walled alleys to Lindos Main Square to pick up his car.

Papadoulis instructed his Sergeant to detail a couple of officers to search all the surrounding areas to the alley slope and the steps, as well as to get two more officers to go door to door further up the slope with the photo of the victim's face.

"Let's find out as quickly as possible just who she is and where she was staying, Sergeant."

3

Late afternoon Tuesday 8th September 2020

The Rhodes Town police lab was much like many others the world over with its antiseptic aroma, its two metal examination tables, its bare walls and range of equipment. It was just after four when Papadoulis put on the required gown, mask and hat in the ante-chamber and then walked through the double swing door to join Christof Costas and the body of the female victim. Without even a courtesy "Good afternoon" or preamble the pathologist launched into what he'd found so far.

"As a general rule of thumb, Yiannis, fractures that involve the upper cervical spine are most dangerous because spinal cord and nerve injury at this level can result in instant death as ability to breathe is tied to nerve responses generated in that upper cervical spine. As I suspected, an x-ray highlighted that her neck was broken. Neck breaks are very high up on the spinal cord, but if the break also damages the spinal cord it can affect the entire lower body, everything below the site of the break. So, the cause of death was her broken neck, which did indeed result in restricting her ability to breathe and instant death."

He paused for a moment, looked across from out of the top of his eyes above his mask at the Inspector and added, "But it looks like you may not have been entirely wrong, Yiannis, and get what you wished for."

Papadoulis shook his head slightly indicating that he wasn't really clear about what he was being told.

"Your murder, you may have your murder after all."

The pathologist quickly put him out of his misery.

"The break was a very, very clean one and very unlikely to have occurred simply from a fall. Almost a precision break in just the most fatal spot. I've seen something similar before in Athens when I was working there. A gangland drugs murder and feud. A precision break produced by a surprise severe and rapid twisting of the neck, a snap twist really, usually from in front of the victim and with both hands on the victim's cheek. A real professional job which leaves no other marks on the victim, not even from the grip on either of the victim's cheeks. In this case, if our murderer was a man, placing his hands on the woman's cheeks gently at first could simply have appeared to her like a movement in preparation for kissing her. Then a quick tighter grip and twist and snap, instant death."

The Inspector shook his head again, this time in a mixture of disbelief and shock before asking, "So, a professional killing? In Lindos, you're sure? We have a professional on our hands, a professional killer to track down?"

"Oh, yes you do, Inspector, but isn't that the sort of case you wanted? That's what it seemed like this morning. And I think we can rule out any idea of her death coming from a fall resulting from too much alcohol consumption after a Lindos night out. There was some level of alcohol in her bloodstream, but nowhere near anything excessive. A couple of glasses of wine perhaps, but certainly not enough to cause her to lose her senses, stumble and fall."

"Shit! Not exactly something you'd expect in Lindos, or even on Rhodes. Athens, yes, maybe, as you said, but not in a tourist village like Lindos. And at the moment we don't even have any idea who she is, where she's from or where she was staying."

Papadoulis was rubbing the back of his neck as he asked, "What about the toxicology report? Anything unusual?"

"No, nothing unusual," Costas confirmed, adding, "No luck with the photo on the door to door with some of the apartments up where the body was found?"

"Nothing yet. Of course, during the day any tourists staying in the apartments up there will probably have been out at the beaches so our officers are going back to check again early evening, around six, plus check in Broccolinos restaurant later when it opens at seven, just in case any of the staff there saw her or anything. I suppose if it's a professional killer that would explain why she had nothing on her, phone or anything to show where she was staying, even any ID."

"Most likely, he or she would have taken any ID she might've had with her, as well as any credit cards, phone and anything like an accommodation key or card. Something else that points to your theory of a professional killer, Yiannis."

"DNA? Finger prints?"

""I've taken a swab and we'll run it through the DNA data base, but unless she has some sort of criminal record nothing is going to show up, but we'll see. I'll send the finger prints over to your Sergeant straightaway at the Lindos station so he can check them with Rhodes and Athens, and I'll email you the full autopsy report by the end of today."

"Ok, thanks. I'd better head off back to Lindos and see if the door to door officers have any luck finding out where she was staying and who she is."

Just over forty-five minutes later the Inspector left his car in the car park by the Atmosphere Bar at the top of the village and strode purposefully down the steep slope path towards the bend at the bottom and beyond it off to the right to the low single storey white building that was the police station. Sergeant Georgiou had already taken up residence in a small office at the rear of the station which the two Rhodes officers had been allocated. Like most of the station it had been only recently classified as updated, although that basically just meant new, much more up-to-date computers and a coat of magnolia paint on the mostly bare, decidedly inhospitable looking walls. The two metal desks in the office had seen better times and had clearly retained their status during the updating not having been replaced. They had been furnished though with considerably more comfortable looking new chairs. The only things that broke up the monotony of the bare walls were the fair sized Incident Board and a new air-conditioning unit high up on one wall which faced onto the outside alley. There was not even a small window through which the bright Lindos sunlight could intrude upon the monopoly of the artificial strip lighting, but at least the air-conditioning unit kept the office at a bearable temperature when needed.

"Anything more at all from the door to door," Papadoulis asked as soon as he came through the office door?

The Sergeant shook his head.

"Nothing yet, sir. The officers said that they couldn't get any reply earlier from many of the places, mostly apartments. Assume they are mostly tourist accommodation, and I expect the occupiers would have been out at the beaches at that time of day. But they said there aren't that many places up that alley anyway, only ten as far as they could see. They are going to go back and check again after six, so in about an hour's time, and they'll check with the staff at Broccolinos then as well as they should be setting up to open at seven then. I've got another Lindos officer trying to track down the owners of the apartments. If our victim was staying up there the owners should recognise her from the photo, have a record of who she is and possibly where's she's from."

Now it was the Inspector who was shaking his head slightly and biting the inside of his lip.

"If she was actually staying up there, of course, but then I suppose why would she be heading up there at that time of night if she wasn't?"

Georgiou simply shrugged his shoulders, indicating that he had no answer to that as his Inspector headed over towards the bare white Incident Board. Instead he informed him, "I got the prints from Christof and sent them to Rhodes and Athens to get them to run an urgent check to see if there is any match on record."

Meanwhile Papadoulis had picked up the black marker pen and was writing at the top of the board, "THE VICTIM". As he finished he turned around to look across at the Sergeant and responded with, "Good, well hopefully that might turn up something. Christof told me he is doing a DNA search from Rhodes and Athens as well."

Turning back to the board he began to add in the centre beneath 'THE VICTIM' 'Female, Caucasian, European?, German?, tourist? Age late 30s, early 40s? Tall, 1.8 metres, slim, worked out, kept fit? Dyed blonde short hair. No phone, no hotel, no accommodation information, no hotel room key card on body, no ID. No distinguishing marks, no tattoos, well dressed, expensive high heel shoes'.

He moved to one side of the board and wrote, 'Body found 7.30 a.m. in alley to right of Broccolino restaurant, around 30 metres up by uneven steps. Time of death midnight - 2 a.m. Cause of death broken neck, clean, precision break, professional killing? No sign of struggle, no gunshot/stab wounds. Some alcohol in body - relatively low level. Lack of identification or where staying on body supports idea was professional killer?'

The Inspector turned around from the board and as he paced slowly back and forth across the office clicking the top of the marker pen on and off he went through everything, repeating everything aloud, that he had just written on the board. While he did so his Sergeant sat in silence at his desk.

After half-a-minute or so he stopped pacing, went back to the board, and wrote at the bottom of the list beneath 'THE VICTIM' 'Who is she? Where was she staying?' He tapped those words on the board with the marker pen and said with emphasis to the Sergeant, "This is what we concentrate on first. First we find out who she is, where she was staying, and then that could lead us to a motive and the killer."

Papadoulis was standing directly in front of the Incident Board and staring intently at what he'd written on it in silence for a few seconds when Georgiou asked, "While the officers are going back to the apartments up the alley from Broccolinos about now should I check the hotels and self-catering complexes at the top of the village, sir, the Krana area, to see if any of the owners recognise her?"

"Let's see if the officers turn up anything from the apartments first. We don't want to be spreading any unnecessary panic amongst the tourists staying up there."

The Inspector scratched the back of his head slightly with his right hand as he added, "In any case that would bring us back to the same question which occurred to me earlier. At the time of night when we believe she was killed why would she be going up that alley and steps where the body was found if she wasn't staying somewhere up there but was staying at the top of the village in Krana? That makes no sense."

"Maybe she actually went up there with the killer, sir," Georgiou suggested. "Maybe he or she, the killer, was staying up there and lured the woman up there for a late night drink or more at their apartment? If that was the case she could still have actually been staying somewhere up at Krana, couldn't she?"

Papadoulis perched himself on the corner of the other metal desk in the office, the one he was using as his, as he said, "That's possible, but if it is, or was, the killer who was staying in an apartment up that alley we have no idea whatsoever what he or she looks like. We only have a photograph of the victim. So, unless the killer had taken the victim back to their apartment on a previous night or occasion no one in those apartments, or even the owners if they are around near the accommodation, are going to recognise the victim from the photo. And if it was similarly late at night would anyone have been likely to have seen them arriving at any apartment the killer was staying in anyway?"

"Well, the places up at Krana might still be worth-"

The Inspector didn't let Georgiou finish, even though the Sergeant seemed persistent.

"No, let's wait and see what, if anything, the officers doing the door to door now up the alley by Broccolinos come up with. If it's nothing, we can get them checking up at Krana tomorrow morning."

As he finished Papadoulis glanced at his watch.

"Just coming up to six. I think we should wait for the officers doing the door to door to report back before we head off back to Rhodes Town, just in case they come up with anything."

"That could be a couple of hours, sir. In the meantime we could try a couple of the bars in the village. See if any of the owners or staff recognise the victim from the photo?"

"Good idea, Sergeant, but I could do with at least a roll or baguette. We haven't eaten anything all day. You sort out some coffees with the front desk and I'll go round to Café Melia in the old Amphitheatre Square to see if I can rustle up some baguettes or a feta cheese pie or something from them, if they have anything left. Then we'll try some of the bars."

4

Sally Hardcastle

"Long time, no see, Yiannis. Just finishing my shift and was wondering if I'd see you, if you'd pay me a visit here again? Heard there was a body found earlier today in the village and thought you might be on the case. News travels fast here."

She was cleaning the display case under the counter, and only intermittently looked up at him with feigned disinterest as she continued to do so. Even though she was leaning into the display case, he could still make out some loose strands of her striking bobbed dirty blonde hair, which he remembered so well, that was just protruding from beneath the white hat of her café uniform. He'd run his hands through it many times four years before. The memory stuck with him of how its appealing shape attractively highlighted her high cheek bones. It was something he noticed instantly when he first met her, along with her slim legs, deeply tanned from the Rhodes summer sun and nicely shaped, perfectly highlighted by some short white shorts. She was now in her late twenties and he remembered telling her many times four years ago that she had, "great legs".

"I wondered if you'd still be here, Sally, as well as if you'd have anything left for me and my Sergeant to eat at this time. We've not had time to eat anything all day."

She finished cleaning the case. As she straightened up from it he was confronted with her broad smile and sparkling eyes, bringing back more memories of why he'd immediately been so attracted to her back then, and that instantly revived those within him.

She had a confident, even cocky, way about her. Something else that attracted him to her, and she knew it. It wasn't difficult at all for her to lure him into starting an affair with her, even though he was a married police officer with two children at the time, and still was. She could easily disorientate him and she liked doing that, even though he was a very experienced Police Inspector, trained to be assured and confident. Right from her initial banter with him it was obviously what she wanted to do, and he couldn't resist it or her.

The affair lasted almost three months in 2016. He would regularly drive over to her apartment in Lardos in the early evening, whether he'd been working at Lindos police station, or even from the Rhodes Town station. She was the one who stopped it. For Sally Hardcastle it was just a bit of fun, nothing serious. Just another Lindos, or rather Lardos, affair during endless summers. He'd actually been growing concerned that she might be getting too serious about it, might actually be thinking he would leave his wife for her. But she wasn't. Very much to the contrary in fact, as she told him firmly when she ended it. She knew she could at any time. She was the one very much in control of it, their affair. And now she was tempting him again, easily. She knew she could. Dragging him back in, back into another affair, or at least restarting what they had before. Another bit of fun.

Her smile was still broad and her deep blue eyes widened as she told him, "I'll see what I can find for the two hard working Rhodes policemen. I'm sure there's a couple of baguettes in the back room. Cheese and tomato ok?"

"Fine, that'll be good."

As she turned to head towards the door to the back room she glanced back over her shoulder at him saying with another cheeky grin, "When I heard about the body I knew you'd come and see me. Glad you did. It was always good to see you, Yiannis, remember?"

He did, but he simply smiled back and raised his eyebrows a little. Just like that time four years ago he was nervous, completely unsure if what he was doing, was about to do again he guessed, was the right thing to do, was wise. Somehow though he couldn't resist it or her, and she knew that perfectly well. In a strange sort of way that was something that also actually appealed to him, attracted him to her, her assuredness and confidence.

She'd been living on the island now for six years, staying even through the winters as well as the summers. She wasn't slow in telling him when they first met that she lived in Lardos, even though she worked in Lindos, because it was better there, cheaper rent-wise. Places in Lindos were more expensive to rent than in Lardos due to the tourist trade, also there were far fewer available for long term lets. The accommodation owners wanted the tourists. That gave them more money, even though it was only for five or six months in the summer. Lardos was better for her, not just rent-wise, but also because there were fewer tourists. She sometimes went into Lindos at night, not that often though, just sometimes to meet friends, Greeks and Brit ex-pats. She had a car, nothing grand, just a small Fiat Uno, and it only took fifteen minutes or so to get from her Lardos apartment to the café for work. For a couple of winters she lived in Rhodes Town, November to early April. That wasn't as expensive during those months as it would have been in the summer. She preferred it back in Lardos though, so stayed there for the other winters. There were a couple of bars and restaurants open, and a few Brit ex-pats living there who also stayed for the winters.

She was born in Manchester. Her parents were both dead and she had one brother from Kilkenny, like her parents. They'd moved to Manchester before she was born. She lost touch with her brother after he came to visit her in Lardos just over four years ago. They never kept in touch much anyway. As she put it, "She had her own life here on Rhodes now."

The apartment she rented in Lardos wasn't large, but there was a separate bedroom with a decent sized double bed. In one corner of the other room was a small kitchenette area with a two ring hob and sink, as well as a sofa and coffee table in another part of the room. Off the bedroom was the shower room and toilet. The apartment was best described as functional, as was its position, just a few minutes from Lardos Main Square. The Inspector got to know it well during many evenings over those three months in 2016, particularly the decent sized double bed.

Papadoulis had no contact with her at all since the affair stopped four years previously. So, he told himself he hadn't deliberately gone to the café that evening just on the off chance she would still be working there. It was just the most convenient, the nearest place to the Lindos Police Station to try and get some filled baguettes or even the traditional Greek feta and spinach pies. In the back of his mind though, he knew that wasn't completely true, reinforced overwhelmingly by the feeling that swept over him when he got to the cafe and saw her.

When she returned from the back room five minutes or so later with a couple of baguettes filled with cheese and salad and proceeded to put each of them in a paper bag with a serviette she was exhibiting another broad cheeky smile. He almost knew what was coming, what she was going to say to him. He'd been there before. Her cheeky confident smile always preceded a suggestion. One that he knew he couldn't resist, just as he similarly was unable to do so four years previously. She knew that too, very well. That was Sally Hardcastle's way. She could play things just the way she chose, in any way she fancied, especially when it came to men. There were plenty who'd tried to chat her up in the café while placing their order, as well as also going so far as to proposition her even in the bars and clubs in Lindos and Lardos over the six years she'd been there. She knew how to choose who to respond to or not. There had been some who managed to break down her barrier, but not very many at all, and even those were short lived. She liked to be in control. She decided who, if anyone, she wanted to do more than just chat with. It was a small select band, a very small select club who got to sample her decent sized double bed at all during her six years in Lardos and Lindos. It consisted of a couple of Brit ex-pats and a young Greek guy who worked in one of the Lardos bars. None of them had lasted very long. In the case of one of the Brit ex-pats it was actually just a one night stand. Of her choosing Inspector Yiannis Papadoulis was one of those members of the club four years previously, and her affair with him actually lasted somewhat longer than with the others.

"So, when should I expect your call, Yiannis? I know you will, call I mean. I'm still in the same apartment in Lardos, if you're interested."

There it was, just as he expected. The thinly veiled invitation they both knew he couldn't resist. It was accompanied by what he'd seen and experienced many times before; her continuing mischievous smile and a sparkle in her eyes as she fixed a piercing, almost seductive stare straight into his while handing him the two bags of baguettes and taking the money he offered to pay for them slowly out of his hand. She was almost stroking it as she did so. Blunt and to the point, as she always had been with him. She knew he couldn't, wouldn't resist her. He would call, and soon.

Before he left her, and the café, his mind briefly shifted from thinking about Sally Hardcastle's personality, as well as her other attributes, and reverted to the case. He produced his phone from his pocket and showed her the photo of the murder victim, asking if by any chance she'd been in the café over the past couple of days or even before. He was out of luck on that as Sally told him almost instantaneously, "No, sorry, Yiannis, never seen her."

As she'd predicted, two hours later he did call her, and then went to Lardos to see her, but not until after he'd visited a couple of the Lindos bars with his Sergeant to check if any of the owners and staff recognised the victim from her photo.

5

Two Lindos bars

Having consumed their baguettes, accompanied by a coffee, the two policemen made their way out of the small Lindos Police Station and down the slight slope of the alley towards the centre of the village. It was early evening, still nicely warm, and the Lindos narrow alleyways were starting to get busy with tourists making their way to some of the many restaurants for an early dinner while others were on their way to the bars for a pre-dinner drink and eat later. Some of the bars, like Yannis Bar in the very centre of the village, were perfect for that pre-dinner drink while watching the world go by in the shape of the many tourists, as was Giorgos a little further on and down an alley off to the right from the main one running through the centre of the village.

As they reached the small square by Yannis Bar and Bar404 with its tree and low white wall, also very popular for later in the evening drinkers to perch upon and watch or chat to others, Georgiou asked, "Where do you think we should start, sir?"

"Courtyard Bar. That's as good a place to start as anywhere, and with the owner, Jack Constantino. I've spoken to him before on a couple of cases, just getting background on a few of his customers. He seems to know pretty much what is going on in the village, as well as quite a few of the tourists, the regular Lindos visitors at least. Let's see if by any chance he recognises our victim."

The Inspector and his Sergeant continued on through the village, weaving through the growing number of tourists heading for their night out. After a minute or so they turned off to the left by Pal's Bar on the corner and up the alleyway towards the two small steps towards the Courtyard Bar. It was a traditional old style Lindian bar with the usual fair share of dark polished wood. All along the length of the back wall was the bar itself, except for a few feet at the end for a doorway and narrow steps down to the toilets. At the opposite end were the music console and a larger and wider area with some tables and chairs and room for dancing, as well as a flight of stairs up to the roof terrace.

Jack Constantino was a very convivial friendly host. A lot of the Courtyard Bar customers were repeat ones who returned to Lindos, particularly the Courtyard Bar, year after year, in many cases two or three times each summer. They spent a lot of time in his welcoming bar. It was particularly popular with families, not only because of its host, but also because of the courtyard that gave it the name. It was a perfect setting for them to sit outside during the warm evenings and yet still be able hear the music drifting out through the open doors of the bar. Usually on Sundays there was live Greek music and dancing as Jack entertained the customers with his considerable various musical instrumental skills. He was a stocky, dark-haired, quite tall man in his mid-forties. Lindos born and bred, he would relate many stories from his youth in the village for the entertainment of his customers. He'd also spent some time in America a few years before he married back in Lindos. Besides his bar, or maybe as well as is a better way of putting it, his passion was his music and he was a great fan of Cat Stevens, or Yusuf Islam as he was now known. Jack Constantino regularly entertained his customers with renditions on his guitar or bouzouki of the songs of his favourite musician.

As the two policemen made their way into the bar there were three couples at tables outside in the courtyard. Constantino was sat at on the customer side of the bar at the far end checking his phone, while two other younger guys were busy re-stocking some of the shelves and fridges behind the bar with bottles of Greek Mythos beer from a couple of green crates on the floor. The bar had only just opened for the evening, at six, and was empty inside, although from the CCTV screens high up on the wall at the far end of the bar the Inspector could see that there were quite a few more customers enjoying an early evening drink up on the terrace as they watched the warm Lindos night rolling in.

As Constantino looked up from his phone Papadoulis went to his pocket to produce his police credentials. Before he could do so, as well as introduce himself and his Sergeant, the bar owner obviously remembered him from enquiries he'd made on previous cases, telling him, "It's ok, Inspector, I remember who you are."

So instead the Inspector produced his phone from his pocket and asked, "Do you recognise this woman by any chance?"

"Is that the woman whose body was found in the alley by Broccolinos this morning?"

Papadoulis ignored the question. Continuing to hold his phone towards the bar owner's face he repeated, "Do you recognise her," followed by, "She was a tourist we think. Have you seen her here in the bar recently at all?"

Constantino peered at the photo for a few seconds. He started to shake his head slightly and initially replied, "No, no, can't say I do, not for certain. She does look a little familiar though. Probably a tourist, as you said, Inspector, definitely not a local, someone living in the village or nearby. I'd recognise her for certain if she was."

Papadoulis went to move his phone away, but Constantino stopped him, saying, "Hang on, let me see-"

The Inspector moved his phone back for the bar owner to take another look.

"Yes, yes, that's right, that's why I thought she looks a bit familiar. I thought she maybe looked a bit like a woman who I remember came in one night last year."

He peered at the photo again then said, "But no, no, I don't think so. I can't remember that clearly. It was last summer, a while ago now. Could be the same woman but .... no, no, don't think so, Inspector, and anyway, you said recently didn't you?"

Papadoulis was quite short with him in his reply. "Yes, I did, recently, I asked if you remember her coming in recently, not last year. So, this is obviously not the same woman you're thinking of."

Constantino turned back towards the bar. Pointing to the two young barmen at the far end and waving them to come over he added, "Dimitris and Cris would know if the woman in that photo has been in here recently. They do most of the serving."

The two guys took a look at the photo, but both shook their heads agreeing they didn't recognise the woman as a customer they'd served.

The Inspector puffed out his cheeks before telling the owner, "Thanks anyway. I just thought there was a chance she might have been one of your customers."

As the two policemen turned away to leave the bar Constantino tried once more. "Is she? Is she the body found this morning?"

But Papadoulis simply glanced back over his shoulder saying again, "Thanks," and they headed out of the bar. As they made their way down the few steps into the alley Georgiou asked, "Where next, sir?"

The Inspector rubbed the back of his aching neck from the long day with the palm of his left hand.

"I hoped Constantino would be able to help us and tell us more, even possibly identify the dead woman." He hesitated for a few seconds as they continued down the alleyway before adding, "Let's try Giorgos. That's a place that's popular with tourists. Perhaps the owner and staff there will be able to help us."

Giorgos Bar was indeed a popular place with tourists, as well as with some of the locals, including some Brit ex-pats. Around twenty metres or so off the main alleyway through the village it was perfectly situated for the passing large numbers of tourists making their way up from Pallas Beach into the village having arrived from Rhodes on the boat day trips. Consequently, it was always busy with lunch customers, and the tables outside were perfect for watching the world go by in the village during the day or in the evening while nursing a cold drink or enjoying some of the good food. In the evenings it drew a good number of regular tourists who came to Lindos year after year. Giorgos was busy, even on that particular September evening as the end of the season approached,.

The two policemen made their way quickly between the outside tables and inside through the doorway. As they approached the bar a young Greek barman asked what he could get them to drink. Once more the Inspector reached into his pocket for his police credentials, introduced himself and his

Sergeant, and asked if the bar owner, Tsamis, was around. Papadoulis had also met him on previous investigations in the village.

"He's in the back. I'll fetch him," the young barman replied.

Tsamis was a dark curly haired Greek, who, like many of the other Lindos bar and restaurant owners, was very popular with his regular year on year returning tourist customers. Couples and different generations of families frequented his bar. Also, like the other bar and restaurant owners, he worked hard, with long hours through the summer season stretching from late April to the end of October. By mid-September the long hours were beginning to take their toll and weariness from the long summer was creeping up on them, not that any of them ever allowed it to show when it came to dealing with customers. The service was always exemplary, and Giorgos was no exception.

When Tsamis emerged at one end of the bar from the back room with the young barman he too recognised Papadoulis immediately.

"What can I do for you, Inspector? I assume this is not a social visit, so I can't offer you a drink."

"No, I'm afraid it's not, much as I'd like a drink, as no doubt would my Sergeant here. Do you recognise this woman by any chance? A tourist, in here recently over the past few days perhaps," Papadoulis asked as he held up his phone for the owner to study the photo.

Tsamis shook his head slightly saying, "No, I can't say I do, Inspector. Don't recall seeing her in here."

With that he waived the young barman over, explaining to Papadoulis, "Let's see if my son does. He's here at other times when I get a few hours off, early evening."

But his son just looked at the photo on the phone for a few seconds and also replied, "No, I don't recall seeing her in here."

They repeated the same process as Tsamis called his young female waitress over, but with a similar negative result. Now it was the Inspector's turn to shake his head slightly, before telling the bar owner, "Thanks," and adding ruefully in some desperation, "I could really do with that drink now, but as we are on duty …"

His voice tailed off somewhat wearily, before he added another, "Thanks again," and motioned to his Sergeant that they should leave.

As they made their way once more through the early evening tourists and along the main alleyway running through the village Georgiou asked, "Should we try a couple more of the bars, sir?"

The Inspector glanced at his watch. "It's coming up to seven, and it's been a long day. I think we'll leave the other bars and restaurants to some of the local Lindos officers for the rest of this evening and tomorrow morning. See if they turn up anything, and whether they have any luck from the door-to-door up the alley by Broccolinos. I just thought Jack Constantino and Tsamis might be our best bet. Let's call it a day for now. I'll hang on at the station here, just to see if the door-to-door does turn up anything tonight. Get one of the officers in the Lindos station to run you back to Rhodes Town."

6

Sally Hardcastle and 'lightness'

Just over thirty minutes after his Sergeant said goodnight to him in the Lindos Station for his police car lift to his home in Rhodes Town Papadoulis was softly knocking on the door to Sally Hardcastle's small Lardos apartment. He rang her as soon as the Sergeant left the Lindos Police Station office. Seeing his number come up on her mobile screen she answered as cockily and sure of herself as ever.

"Good to know I haven't lost it, Yiannis. I said you'd call. When should I expect you? You're obviously coming over. Coming over to catch up on old times, if you know what I mean?"

He did, as a small smile spread across his lips in reaction to her cockiness and self-confidence. He remembered that very well from their affair. He'd loved it. It was one of the first things that attracted him to her, and now he was glad to hear she hadn't lost it.

"About half-an-hour, I'll be there in about half-an-hour. I can't stay too long though. Got to get back to Rhodes Town. It's been a long day, and tomorrow could be even longer."

"You found out who the victim is yet," she asked.

He ignored her question.

She got the message from his lack of response, telling him, "Ok, see you in half-an-hour," and rang off, more confident than ever he'd come running over to her as quickly as he could.

She opened the door to her apartment wearing bright green tight fitting shorts - very short and very tight - showing off to their best her tanned, shapely legs. He'd often wondered before how she managed to get and maintain such a great tan, given that she worked in the café six days a week throughout the whole summer with only the one day off each week. He asked her once and she simply told him she tanned easily. On top of the shorts she wore a sleeveless vest type white t-shirt, as well as flip flops at the end of her tanned legs. She'd obviously showered on her return from work in the café and washed, dried, and brushed her bobbed dirty blonde hair into an attractive shape. All of that displayed her self-confidence that he would, indeed, come over to see her to, "catch up on old times."

Her eyes widened and her smile was broad as she was unable to resist telling him yet again in a confident tone, "I knew you'd call, knew you'd come."

He just smiled back and raised his eyebrows a little.

She knew he couldn't resist her confident, self-assured way with him. Her belief in that was quickly confirmed. They hardly bothered with small talk, or any preliminary sparring on the sofa in what passed as her lounge. She never even bothered to offer him a glass of wine as she had done initially on the first night in her apartment of their previous affair in August 2016. Instead, from the doorway to the apartment she just caught hold of his hand and led him firmly straight across the lounge and into her bedroom with its good sized double bed.

Even now somewhat surprised at her blunt directness, despite having seen something similar from her previously, he started to say, "I-"

She never let him finish. She put the index finger of her left hand to his lips signalling him to stop talking and simultaneously began to unbuckle his trouser belt with her right hand, telling him, "On the phone you said you couldn't stay long, so let's not waste time, Yiannis."

Sally Hardcastle was a woman who always knew what she wanted and how to get it as quickly as possible. This, and Inspector Yiannis Papadoulis, was no different from many other things she'd wanted at precise times in her life. What she wanted now was him in her bed again and sex, just as she'd done over three months in the summer of 2016. So, that's what she got. She usually got what she wanted.

She almost ripped the rest of his clothes off him and then pulled her t-shirt off over her head to reveal her perfectly formed naked breasts above her bronzed flat stomach. Seconds later her unfastened shorts fell to the floor beneath her feet revealing her bright white thong.

Within seconds they were exploring each other's naked bodies in her large double bed. Unlike him, wearing the odour of his day investigating in the hot Rhodian sun, she smelt fresh and clean. Her aroma was added to by her Armani perfume as it swept over him and engulfed his senses. She remembered that he loved it and couldn't resist her when she wore it. He had told her as much many times in the past. Her body was firm and untouched by child birth. In anticipation and excitement of what was to follow, where he was headed, she let out a small moan as he caressed and kissed her toned flat stomach. He knew she loved that moment of anticipation. Her hand reached down to the top of his head to direct him to where she wanted him to go.

For an hour they enjoyed each other's bodies. For her it was just fun. Not anything signalling they were making love. It was just sex. She enjoyed it that way, loved the 'lightness' of it without any responsibility whatsoever.

He wasn't as sure as her about it though. Wasn't as clear in his mind just what it was that they were doing. What it meant. He knew what it meant to her, what it was for her. She'd told him that towards the end of their previous affair four years ago.

"Just fun, Yiannis. I'm perfectly happy the way it is," she told him very clearly and firmly one evening after they'd had sex again in her bed. She said it in a very dispassionate matter of fact way, almost as if she was telling a customer in the café what baguettes they had left. He remembered being surprised then, thinking beforehand that she might be wanting more, more of the 'weight' of a permanent relationship. Not long after that the affair ended. He wasn't even clear whether it was him or her who ended it. Either way she didn't seem very bothered or upset when it did end. It was after all, "Just fun," and all fun eventually comes to an end, a conclusion, appeared to be her attitude. That was, after all, Sally Hardcastle's life, her outlook and philosophy on life. Looking back on it he realised that their affair and her attitude over it ending fitted completely with her general approach to life - a 'lightness' and virtually no responsibility. That was seemingly why she'd come to Rhodes to live and work in the first place, to experience and live life to the full.

Despite that, what he knew was that when he was with her back then four years ago, as well as seemingly now, there was no guilt, neither on her part or his. He felt no guilt over what he was doing when he was doing it, no guilt over his wife and his marriage. He knew he should have, even wondered why there wasn't, but for those moments he was with Sally he felt no guilt. There was a 'lightness' in his life while he was with her. He knew that would evaporate later and the 'weight' of responsibility would return. The guilt would sweep over him like a dark Rhodian storm cloud during his hour's drive to Rhodes Town, his home, and his wife's bed.

There were problems in his marriage, problems between him and his wife. He convinced himself it was because of his job as a Police Inspector and the often long hours. Maybe it was more than that though, other things that made his wife unhappy. During his guilty drive back to Rhodes Town late that night he tried to convince himself he could stop this thing with Sally Hardcastle again at any time he wanted, especially if she looked upon it simply as "fun", as she'd told him many times. In reality though, he knew it was her who would stop it when she wanted, not him.

7

Wednesday 9th September 2020

The next morning Papadoulis arrived at the Lindos Police Station early, just after eight. His Sergeant hadn't arrived yet, but as he sat at his desk staring across at the white Incident Board one of the local Lindos Station officers came into the office to report they'd had no luck from the door-to-door enquiries the evening before in the alleyway where the body was found. No one in the apartments up there recognised the victim from the photo. The officer reported it was mostly tourists, but also some of the apartment owners living up there didn't recognise her either.

As the local officer left the office the Inspector got up from his desk and walked across to add on the Incident Board the words, 'victim not staying where body found'. As he took a pace back and stared at the quite sparse amount of information on it his Sergeant finally arrived with better news than the local officer had brought, and with considerably more enthusiasm in his voice.

Unable to contain himself, he announced as soon as he came through the door, "Found her, sir."

He was so anxious to give his Inspector what he believed was a breakthrough that the way he expressed it didn't really make sense.

Papadoulis spun around to face him and with a frown and a confused look across his face asked, "Found who?"

"The dead woman, sir. I meant we've found someone who recognised her. At least someone in the village who remembers her being in his restaurant, Gatto Bianco, two nights ago, on Monday night, the night she was murdered."

"So, who is she?"

"The restaurant owner, Valassi, said he didn't actually know her. He said she wasn't a local. But he heard the man she was having dinner with call her Sophia, and he knew the man, David Alexander. He's been in his restaurant quite a few times and has been staying in Lindos for the past two summers."

"Two summers? Did the owner have any idea where this guy Alexander stays in the village? Does he live here permanently?"

"He said no, only for the last two summers, and he thought it was near the restaurant, a flat in the alley coming down from between Yannis Bar and Bar404, although he couldn't be sure which one. According to the local officers there aren't many along there though, so we could check each one."

"Did he say what this guy Alexander does here if he stays all summer? Or is he just a long term tourist?"

"He wasn't sure. He thought that maybe he'd heard somewhere in the village that he was a writer, but he couldn't say for certain."

"Ok, we need to go and find him. Did you get any sort of description of him from the owner?"

Georgiou checked his notebook before replying.

"Yes, he reckoned he's late thirties, tall, around six feet, light brown shortish hair, and a relatively slim figure."

"Not much to go on, but some help I suppose. What about the woman, our victim? Did he think Alexander knew her well? Maybe they worked together on something here, a book maybe? Or perhaps back in England?"

"Valassi said it didn't seem like they knew each other that well, although he couldn't really say, but he did notice her reach across the table and take the guy's hand at one point during their meal. He had no idea if they worked together though, or had worked together in the past, and he obviously had no idea what she did work-wise."

The Inspector hesitated for a moment, glancing at his watch and then rubbing his chin. Without saying anything he turned and went over to the Incident Board to write the names 'David Alexander' and 'Sophia' on it, with a question mark after the woman's name.

"Hopefully this guy Alexander can give us her last name," he said as he turned back towards Georgiou. "It's just gone nine. Let's go and see if we can find Mr. Alexander. See if he's a relatively early riser. If he's not just a one or two week tourist, as the restaurant owner suggested, then I'm guessing he won't be off to the beach every day. So, hopefully we'll find him in."

Five minutes later the two policemen were making their way up the few steps at one end of the alley the Gatto Bianco owner thought the flat David Alexander stayed in was located. There were three large wooden doors on the left hand side of the alley. On the right hand side there was a short alley with a dead end. There were two more doors within that and at the far end of the alley was another set of double doors with three steps leading up to it.

"You take the right hand side and I'll start with the three on the left," Papadoulis told his Sergeant.

While Georgiou disappeared off down the short side alley to begin knocking on those doors the Inspector did the same, knocking hard on the first set of large wooden double doors on the left. He got no response, so he tried again after a few minutes. When there was still no response he moved along the alley to the second set of doors with their large faded brass knocker.

This time he had more success. The second time he banged the knocker a young, bleary eyed, dark curly haired guy in a white vest, shorts and flip flops opened it. He looked Greek. Papadoulis produced his police credentials and introduced himself. The guy was obviously too young to be David Alexander, and certainly not English. So, the Inspector asked who he was and if the guy lived there.

"I do. There are three flats here, two here in the courtyard and another one up the stairs. I live in that one."

He half turned and pointed to the open door at the far side of the high walled courtyard. Before he could answer who he was Papadoulis asked, "Do you know whether a guy named David Alexander lives in one of the other two flats?"

He got the answer he was hoping for, well half of it at least.

"There's an English guy called David who lives in that one, but I don't know his full name. I only know him as David."

The guy half turned again and this time pointed to the doors to the left of the courtyard just beyond the bottom of the wrought iron stairs.

Papadoulis moved to go past him towards the doors as he asked, "Do you know if he's in?" But he stopped as the guy told him, "No, he left early yesterday morning. I saw him leaving as I was getting ready for work down at St. Paul's beach. I had an earlier than usual start yesterday as we had an early delivery at the restaurant there at seven. Today's my morning off or I'd be down there now working, like on most days through the summer. Anyway, he said he had to go away for a few days."

"Did he say where?"

"No, and I didn't ask. It must have been before six and I was still half asleep when I heard his flat door closing. I thought maybe he was only just coming back from one of the clubs, but when I opened our flat door I saw he had a bag and was leaving, I assumed to England. That's where he's from, London I think."

"Do you know what he does here in Lindos? Just a tourist? Although we've been told he's been here for the last two summers."

"He told me he was a writer. Well, trying to write some sort of novel, I think, as he said he hasn't had one published yet. I heard in the village that he used to work at a university in England, although he never told me that himself. I never asked."

"Right, I see."

The guy turned towards the white plastic table and chairs in one corner of the courtyard and went over to sit in one of the chairs.

Papadoulis joined him while stroking his chin briefly and then taking out his phone to show the photo of the victim's face to the guy.

"Do you know this woman? Have you seen her with this guy Alexander, perhaps in the courtyard here or going into or out of his flat, or maybe around in the village?"

The guy took a quick look and almost instantly replied, "No." But then a few seconds later as the Inspector went to put his phone away he added, "Wait a second. Let me look again. He peered at the photo for a few more seconds and then said,

"Yes, yes I think I recognise her, or at least I've seen her before."

"Here, with your neighbour, David?" Papadoulis interrupted, his voice heightened.

"No, no, not here. I think I saw her one evening towards the end of the season last year in the bar I work in, Antika. David was in there that night too."

"Together? They were in the bar together?"

"No, well not at first. She was asking me about what cocktail to have and David was standing close by at the bar and started talking to her. I remember I think I heard him say to her he recognised her from somewhere-"

"Where?" Papadoulis interrupted.

"I didn't hear that part of the conversation. I was busy making the cocktail and some other drinks orders."

"Any idea where she was from? English?" Papadoulis pressed him.

"From her accent I'd say Eastern Europe somewhere, maybe even Russian. Definitely not English, although from what I heard and what she said to me, her English was good."

"Did you overhear her name?"

"While they were chatting at the bar over their drinks I think I heard David call her Sophie. Something like that anyway, but we were very busy that night if I remember, so I didn't hear much at all of what they were talking about."

"Sophia? Could it have been Sophia? And that's all, no last name?"

"It could have been, Inspector, but as I said we were very busy that night and when that happens, and with the loud music, you don't really overhear much of the conversations. So, I didn't hear whether either of them mentioned her last name."

"You said it was towards the end of the season last year. Any idea more precisely when that was?

"Well, I remember it was not long after David told me one night in the bar that he had to go back to England. Something to do with an agent and a publisher in London, he said. Towards the end of October maybe."

"But you haven't seen him with her this summer at all?

"No."

The guys bleary eyes had completely cleared now and he told Papadoulis, "If that's all I have to get ready for work soon, Inspector."

"Yes, yes, of course. You've been very helpful, thanks, but just a few more questions. I didn't get your name."

"Ledi."

"Greek, are you Greek?"

"No, Albanian." He became very defensive as he added, "But I have all the necessary papers, if that's why you're asking."

"No, no, I'm sure you have. It's just for my records. Do you live here alone and do you know who lives in the flat upstairs?"

"It's empty. No one lives there. It's been empty for the last two summers. And I live here with my girlfriend, Gloria. We've lived here for the last three summers and most of the winters, except when we go back to Albania to see our families for a few weeks over Christmas. She's from Albania too, and also has all the necessary papers to live and work here."

"Yes, yes, I'm sure she has. Don't worry, that's not why I'm here at all. As I said, it's just for our records concerning the case we're investigating relating to Mr. Alexander."

Papadoulis continued to scribble notes in his police notebook, just as he had throughout their conversation.

Ledi looked a little concerned as he said, "Investigation? Is he in trouble? Nothing to do with us is it?"

The Inspector shook his head quite vigorously as he reassured him.

"No, no, not at all. It's just background and you've been very helpful. But what about your girlfriend, Gloria you said her name was?"

"Yes."

"Could she have possibly seen this woman here I asked you about, Sophia, going into David's flat at any time? Is she here at the moment?"

"No, she's already at work, down at St. Paul's. She works there too, with me. But we are both out working throughout the day at the beach and then in the evenings in the bar, Antika, every day and evening through the summer. So, usually we come and go to our flat here together. I'll ask her, but if I haven't seen the woman here I'm pretty sure Gloria wouldn't have. I'll check with her, but I really doubt it."

"Ok, let us know at the station if she does recall seeing the woman here. What about the flat though. Is it owned by the same person who owns yours?"

"Yes, all three flats here are owned by the Greek couple who live next door. But I really have to get ready for work now, Inspector, and get off down to St. Paul's soon."

Papadoulis closed his notebook and put it away, taking out his phone in its place as he nodded slightly saying, "Of course, thanks for your help."

As the Albanian disappeared inside his flat the Inspector called his Sergeant.

"I'm pretty sure I've found where Alexander stays. It's in one of three flats in a courtyard through the second set of doors on the left hand side of the alley. Come and join me here."

Half-a-minute or so later the Sergeant emerged into the courtyard through the wooden doors. Pointing with his left hand Papadoulis told him, "It's that flat there, but he's not in."

He pointed again and added, "The Albanian guy who lives in that other flat in the courtyard there with his girlfriend told me an English guy called David lives there, but left very early yesterday morning, before six. The Albanian guy saw him leaving as he was going off to work and he told him he was going away for a few days. He also remembered our victim being in the bar the guy works in, Antika, one evening towards the end of the season last year. Apparently, this guy, David, presumably David Alexander, was in the bar that evening as well and was talking with her. They weren't together, but he started a conversation with her at the bar while the Albanian guy made her a cocktail. He said he thought he overheard David saying to her that he recognised the woman from somewhere else. At first he told me that he thought he heard him call her Sophie, but when I asked if he thought it could have been Sophia he said it could have been. He also said she had what he thought was an East European accent, but could have been Russian."

"So, should we have a look now in this guy David's flat, sir," Georgiou asked?

"Yes, we need to. As I said before, according to the Albanian guy, David told him yesterday morning he was going away for a few days. It would be interesting to see if he has left many of his clothes in there. Whether he intends returning? That would certainly give us a big clue whether he is our killer. Apparently the owners of the flat live next door."

"But we'll need a warrant, sir?"

"Let's see. Let's go and ask the owners if they'll open the flat up for us. They are the owners, so-"

"But if this guy, David, is renting it and living there surely we will need a warrant, sir?"

The Inspector glanced sideways at Georgiou and then shrugged his shoulders before replying, "Well, maybe Sergeant, but if the owners don't ask for one then …"

His voice tailed off as he turned towards the courtyard doors.

The set of dark brown wooden doors next door were very similar, even down to the large faded brass knocker that the Inspector banged twice with. After half a minute or so an elderly Greek man with swept back greying thinning hair wearing a white vest and dark blue baggy shorts opened the door. Papadoulis again produced his police credentials and explained that they were looking for an English man called David who they understood was staying in one of the man's flats in the courtyard next door.

"Yes, David Alexander you mean. He's rented one of our flats in the courtyard next door for the whole summer," the man told him.

"We understand he's gone away for a few days?" the Inspector asked, having been pleased to at least have got confirmation that it was where the man they were looking for, David Alexander, had been staying.

But the owner of the flat simply shrugged and it was clear he didn't know that was the case. The Inspector anticipated the answer, but still asked if the owner knew where Alexander had gone. He was right. The owner simply shrugged again and shook his head slightly. Papadoulis was also right about there being no need for a warrant, or at least that the owner wouldn't raise it. When he asked if he could open up the flat to let them in the owner agreed straightaway, without any mention of a warrant, telling the policemen he would go and get his key.

The flat wasn't empty. There were still some clothes in the two built in wardrobes, one in the lounge and one in the double bedroom. They were clearly men's clothes, and as Papadoulis commented to his Sergeant, they were presumably Alexander's. Overall, there was nothing out of the ordinary in the flat, nothing to suggest a person living there wouldn't return. There were no toiletries or razor in the bathroom, but the Inspector presumed that a man going away for a few days would take those with him. In the bedroom there was a chest of drawers and on either side of the bed a small table with one draw. As Georgiou checked inside them he confirmed to his Inspector that there were a few clothes in the chest of draws, but nothing in the draws of the bedside tables. Papadoulis stood in silence at the end of the bed rubbing his chin with his right hand and shaking his head slightly.

Eventually, he asked Georgiou, "What do you think that tells us, Sergeant?"

"What, sir, what what tells us?"

"No passport. He's taken his passport. So, he's leaving Greece, whether for a few days or more."

"Well, the guy in the flat across the courtyard told you he presumed Alexander was going to England, so-"

Papadoulis didn't let him finish.

"He did, but we can be pretty sure now he was at least leaving Greece. Whether he was going to England though or …"

He stopped for a couple of seconds. Then scratching the back of his head added, "It's probably too late as he left yesterday morning, but anyway we need to get an alert out for him at the ports and airports straightaway, plus do a social media and financial search on him, as well as a check to see if there are any police records on him in Greece and the U.K.. Later we'll go back and see some of the bar owners again. They may be able to give us some background on him if he's been here for the last two summers."

8

Invisible David Alexander?

It looked like they'd made a breakthrough by at least identifying the first name of the victim, Sophia, and even perhaps her nationality, Eastern European or maybe Russian. Then there was the fact that she was seen having dinner with David Alexander on the very evening she was murdered. The Inspector's optimism about the case was stalled though when his Sergeant reported what his search for David Alexander's social media had discovered, or rather didn't discover.

"Nothing, sir. Nothing at all. Bloody nothing at all. The man's invisible in terms of any social media activity or profile."

Papadoulis had just finished writing all they had discovered earlier about Alexander on the Incident Board – the time he'd been in Lindos, the two summers, what he supposedly was doing there during that time, his dinner with Sophia in Gatto Bianco, and where he stayed in the village – as well as adding under the name 'Sophia' the words 'Russian or Eastern European'. He spun around on his heels from the board and clicking the top of the black marker pen on and off he repeated, "Nothing, nothing at all?"

"No, sir."

The Inspector scratched the back of his head briefly.

"Perhaps he's just not that sort of person, not into social media. Not everybody is, Sergeant."

"That's true, but if he's a writer, as the restaurant owner suggested, you'd think he would be, if only to publicise what he's writing, his novel, I suppose. Plus, didn't his next door neighbour say he heard around the village that Alexander used to work at a university in England? Doesn't mean he'd need to be on social media though, but I could do a check on that anyway."

"Yes, although even if you find him, find anything on university sites, it might tell us something about his past, but unlikely to give us much on where he might be now. Worth a try though, I suppose. What about financial stuff or any police record?"

"One of the local Lindos officers is still checking those, but so far he said there's no trace of Alexander having any Greek bank account, nor any police record. I put a call in to London to see if they could help on the financial stuff and any police record in the U.K. I only spoke to a Sergeant at New Scotland Yard, a contact of mine there. He said it was all above his pay grade so he'd have to check with his superior officer about running a thorough check on Alexander. He's going to get back to me later today or in the morning. And I put an alert out at all the ports and airports for him, but nothing so far. As you said, he's probably long gone. Disappearing straight after the murder, or at least the next morning, makes him our most likely suspect though, doesn't it?"

Papadoulis never answered. Instead, he simply rubbed the back of his neck as it was aching again from growing stress and tiredness, the result of trying to lead a double life in his personal matters. His mind had been wandering regularly to when he might be able to pay another visit to Lardos and Sally Hardcastle. He hoped it would be that evening, but that would depend on the case and any further developments. He'd already had one text message from her earlier simply saying, "Again tonight?"

"So, why the phone, sir?"

"What?"

Georgiou startled him, disturbed his thoughts. For a very brief moment he actually misunderstood the point of his comment and thought he was referring to something to do with Sally Hardcastle texting him.

"Her phone, sir, the victim's phone. Why would the murderer take that? We haven't thought about that. It can only be to prevent her being identified. Unless she left it where she was staying in the village she would surely have had it on her. Not many people go out without their phone these days, especially with so much stuff stored on it, even credit card links to pay things."

The Inspector stood in front of the Incident Board, gazing at it and stroking his chin with his right hand before agreeing with his Sergeant.

"That's true. It can only be to stop an easy identification of her. So, we can conclude from that it wasn't a spur of the moment murder, committed in an act of rage during an argument. It was pre-planned, premeditated. Christof thinks it could be a professional killer we're looking for."

As he finished speaking he picked up the marker pen, clicked off the top and added the words 'PREMEDITATED', PROFESSIONAL? and 'phone?' to the board.

"Unfortunately, as we don't have her full name there is no way of trying to trace her phone," he added as he finished writing.

"And then there's the fact that she had no card or key indicating where she was staying in the village, sir. That also suggests the killer was keen to ensure she couldn't be easily identified. Christof's right, it's all increasingly pointing to a professional job."

Papadoulis nodded slightly in agreement and rubbed his chin once more still standing in front of the Incident Board and peering at it intensely.

"From the lack of any result on the door-to-door up there it looks like we can assume the victim wasn't staying near where the body was found, where she was killed we assume. The killer could have been staying up there of course and persuaded her to go back to wherever he was staying. Although we've no way of checking that as we don't have any identification of the possible killer, except for David Alexander, and we know he wasn't staying up there. But if our killer is Alexander what was the victim doing up there with him, and at that time of night? His flat is on the other side of the village."

Georgiou walked over to join his Inspector in front of the board, asking again as he did so, "Krana, sir? What about Krana at the top of the village, and the hotels up there? She could have actually been staying somewhere up at Krana couldn't she, or even the Memories Hotel or the Acquagrand hotel just outside

Lindos? Judging by what Costas said about the expensive looking high heeled shoes on the body yesterday morning she doesn't appear to be a woman who would stay in a self-catering apartment in the village. Isn't it more likely she was staying in one of the more expensive hotels like Acquagrand or Memories."

"Fair point, Sergeant," Papadoulis agreed, nodding once again. "Get a couple local officers to check those out with her photo."

He glanced at his watch and added, "Meanwhile, let's go and see what Jack Constantino at the Courtyard Bar can tell us, if anything, about Mr. Alexander."

It was just after six again when the two policemen made their way into the Courtyard Bar. It had only just opened for the evening and so was empty, at least it was in the downstairs bar. Jack Constantino was sitting on a stall at the far end of the bar checking his phone as he was when they went there the evening before, while the two younger barmen were again busily restocking the shelves behind the bar ready for the evening customers. As he looked up from his phone the owner said, "Back again, Inspector. Is this police business or can I offer you a drink?"

"No, thank you, it's police business, I'm afraid, something more I hope you can help us with. A British guy called David Alexander. Do you know him? Does he drink in here much, regularly?"

"David, yes, he comes in quite regularly over the last two summers. Is this also connected to your investigation of the body that was found by Broccolinos? What's David got to do with it?"

Papadoulis again ignored the question, instead asking, "When was the last time he was in here?"

"Not sure. At this time towards the end of the season I don't always come in every night. The boys might know. They are here every night."

He shouted along the bar to the two younger guys stocking it up.

"Dimitris, Cris, any idea when David was in last?"

The slightly older of the two looked up and replied first.

"David Alexander?"

"Yes."

"Four or five nights ago, I think. Sunday night maybe?"

The younger one nodded in agreement.

"Is that unusual?" the Inspector asked, "for him not to come in for four or five nights?"

"Not really. People tend to go to a few different bars in the village on different nights, especially those who are here for a longer time than just a couple of weeks on holiday."

Constantino tried again.

"What's he got to do with the body that was found? Have you managed to identify it yet?"

Papadoulis once again ignored his questions.

"But he is a regular though, and has been over the last two summers? Always alone?"

"Yes, as I said, he's been a regular over the last two summers. A writer, he said. Cris said he heard in the village that he used to work at a university in England before. Sometimes he's been in with other people, a group. I guess he's got to know quite a few of the bar and restaurant workers in the village. A lot of them come here after they finish work, around one, sometimes later, for a wind down drink before going to bed. So, sometimes he'd come in with a few of them, or he'd already be in here when they arrived."

"Mostly men? Any women?"

"Mixed really. Mostly Greek men, but a few Albanians, and even a few Brits, and a few women."

The Inspector produced the photo of the victim on his phone again and asked, "Are you sure she wasn't one of them, in here drinking with Alexander, and maybe some of those workers, this summer or last, maybe was even one of them?"

"As I said when you showed me that before, Inspector, I thought she might have been a woman who I vaguely remembered came in last summer, but I don't think it's the same woman, so no, I'm pretty sure I've never seen the woman in the photo in here or anywhere in the village. David did used to drink with a woman in here quite regularly last summer and for the first part of this one, late after she finished work in one of the restaurants, but it wasn't her. That was a British woman who'd worked here for a few years, Alice, Alice Palmer."

"Is she still in Lindos? Perhaps she might know where we can find him. We need to talk to him."

"No, Alice left earlier this summer, July, mid-July I think it was, quite suddenly as it happens."

"Why? Do you know why she left? Anything to do with David Alexander and do you know where she went when she left?"

Constantino shook his head.

"No idea, I assumed she went back to England. Don't think it was anything to do with David, her leaving, but I don't really know. She never even came to say goodbye. She was quite a regular in here, and stayed through the winter as well. But I didn't even know she'd left till one of the boys here told me, and David never mentioned she'd gone."

"Hmm ... that was a bit odd wasn't it, given that they, Alexander and this Palmer woman, seemed to be good late night drinking friends in here? But Alexander stayed in Lindos after she left around two months ago?"

Constantino shrugged his shoulders as he replied, "Yep, it was a bit, but people come and go here working, sometimes for two, three, or even four or more years and then just decide they've had enough and want to move on. I assumed that's what Alice did. And it's not as though she was one of the youngsters who come to work here for just a summer or two. She was older, mid to late thirties I think. I guess after a few years she'd just had enough and just decided to leave on the spur of the moment, which is why she never said goodbye I suppose. All a bit sudden, or maybe there was something back in England she had to get back to, family issue or something like that."

While the Inspector scratched the back of his head briefly his Sergeant asked, "But you never saw Alexander and her have any sort of an argument?"

"No, on the contrary, they seemed very close, if you know what I mean."

Hearing that remark by Jack Constantino one of the young barmen, Dimitris, looked up again from further along the bar and grinned broadly in agreement.

The two police men knew exactly what Constantino meant.

"Oh, I see," Papadoulis nodded slightly again before asking, "What about David Alexander generally though? Any problems, arguments that you saw or heard about in the village. Anyone he fell out with, locals or Brit ex-pats for instance over the two summers?"

"No, not in here, and not that I heard about in the village. He's just a regular, ok guy."

From that reply Papadoulis realised that Constantino didn't know that Alexander had left the village. He probed a little to see if he knew anything more about Alexander and Alice Palmer's relationship.

"Did he stay here through last winter as well, like you said Alice Palmer did? Did he stay with her?"

"No, I don't think so, Inspector. I don't live in the village and so am not in Lindos that much during the winter when almost everything is closed up, just the odd days when there is something to do in the bar, maintenance and any alterations. So,-"

"He didn't," the other young barman, Cris, interrupted.

As Papadoulis looked along the bar at him he added, "He left. Went back to England I heard and came back sometime early March this year I think, just before the season started in mid-April. I also heard he'd been to Athens, but I don't know if that was on his way back to England at the end of last summer or on his way back here in March."

"How did you hear that? Why did he go to Athens? Did you hear why?" Georgiou rattled off the questions.

"No idea, maybe just availability of flights. Most of the airlines stop direct flights from England to Rhodes towards the end of October and then don't start them again until early to mid-April. It was just something I heard around the village in passing. Just gossip I suppose, about people who stay here for whole summers. Just something I heard. Don't know if it's true of course."

As Cris finished speaking the Sergeant took out his small notebook and wrote 'David Alexander Athens, October - November 2019/March 2020?"

While he did that Papadoulis asked, "Is he much of a drinker, Alexander, enough to sometimes get angry perhaps?"

The tense of his question betrayed to his Sergeant that he still wasn't letting Constantino know that David Alexander had left Lindos.

"No, not really. A few bottles of Mythos, three or four at the most, and I never saw him angry. As I said before, never even saw him having an argument with anyone in here, nor heard he'd had any trouble in the village. We usually do hear if anything like that happens, village gossip you know."

"Ok, thanks, that's helpful. We'll let you get on preparing for your evening customers," Papadoulis said as he indicated to Georgiou they should leave.

"Ok, Inspector, no problem. If David comes in later I'll tell him you are looking to speak to him."

Papadoulis half turned towards him and hesitantly replied.

"Yes, erm ... yes, thanks."

As they walked down the three small steps outside the bar into the alley the Inspector told his Sergeant, "Get one of the local officers at the station to check with the airlines for passenger lists from Rhodes to Athens in October and November last year and from Athens to Rhodes this March, and whether there were any direct flights from Rhodes to England and back during those months. Maybe the barman is right and there were no direct flights, but if that's not the case why was David Alexander going back to England via Athens? Who, or what, was he going to meet or see there?"

As he finished saying that his phone pinged. When he glanced briefly at the screen there was simply one word in capital letters, "LATER???"

He didn't need to look at the sender, He knew who it was.

9

Sophia who?

As soon as Papadoulis and his Sergeant got back to their small office in Lindos Police Station he took out his phone, stared at the screen for a few seconds trying to decide how to reply. He knew he wanted to go to Lardos again, to Sally Hardcastle, and had been tussling with that dilemma in his head, over the wisdom of it or not, as the two policemen walked through the village and back to the station. Besides the fact that the thought of her was clearly messing with his head, and his marriage, there was the case and its developments to consider. He knew he should be totally focussed on that, but he just couldn't get the thought of spending another couple of hours in her bed out of his head. Eventually he sent her a simple one word message in reply, "Possibly."

While Papadoulis was wrestling with his conscience and his sexual urges Georgiou was adding the relevant information they'd obtained from their latest interview with Jack Constantino to the Incident Board. When he finally got his mind focused fully back on the case he checked his computer screen and then looked across at Georgiou, telling him, "And you can add under her name 'no fingerprints match or DNA match on Greek data bases'. There's a couple of emails confirming that, one from Costas on the DNA and one from Athens on the fingerprints. No record of our mysterious Sophia on either of them."

"So, we know she doesn't have a criminal record then, at least not in Greece," Georgiou commented as he briefly turned around from the board having finished writing.

The Inspector got up from his desk and walked over to join him in front of the board, once more rubbing his chin with the fingers and palm of his right hand. It was a small mannerism he'd developed, a habit, when confronted with a puzzle or in this case a murder mystery. It helped him think and go over and over what they knew about the case and its victim, plus any suspects. His predecessor, his former boss Inspector Dimitris Karagoulis, used to do his thinking aloud whilst constantly walking back and forth across the office he happened to be in, whether in the small office of the Lindos Police Station or the much larger one at the Rhodes Town Station. Papadoulis noticed that quite soon after he started working with him. He reckoned all good detectives had their little quirks, little thought process mannerisms, and his was his hand and rubbing his chin. He couldn't recall how or when it started; maybe it was when he was working with Karagoulis. All he knew though was that the rubbing somehow helped his brain and thoughts when it came to cases. He did it almost automatically now.

Eventually the Inspector stopped rubbing his chin and did something else that he always did on cases - go over and over what was in front of them on the Incident Board, going through everything they knew so far about the case, what was in front of them.

He pointed to his name and said, "So, what exactly do we know about this guy David Alexander?"

It was a rhetorical question. Georgiou knew the process. He'd seen it plenty of times now, his Inspector's thought process, and he knew precisely how to go along with it.

"Well, we've heard from a few different people that he's been staying in Lindos for the past two summers. Jack Constantino and the owner of the Gatto Bianco restaurant told us that, plus the Albanian guy, Ledi, who lives in the flat next door with his girlfriend." Georgiou began their little process. "And they all seemed to think he is a writer," he added.

Papadoulis picked up the marker pen and pointed to the words 'Antika Bar, Ledi and Gloria – neighbours' saying, "This guy, Ledi, told me he never actually saw Alexander going into his flat with Sophia, but said he did remember her and Alexander talking to each other in the Antika bar where he works, introducing themselves to each other, towards the end of the season last year. He said, as Alexander was his next door neighbour and regularly came into the bar for a drink in the evening he remembered that evening in particular because he usually drank alone. He even told his girlfriend Gloria about Alexander having a drink with the woman. It was her, Gloria's night off, so she never saw it apparently."

He stopped for a moment, clicked the top off the marker pen and wrote under 'Antika' 'Alexander regular, usually drank alone', then continued.

"Ledi said he thought the woman was, Sophia, although at first he told me he thought he heard her name as Sophie. Anyway, the barman thought she was a tourist, from Athens. He thought he recalled her telling him that after he asked when she first came to the bar that night. He was sure she wasn't Greek though, thought she was Russian, or at least from some part of Eastern Europe. Alexander started talking to her at the bar when she asked Ledi what was a good cocktail, what he recommended. That's when he was sure he overheard Alexander tell her he thought they'd met before. But the barman just thought that was some rather elaborate chat up line. So,-"

"Yes, that's odd. I'd almost forgotten about that," Georgiou interrupted his Inspector's growing dialogue of his lengthening thought process, which drew a swift sideways glare in his direction from Papadoulis who now began to rub his chin again in the interval.

Georgiou wrongly took that as an indication he could continue what he was saying and started to add, "But why would Alexander-"

That drew another glare from his Inspector and the Sergeant stopped dead with what he was saying.

"Why would he not remember her name, Sergeant? Is that what you were going to say?"

Georgiou nodded in silence at his Inspector finishing his sentence, knowing better than to try and answer that rhetorical question. The Inspector's facial expression told him he was definitely not being invited to, before he added, "Perhaps he simply didn't remember. Sometimes the obvious explanations are just that, obvious."

Papadoulis turned his head back towards the board, stood staring at it for a few seconds and then continued, repeating some of what they'd just gone over.

"So, the barman initially thought he heard her say Sophie, but he never heard either of them use her last name."

He rubbed his chin again a couple of times before adding in a lower quizzical tone of voice, "So, Sergeant we still don't know the full name of our victim, or where she was staying. Nor do we know why our chief suspect suddenly up and left the village immediately after the murder."

"Obviously unless he's our murderer, sir."

The Inspector once again cast a glance sideways at his Sergeant, this time with a frown across his face as a result of the puzzle before them. He shook his head slightly before instructing his Sergeant, "Right, let's get a couple of officers asking some more of the bar owners in the village and see if anyone knows anything more why he left, and so suddenly? See any of them knows if he had any legitimate reason? Plus get an officer out to the Lindos Memories and Acquagrand hotels just outside the village to check if they have had a woman named Sophia staying there recently?"

The Sergeant initially simply responded with, "Ok, sir," but he wasn't about to leave it at that. By now he was more convinced than ever that David Alexander was the killer and he repeated his previous supposition.

"But doesn't it seem obvious, sir. Alexander left because he's our killer? He was the only person we know was seen with the victim on the night she was killed, having dinner with her earlier, and then he left immediately before or just after the body was found. Doesn't that seem suspicious, sir? That can't just be a coincidence can it?"

Papadoulis rubbed his chin yet again and stared at the board in silence for a few moments realising it was difficult to argue with his Sergeant when they had identified no other suspect as yet.

"Ok, yes it does appear obvious, Sergeant. And he is our only lead at the moment. No one else seems to have been seen with our victim and we don't even know at this point where she was staying or for how long. Perhaps Alexander was seen with her there, where she was staying? So, we need to find that out first, as if he was seen with her there it would tie him into her even more. Plus, hopefully we might get more background on him and his stay here from what the officers can pick up from more of the bar owners. He's been here for two summers so some of them must know more about the mysterious Mr. Alexander."

"And there's London, sir," Georgiou added. "Perhaps they'll come back with more on him, if there is anything on their police records of course."

The Inspector had walked across to sit at his desk and was looking a bit detached, prompting Georgiou to repeat, "Sir … perhaps London will have something on him"

"What? Oh yes, possibly. Let's see."

For some reason though Papadoulis still wasn't entirely convinced that David Alexander was their killer. He continued to stare across at the Incident Board from his desk as he shook his head briefly and added, "It's just all a bit too obvious though. What's the motive? We have no idea at the moment about that. Perhaps, that guy Ledi in the Antika Bar can give us some clue?"

He rubbed his chin once again as he continued, "What if they were back in his bar the night of the murder and had some sort of argument?"

He was clearly grasping at straws in frustration, but the Sergeant wasn't going along with his Inspector's speculation.

"Maybe, but surely he would have told us if that was the case, sir? He'd hardly forget that happening in his bar when we were asking him about one of the people concerned being murdered, would he?"

Papadoulis let out a long sigh in exasperation. He knew his Sergeant was right.

"That's true. Of course he would have remembered something like that and told us. So, if not that, not an argument, what's the motive for Alexander to kill her?"

Papadoulis got up and walked over to the board again and stood staring at it for a long silent minute before turning back to face Georgiou.

"And Costas said it was definitely a professional, a professional killer."

He shook his head again slightly, displaying his disbelief and lack of conviction before half turning to point at the name

David Alexander on the board and adding, "But this guy Alexander seems anything but a professional hitman, a professional killer. All we've heard in the village is that he was a writer, or at least claimed to be writing a novel, plus some rumours that before that he worked at a university in England. A lecturer, doesn't seem even to be much of a likely cover for a professional killer does it?"

He was shaking his head again slowly, before saying nothing more for a few seconds, then he puffed out his cheeks and said, "So, what if what seems so obvious isn't, Sergeant?"

Georgiou frowned but didn't answer.

The Inspector glanced back at the board once more and let out a small sigh, yet again betraying his exasperation, before continuing.

"Right, we need to find out as much as we can on Alexander as our prime suspect, but we need a motive, or at least have some idea what happened between the two of them that night in the alley where her body was found."

He stopped halfway back across the office, turned around to stare at the board again.

"No idea at the moment how we are likely to find out that, but in the meantime we need to continue to challenge what seems obvious, that Alexander is our killer."

Papadoulis' meandering exasperation was interrupted by a local officer from the Lindos Station entering the office to inform them that he'd identified that David Alexander was on an Aegean Airlines Passenger Manifest for a flight from Rhodes to Athens on the 25th of October last year and was also on one for a flight from Athens to Rhodes on the 2nd of March earlier this year. However, he added that there was no trace of him on any flights from Rhodes airport in the past week.

"So, if he's left the island, sir, he must have gone on one of the ferries from Rhodes Town," he added. "But he could have just turned up and bought a ticket just before the ferry left for one of those, so there's no passenger list."

While Georgiou went over to add all that information to the Incident Board the Inspector asked the local officer, "When do the direct flights to the U.K. from Rhodes stop for the winter?"

"End of October, sir, the last one is usually the 31st, and then they start again around about the 1st of April."

"Right, thanks, Officer, good work," Papadoulis told him. As he left the office the Inspector went over to stand next to Georgiou by the board. Pointing to what his Sergeant had just written he said, "So, Sergeant, if there were direct flights to the U.K. from Rhodes up until the 31st of October last year why did Alexander go back there via Athens? Why was he on a flight from Rhodes to Athens on the 25th? What was so interesting for him in Athens? I think we can safely assume it wasn't a tourist visit. And I'm sure two flights to London, via Athens, wouldn't have been cheaper than one direct."

"Maybe that's where the woman Jack Constantino told us Alexander spent a lot of last summer with, Alice Palmer, was living then?"

"Couldn't have been her," Papadoulis said as with a frown across his face he glanced sideways at his Sergeant. "She stayed here all last winter. Constantino told us that. So, who was it? What did he want in Athens? We can assume he came through Athens on his way back here at the start of this March simply because there were no direct flights from the U.K. at that time, but there were some still going direct to London the previous October."

The Inspector took the marker pen out of Georgiou's hand and wrote on the board, 'Why Athens 25 October? Who?'

He rubbed his chin once again in silence for a couple of minutes while staring at the board before he eventually said enthusiastically, "What if it was our victim who he was going to see in Athens, the mysterious Sophia? That Antika barman, Ledi, said he thought he heard Alexander saying to her last October that he thought he knew her, and that they ended up drinking together that night in the bar? And we know from the owner of the Gatto Bianco restaurant that they had dinner together in there the night she was killed."

He started agitatedly pacing back and forth across the office, in a way reminiscent of his previous boss, Inspector Dimitris Karagoulis.

"So, what if he went to Athens on his way back to the U.K. last October to see our victim, Sophia, and that was where she lived?"

Georgiou took a deep breath before he responded.

"That's a possibility, sir, but we don't even know her full name, so we can hardly check on everyone called Sophia in Athens and see if any of them are missing. It's quite a popular name."

Papadoulis spun around to glare at him.

"No, Sergeant, obviously we can't. But we can get an officer checking with Athens for any missing persons reported in the past few days, anyone called Sophia. Get an officer on it now."

Georgiou wasn't convinced by his Inspector's logic, but he simply said, "Ok," and went out to the front desk to get that sorted. Just as he reached it though his mobile phone rang.

"Found where she was staying, sir, the Acquagrand. We've sealed off the room and there's a forensics team on their way from Rhodes. According to the receptionist she checked in with a British Passport as Sophia Orlova."

"Ok, I'll be out to you with the Inspector straightaway," Georgiou told the local Lindos officer and went straight back to the office to tell the Inspector.

Around fifteen minutes later he arrived with Papadoulis at the Reception of the Acquagrand hotel just under a mile from the village. The hotel was quite expensive, large and relatively new. It was situated in a beautiful picturesque bay at the end of a road leading down from the main Lindos to Pefkos road. The bay was known by locals as Navarone Bay as some scenes from the 1961 war movie 'The Guns of Navarone' were shot there.

The same officer took them straight to Sophia Orlova's room. It was large, with a king-size bed as well as a good sized modern looking couch and a light wood coffee table. There were floor to ceiling glass sliding doors at the far end leading onto an equally large patio facing out to the bay with its sparkling clear blue water. It clearly wasn't a cheap room.

"What did the receptionist tell you about her?" the Inspector asked the officer.

"Not much more than I told the Sergeant on the phone, sir. She arrived on Sunday and was booked in for three nights, although she told the receptionist when she checked in that she might stay a bit longer if they had rooms. He said he told her that would be ok as the hotel wasn't full. Apart from that the reception staff said they never really saw her. As I told the Sergeant on the phone, she had a British Passport, which the receptionist took the details of for registration when she checked in, although he did say she didn't have a British accent. He thought she sounded like she was from Eastern Europe or possibly Russia."

"That fits with what the Antika barman told us, and the Gatto Bianco owner," Georgiou commented.

"I got the Hotel Manager to open the room safe in the wardrobe for us, but there was only her passport and some euros in there, two hundred and eighty," the officer added.

"No sign of her phone?" Papadoulis asked.

"No, sir, just her laptop on the desk."

He pointed towards a desk against one wall a couple of yards away from the end of the bed.

"Ok, get it bagged up and get some of the tech guys back at Rhodes Town working on it tonight. Let's see if there's anything interesting on it."

Papadoulis quickly scanned the room before him and added, "The hotel must have a permanent home address for her, in the U.K. presumably? She would have had to fill that in on the registration form when she checked in."

"No, sir, I mean yes she had to provide a permanent address when she checked in. But when I checked with the Manager just after we found she'd been staying here he looked in their records and the permanent address she provided was in Athens, in Glyfada. So, no, I meant not the U.K., sir."

The Inspector stopped looking around the room and immediately looked across at his Sergeant saying, "Athens. She was living there, and in Glyfada, very nice, and not cheap. So, perhaps that was why Alexander went back to the U.K. via there at the end of last October, Georgiou. To see her."

"Seems likely," the Sergeant agreed. "And that means it seems they knew each other a lot better than we thought."

"We did a quick check online of her address in Glyfada while we waited for you to get here, sir. It's in a very smart area, in a very expensive looking apartment block," the officer added.

"Interesting. Get on to Athens, Georgiou, and tell them to get a forensic team checking out her apartment. Let's see what they can turn up from there about her. So, it seems she was pretty well off, this Sophia Orlova. See what you can turn up in a financial check on her, bank account, credit cards and the rest. Maybe the laptop will tell us what she did for a living, and how she came to be well off enough to live in Glyfada and stay in the Acquagrand. Perhaps, even how she came to meet David Alexander, who claimed to be a writer. That doesn't-"

"The barman in Antika told you he overheard Alexander say to her that he thought he recognised her when they were both in his bar towards the end of the season last year, in October wasn't it?"

Georgiou's interruption of his Inspector wasn't welcomed and he snapped back at him. "Yes, he did, but he never heard where Alexander thought he recognised her from."

"Alexander did claim to be a writer, or at least was trying to write a novel in Lindos, but Jack Constantino said one of his barmen heard he used to work at a university in England, sir. So, maybe that's how they met, perhaps even at an academic conference?"

Papadoulis was slowly shaking his head slightly.

"No, I can't see that being how they met, Sergeant. Perhaps her laptop will tell us more on that, but from what I know of Glyfada, and property there, and from what the officer has just told us about the apartment block she lived in there, I can't see her being an academic. Universities in Greece don't pay that well, not that sort of money. And there's also the high heeled shoes she was wearing the night she was killed. Costas reckoned they were very expensive, or rather, his female assistant did. But anyway, if that's right they didn't seem the sort of shoes an academic could afford, a Greek, Russian or a British one."

As he finished his phone pinged again. Just like before he knew who the message would be from. He was right, and her message suggested she was growing impatient.

"You coming or not???? Even if you are stressed with the case you know I can make you feel better."

It was coming up to eight-thirty. He knew that if he was going to see her in Lardos he would have to go now or not at all that evening, or else it would be far too late, even if he could put Sally off for another hour or so. Anyway, she knew he'd come. He always did when she wanted to see him. He was struggling with trying to reconcile love and infidelity. He told himself he loved his wife, but if that was the case why was he engaging in infidelity with Sally? He knew he didn't love her. He was sure of that. He loved his wife. He kept telling himself that repeatedly. But he enjoyed being with Sally, enjoyed the sex and the excitement. So, he knew he'd go and see her that evening, enjoy being with her, and then the guilt would descend on him again like an intense dark Lindos storm cloud as he drove back to Rhodes later. His personal life was spiralling into uncontrollable chaos and confusion, spilling over into, and invading, his work life. That wasn't the way his professional life as a police officer was meant to be. It wasn't the way he always tried to ensure he managed his work as a police officer. But deep down he knew he'd eventually give in to the temptation and the excitement and would go and see her that evening.

"Be with you in 45 minutes," he tapped out on his phone and hit 'Send'.

As he looked up from it his Sergeant and the local officer were checking the wardrobe as well as the draws of the desk and the bedside tables

"Nothing, sir. Nothing in any of the draws or the wardrobe," Georgiou started to tell him. "Looks like the only way we are going to find out more about her are if there is anything interesting on the laptop, or anything on our Greek or U.K. police records now we have her full name."

"Yes, ok, let's leave the rest of the room to the forensic team for now. You get a lift back to Rhodes with the officer here while he delivers the laptop to the tech boys. I'll see if the Hotel Manager and the receptionist can tell us any more about Sophia Orlova while I hang on for the forensic team to arrive. They shouldn't be much longer."

10

Lardos again

Papadoulis was right. The Forensic team from Rhodes arrived ten minutes after Georgiou left with the local officer and the laptop. During those ten minutes he spoke to the Hotel Manager briefly, as well as the receptionist, but they couldn't add anything to what he already knew about Sophia Orlova. What he knew was still actually very little, except that she had a British passport, but not a British accent, and was very dead.

When Sally Hardcastle opened the door to her flat in her long white shirt dress and flip flops thirty minutes or so later he asked straight away, "How did you know I needed to feel better?"

She was a little taken aback by his somewhat unusual greeting, even though it wasn't said in an aggressive way, more out of curiosity.

"Oh, good to see you too, Yiannis," she replied sarcastically as she turned to head towards the small kitchenette area in one corner of what could be described as the lounge. On her way she picked up her almost empty wine glass from the coffee table and added, "Do you want some wine?"

He attempted to calm her uneasiness over his abrupt greeting by trying to explain, asking in a much softer way, "I just wondered, that's all. But yes, only a small glass though, got to drive back to Rhodes later."

She glanced back at him over her shoulder as a small smile crept across her lips. She always knew exactly how to unbalance him, throw him off guard. Destabilise him, might be too strong, but it always gave her the upper hand with him. It had become almost too easy. Initially she'd played it, played him, as a sort of a game, but it had become so easy she almost wasn't sure how much she enjoyed it now. This time she'd done it straightaway, as soon as he arrived. Usually she'd wait for half-an-hour or so, maybe even longer if she decided to do it after they'd had sex. She knew he would be aiming not to stay long though this evening, so she'd started her game earlier, immediately. She wanted to ensure she was in full control of the next couple of hours that he aimed to be with her. That was the way she liked it to be, not just with him, but with any man. And in any case, she was determined on this particular evening to get him to stay with her longer. Not long term, not to move in or live together. That wasn't part of Sally Hardcastle's character or plans at all. She just wanted him to stay all night and not leave until after breakfast. She wanted to see just how he would cope with that, cope with even the suggestion of it, which she certainly wouldn't make until after they'd had sex. It was a sort of a test which she'd concocted in her head for him. There wasn't even any real point to it. No grand long term plan about them being together as such. She decided to do it just because she knew she could, and she knew that to some extent she would still enjoy doing it. That was Sally Hardcastle. That was what she did, played games with people and their lives. And more than anything the best thing about this particular game for her was that it would put him on the spot having to explain to his wife just where he'd been all night. That she would enjoy a lot.

All that, her game playing with him, would come later, after they'd had sex. Bringing any of that up now, immediately after he arrived, that he should stay the night, would only put him on edge. It might simply lead to a disagreement between them, possibly even an argument, resulting in no sex, which was the last thing she wanted to happen. Her game playing and his test could wait until later, until after she got what she mainly wanted, the sex. In her mind, the rest of it was like a dessert after the main course. That could wait.

"I just assumed you'd be stressed that's all, with the case I mean, if it was proving difficult," she started to answer his question as she handed him his wine as he sat on the sofa.

"Oh, well yes, but you know I can't talk about that," he replied as she sat down next to him.

He was starting to feel a bit more relaxed after having got a little uptight over her initial question.

However, she didn't want him too relaxed just yet. She couldn't resist deliberately adding with something of a fake sympathetic smile as she simultaneously tenderly placed her right hand on his thigh just above his knee and gave it a little squeeze, "As well as over your marriage, of course, stressed I mean."

That sort of comment from her only contributed to his stress, and his guilt. He took a gulp of the wine and tried to dismiss it.

"I can't, don't want to, talk about that either, Sally. You know that too. We've talked about it in the past."

"Only briefly, we talked about it very briefly," she told him, accompanied by another squeeze of his thigh.

She didn't actually want to talk about it. That wasn't the purpose or aim of her comment about his stress and his marriage. She certainly didn't want to hear what she thought were just the latest day-in, day-out, dreary details of his marriage. She knew enough of their background. He'd told her all that one night in her bed when they first met back in August 2016, and started their affair the first time. She knew he'd met his wife, Dimitra when they were both training at the Hellenic Police Officers School and like him she was from Rhodes Town. They had two teenage children and been married for nineteen years. She gave up her career in the police service when she became pregnant with their first child and now she had a part-time job in an office in Rhodes Town dealing in, and marketing, computer software. For many years before that following the birth of their first child she devoted her life to Yiannis and the two children. Sally Hardcastle had heard all that from him before.

On another evening, during some more talk in her bed, he'd told her his wife's focus was very much on her family, He said that having trained as a police officer she fully understood the pressures and demands of the job on his time, particularly after he was promoted to Inspector. However, that seemed to be increasingly less so. She'd become increasingly less understanding of the demands of his job and how it affected their family life. At least, that was the way he saw it, how it seemed to him. As a result things were not so good between him and Dimitra.

Having said he didn't want to talk about it now though, his marriage, the only thing that Sally could get out of him this evening about it was that he was feeling increasingly guilty over what they were doing again. He knew he should stop, but he couldn't.

Now he was more confused than ever. Why was she asking about his marriage now? She'd always made such a point of telling him a number of times before what was between them was, "just fun". She was always very firm, adamant, about that. That was the way Sally Hardcastle was. She clearly liked, very much enjoyed, the 'lightness' of what they were doing, what she did generally with any men now in her life.

Because of what she'd just said to him about his marriage and stress though, a small part of him started to wonder if that had changed in some way. Was this beginning to be no longer "just fun" for her? And what would that mean for his marriage? That would definitely add to his stress. And what did he want anyway? Was he thinking too that he wanted this to be more than "just fun", or at least starting to think that way?

She could see from the confused look on his face that she'd achieved precisely what she'd set out to do, disorientate and unbalance him. There was no way she wanted anything more out of their relationship, if that's what it was, than she had right now. Maybe their affair was a better way of describing it. She just wanted to plant a little seed of doubt in his mind over that, ensuring that he wasn't too comfortable with what they had. That was what she always did with men, had done in the past, and very well. She was an expert at it. Although she would never acknowledge it, to some extent it was her self-defence mechanism when it came to men and relationships, or affairs, with them. It was a sort of reverse psychology, self-inflicted or imposed of course. Bizarrely, by asking certain questions about his marriage, and the stress of their affair on it and him, she was deliberately casting doubt in his mind about what they were doing, their affair, and thereby constructing her own self-defence mechanism in order to protect herself and prevent any chance of her changing her view of it from "just fun" to something more serious. Something she was convinced she never wanted. The doubt and guilt she planted in his mind with her 'stress over his marriage' question, along with the squeeze of his thigh, was designed not to sympathetically hear and listen to him recounting the detail of that stress and his marriage, but to simply subtlety exacerbate his guilt, prevent him wanting more with her, something more permanent. Thereby to simultaneously protect her from falling into what she regarded as that emotional abyss.

So, "just fun" was the phrase she kept prominently at the front of her brain, not just that evening, and not just with him, but at all times with men. "Just fun, Yiannis. I'm perfectly happy the way it is," she told him very firmly and dispassionately quite a few times on previous evenings after they'd had sex again in her bed during their previous affair.

He wasn't going to talk about the stress in his marriage on this particular evening though. And neither was she. After all, that wasn't the reason why she sent him those text messages earlier asking was he coming over, and it definitely wasn't the reason he did, even if it was somewhat later than she wanted. She'd succeeded in what she initially aimed to do, plant the seeds of doubt and guilt in his head with her stress and his marriage question, and now it was time to move on to the main course of the evening, before her bombshell dessert later. She stood up from the sofa, reached down and took his hand and softly told him, "Let's go to bed."

Guilt or no guilt, she knew he couldn't resist. And he didn't. As soon as they made it into the bedroom she pushed him down on his back onto her double bed and then stood over him while she peeled her long white shirt dress over her head to reveal her completely naked body, perfectly naturally bronzed from the long Rhodes summer sun days. As he kicked off his shoes she reached down to unbutton his shirt, pull it off him and then unfasten his trousers to remove them. She softly kissed his naked flat stomach and then removed his boxer shorts. He lay motionless, allowing her to do exactly as she wanted until finally she climbed astride him. There was an electric silent atmosphere as neither of them spoke a word. She gazed down at him for a long ten seconds or so as she sat on top of him with her knees bent either side of his lower body. It was as though she was building up her energy, her desire, as she slowly felt him precisely where she wanted him. She held him motionless there for a long minute, her deep brown eyes gazing down, piercing into his face as she sat above him. She slowly raised her left hand and pushed a few loose strands of her hair off her face, accompanied by a small pleasant smile creeping across her lips. Another ten seconds or so passed while she held him in the same motionless position before he tried to instigate a rocking motion. She leaned down and placed the palm of her right hand on his chest preventing it and telling him softly, "Wait".

Another smile spread across her moist lips. This was a much more mischievous one, immediately preceded by running her tongue along them slowly.

"I want to see just how much self-control you have for me."

She kissed him gently on the cheek and then sat back up again. She liked to be in control. That excited her. The fact that it was a policeman below her made it even more exciting to be in control, in control of him. Earlier she'd already made sure she controlled his mind, his thought process, what was going through it about his marriage, his guilt and their affair. Now she wanted to control him physically, control his body. She'd played with his mind, now she was going to play with his body. That was what she enjoyed, the play, the dance between their bodies and their minds, or more accurately the dance in her mind and body, and the 'lightness' of it all. She would make him wait a little longer, until she was ready. Even that, the wait, was making her more and more excited by the second, and from what she could feel it certainly wasn't having a bad effect on him.

She raised herself to the full height of her upper body while remaining sitting astride him. He felt her tense up and her body tighten while she stretched her neck backwards slightly at an angle and lifted her head upwards. Her eyes at first rose to look away from his face and up at the white ceiling above them and then closed completely. She was enjoying the moment fully, as though in a trance of complete enjoyment.

He lay motionless, peering up at her body and her taught neck for a good ten seconds. He was waiting for her, just as she'd told him to. He was just about to try and move again, begin to rock back and forth beneath her, when she beat him to it. She exploded above him. Her whole body burst into a furious rampant energetic motion. She was so forceful in what she was doing, what she wanted to do, that he was again rendered motionless. He couldn't move. She knew exactly what she wanted. She'd built up to the moment by making him, as well as herself, wait until she was completely ready to get maximum enjoyment out of what she was about to do. For her the delay and build up, the control, was part of the enjoyment and fulfilment. Now she was going to have precisely what she wanted, had aimed for, him, and not just the once that evening.

Her fulfilment didn't last very long at all during that initial time when she decided to get to the final part. However, just when he thought that might be it, and he could think about leaving to go back to Rhodes Town with his guilt to his wife, she aroused him and climbed on him again. That was the second time that evening, and then there was a third. She was, indeed, rampant, and demanding.

When he'd eventually got to her place in Lardos earlier he'd been stressed and weary from the case, as well as over the issue of his marriage. Now he was completely shattered.

She knew that, was well aware of it. What they'd just done was exactly what she'd planned, what she wanted to do that evening, exhaust him and add to his weariness. She'd succeeded. He dozed off easily, drowsy, half conscious, half sleeping, for what seemed to him like a few minutes, but was more than an hour. She lay beside him and watched him while not remotely overcome by sleepiness herself.

It was just gone eleven-thirty when he sat up with a start and peered through his blurred eyes at the alarm clock on her bedside table.

"I should-" he began to say.

But she didn't let him finish. Instead she reached up and placed her left hand on his cheek and drew him back down and into her kissing him firmly on the lips. As she tried to roll over on top of him again, clearly intent on continuing what they'd done earlier, he stopped her and told her, "No, no, Sally. I really do have to go. It's late."

It was almost an hour's drive to Rhodes Town and his home. It would be almost one by the time he got into bed alongside his wife, Dimitra. His exertions over the last couple of hours, well an hour of them anyway, as well as the late night and another early morning the next day at Lindos Police Station after another drive of forty-five minutes would do nothing to alleviate his weariness. And that was without the difficulties of the case adding to it.

He needed to leave her now, but in her own particular unpredictable way Sally Hardcastle surprised him yet again.

"Stay," she started to tell him softly, but he misunderstood what she meant.

"I can't. It's late and it'll be nearly one by the time I get home."

She ignored what he said and once more placed her left hand on his cheek, kissed him tenderly, and then stared straight into his face with her piercing deep brown eyes before adding softly yet again, "So, stay here, stay the night. Don't you want to wake up with me for once?"

He didn't answer. He just got up from the bed and began to pull on his boxers and trousers with his back to her while she remained laying on the bed naked. Consequently, she couldn't see the frown across his face signalling his confusion. What was she up to? She'd never suggested that he stay before, never seemed remotely interested in that happening. So, why now? Was her whole attitude to what they were doing, her feelings for him, changing into something more serious? Up to now she always appeared to be not really too bothered about any of that. That was always the impression she gave and expressed over what she wanted between them. So why suggest his now, something that would certainly move things on between them. He always knew she just enjoyed the sex. She'd told him many times that was all she wanted, the 'lightness' of what they had. It was only about her enjoying the sex. Why would she want the 'weight' of more now, and did she really, even them together permanently and the 'weight' of fidelity? Surely not? He couldn't believe she really wanted that. He was sure he didn't, or at least thought he didn't until that moment when she'd said what she did and confused him.

While he buttoned up his shirt, still with his back to her, he kept quickly going over and over in his mind that phrase he'd heard from her many times.

"I just want to have sex with you, Yiannis, that's all, nothing more, just some fun," was what she was fond of telling him.

Even though he was a detective he hadn't figured out that there was another more sinister part to her agenda within what she'd just said to him about staying the night. She knew very well that if he stayed with her overnight it would cause even more problems between him and his wife Dimitra, even more than there was already. That was not even because Sally thought it would lead to him leaving his wife. That wasn't what she wanted at all. She just couldn't resist it, suggesting he stay the night, simply because she knew it would create problems and she enjoyed doing that in his and his wife's life. Not as much as the actual sex with him of course, but it was just another enjoyable game she liked to play. That was the way Sally Hardcastle was.

He decided the best thing was to ignore her suggestion that he stay. Instead, as he sat on the edge of the bed to put on his socks and shoes he changed the subject, thinking it best maybe to confuse her. For no reason at all he asked, "Do you have many friends on the island?"

She sat up and now it was her face that wore the confused frown.

"What? Friends?" Why you asking that?"

"No reason. I just wondered. I never see you out with anyone in Lindos that's all."

"But you never see me out at all in Lindos, Yiannis. Why would you? Except at work in the café."

She was frowning straight at him as he stood up above her still lying naked on the bed. She rubbed the index finger of her right hand down her chest and over her stomach as she tried one more time, telling him enticingly as she gazed up into his eyes, "You sure you won't stay?"

Exercising immense self-control, he ignored her invitation yet again.

"So, what about there then? No friends at work to go out with?"

"No, not really. Why you so interested?"

He wasn't actually. He was just trying to get her off the subject of him staying over by making small talk while he finished dressing. Again he ignored her question.

"Is that because you rub them up the wrong way? You can come across as aggressive sometimes you know?"

That at least stirred her into getting up off the bed and pulling on a nearby t-shirt and her pants while she let out a small chuckle. She walked around to the side of the bed where he was standing, smiled slightly and then told him, again in a soft seductive tone as she once more looked straight into his eyes, "But I thought you liked that, Inspector, my aggression? It certainly seemed like you do."

"I ... err ..."

He was desperately trying to ensure his resolve to leave didn't weaken as she pushed her body close to his.

She didn't let him finish, even if he had known just what his reply to that would have been. He didn't.

Her tone changed and the softness in her voice gave way to a harder, firmer one.

"Look, Yiannis, I know some of the people at work think I'm awkward. I realised that a while ago. I suppose they look upon me as different, someone with a different attitude. Ok, maybe just an attitude. I guess you do too, and in a way I think that's actually why you like me."

She stopped and fixed another stare at him with those piercing deep brown eyes, waiting to see if he would respond.

When he didn't she let out another slight laugh and added with an edge of disdain in her voice, "So, yes I'm sure the people at work look upon me, down on me, as different, which is funny really because I look down on them as all the same."

An interesting comment, he thought. But this wasn't really the direction he intended the conversation to go when he made that casual comment asking if she had any friends on Rhodes. It was just meant to be small talk as he dressed while he laid the ground for him to leave. It didn't work out quite as he wanted, and she wasn't letting him go that easily.

She locked the fingers of both her hands around the back of his neck and kissed him passionately. Her warm naked body pressed firmly against him through her t-shirt, tempting him yet again.

"Are you sure you won't change your mind now, Yiannis, sure you won't stay," she asked seductively as she removed her lips from his but kept her hands locked behind his neck and her body pressed even further into his, if that were possible.

He almost weakened. She almost got exactly what she wanted. This time Sally Hardcastle didn't though. His better judgement won. He resisted, kissed her back much less passionately and left.

At first as he made his way on the dark road out of Lardos he couldn't get thoughts of the sex with her that evening out of his head. He was definitely very weary from it after a long day on the investigation, but he decided it had been better than ever. She'd been rampant, insatiable. In all the times they'd been together he'd never known her like that. Indeed, there was no end to her ability to surprise him. For the first fifteen minutes or so of his drive she remained inhabiting his brain and he seemed unable to remove her. No doubt that would have pleased her, although not what happened after that initial fifteen minutes. Guilt engulfed him.

He loved his wife. He knew that, tried to convince himself of it over and over in his head. So much so that at one point he angrily slammed his right palm into the steering wheel while exclaiming, "Stupid! Stupid!"

The problem was that he also knew that he couldn't resist Sally, or he had to admit, more accurately, what they did together. He couldn't resist the excitement of being with her. In part, it was the excitement of his infidelity, as well as the excitement of the sex they had together, which of course was a major part of his infidelity. He loved his wife he kept telling himself, but what sex they had occasionally wasn't anywhere near the same as what he had with Sally. Not the same level of intensity and excitement, and sometimes he felt there wasn't any excitement at all. There certainly had been for the first few years of their marriage. Perhaps not the same as he had with Sally now. But certainly it was a lot more exciting between him and Dimitra during those first few years than it is now. But then maybe it was just the intoxicating mixture of the sex with Sally and the infidelity it represented that made being with her more exciting than being with his wife, and having sex with her.

His head had been filled with all that, going over and over it in his brain, until he entered Rhodes Town and was nearly home.

How could he possibly reconcile the two, love and infidelity?

11

A rapidly disappearing David Alexander

It was just before one when Papadoulis gently manoeuvred himself into bed beside his wife, being careful not to wake her. He succeeded. When he woke early next morning she was already up and making coffee in the kitchen. His wife may not have been in bed beside him, but his guilt definitely still was. His brain was wracked with it. He thought the way to deal with it, as he had at times in the past, was to throw himself into the investigation. It wasn't quite that easy this time though. First, he had to get through breakfast with Dimitra.

While he took a quick shower and dressed she remained in the kitchen preparing some breakfast for herself. As he finally appeared the already warm bright recently risen Rhodes sun was streaming through the open balcony doors into the lounge and she was sat outside at the small ornate wrought iron white table enjoying her coffee and some scrambled eggs. Seeing her there looking relaxed, contented with her world in the Rhodes early morning sun eating her breakfast did very little to ease his conscience and his guilt.

"Morning, do you want some eggs?" she asked.

He shook his head slightly and momentarily thought about going to kiss her on the forehead. It was not something he usually did and so, thought for some reason it might arouse her suspicion, display some of his guilt. It wasn't quite the same in terms of a display of guilt as, for instance, turning up with flowers for her, but as it was not something he usually did in the morning he thought it might get her wondering. He thought better of it.

"Just coffee and one of those croissants will be fine."

He pointed to some croissants on a plate the kitchen worktop and went over to help himself to one and some coffee, adding, "I should get off to Lindos as soon as possible. There's a lot going on with the case."

He thought that would enable him to leave what might turn out to feel like a difficult situation for him, and get out of her company quickly before she could ask too many awkward questions. He was wrong though. Well, at least not entirely correct.

"You were late last night, even later than usual," she asked as he joined her at the table with his coffee and croissant.

"What? Oh, yeah, pretty late. Not that late though, I think. The case, you know how it is," he replied as he stirred some sugar into his coffee trying to look unconcerned.

"Well, I read for a little while and it must have been gone twelve before I stopped and went off to sleep. So, after-"

"Yes, as I said, the case, it's getting messy," he interrupted. "You know how it is," he repeated, adding, "can be, especially with a murder investigation."

She did, indeed. She used to be a police officer. There was a sharp, edgy, tetchy tone in her voice as she told him, "I do, of course I do, not that you ever say anything about it anymore."

"Say what, about what?"

"About the cases, Yiannis, you used to tell me a lot more. Not the detail, of course. I understand you can't do that, can't go into detail. But at least you used to talk to me about how you were feeling about it, how you were coping with it. Now regularly you come home after I've gone to bed and to sleep. You never wake me, and in the mornings, like now, you can't wait to get away. We never-"

Her voice was breaking up, and her eyes were tearing up slightly, but he simply interrupted her in a raised voice.

"Look it's the bloody case, Dimitra. What can I do? I can't do anything about that can I, other than solve it, which is what I'm bloody trying to do."

All the stress was flooding out of him in his raised voice, but it wasn't just the case. He knew that. He took a gulp of his coffee then got up and left while she slumped forward and sunk her forehead into her hands.

On his drive his black cloud of guilt returned. As he passed the high walls of the open air Amphitheatre Club on the bend of the road and the village of Lindos came into sight below its multitude of white buildings contrasted vividly with the growing darkening early morning sky above. The Aegean Sea was getting angry at the fast approaching gradual fading of another hot Rhodian summer. Within seconds a storm came rolling into the village. The streaks of lightning flashed out over the sea in the bay, displaying the storms anger as it whipped up the waves, while the booming thunder claps felt as if they were directly over the village. It felt like the Greek gods were telling him something through nature, and it wasn't a good thing, not a good sign at all. Like most Lindos storms it didn't last long. He knew it wouldn't and so sat in his car at the top of the village in the car park opposite the Atmosphere Bar for the final few minutes of it until the rain stopped and he could make his way down the slope towards the police station.

He knew he needed to think about what happened between Sally and him the night before, particularly her suggestion about him staying over. He couldn't get that and what it could mean out of his head. Was it going to be a more regular suggestion from her from now on, and how would he handle it if that was the case? Was she getting more serious? Was that what she actually wanted, despite what she constantly told him about it being "just some fun" as far as she was concerned? And what did she mean by her comment about him being stressed over his marriage? Rather than anything to do with the case, it was all those things and questions that had buzzed around in his head on the drive and while waiting in his car for the rain to stop and the storm to pass. After ten minutes or so it did. Obviously the Greek gods couldn't stay mad at him for long.

He'd messaged Georgiou to take his own car to Lindos and he'd meet him at the station. When he entered the small office at just after nine his Sergeant was already there. As he made his way towards the kettle in the corner to make himself a coffee he asked, "Anything back from London on Alexander and Sophia Orlova's finance checks, or anything on record with the U.K. police for either of them?"

"Not yet, sir, and nothing yet on Orlova's Greek finance checks. Sometime today hopefully, but thanks, I'd love a coffee," Georgiou replied sarcastically.

The Inspector looked around at him blankly as he told him, "Oh, what, yes, ok." His face betrayed the fact that he definitely wasn't in the mood for sarcasm, especially from his Sergeant.

After he handed Georgiou his coffee he took his over to stand yet again staring at the Incident Board and all the various bits of information on it. Standing there for a good three or four silent minutes in between periodically sipping his coffee he frowned and shook his head slowly intermittently, displaying his frustration and bewilderment.

Eventually the Sergeant asked, "Anything more from the Acquagrand Hotel Manager after I left last night, sir, anything more about Orlova?"

Papadoulis turned around to face him, once again slightly shaking his head as he replied, "No, nothing more really, from him nor the reception staff. She seems to have kept herself pretty much to herself, and anyway she wasn't actually there at the hotel very long before she was killed. So, the reception staff presumably wouldn't have come into contact with her much. They said she checked in mid-afternoon on Sunday, and according to Christof she was murdered on Monday night. One of the receptionists recalled that she left the hotel that evening around seven-thirty alone. Orlova got her to call a taxi for her into Lindos Main Square. Presumably she was off to meet David Alexander for dinner at Gatto Bianco. If that was the case, I suppose it suggests it was pre-arranged."

He was back to rubbing his chin as he added, "And that they knew each other before. Bears out what that barman, Ledi, told us about them meeting last year towards the end of the season in Antika, and that he thought he overheard Alexander tell her that night in the bar that he knew her from somewhere even before that."

He glanced back at the board before asking, "What about forensics, anything on Orlova's room at the Acquagrand or on her laptop from tech at Rhodes Town?"

"Nothing from the room, sir. They are still working on the laptop from last night, but so far tech said there's nothing really. A few emails, but all pretty mundane."

"What about social media, anything of hers on there?"

"I ran a check on that, but that's the odd thing," the Sergeant started to reply.

"Odd, how?"

"Well, odd in that's there's nothing, sir. Nothing at all for a Sophia Orlova based in Athens. There are a few women of that name on the various social media sites, but none of them look like our victim in their photos. It was the same with David Alexander remember, nothing."

"Odd, Sergeant? You say that, but not everyone is a slave to social media. It tends to be mostly young people doesn't it, teenagers? Our victim is a little older than that, as is Alexander."

Georgiou shrugged his shoulders slightly as he added, "I guess so, but in her case it's almost as if she didn't exist."

That drew a slight chuckle from the Inspector as he commented, "What, if you don't have a social media presence then you don't exist? Interesting deduction, Sergeant."

"Well, it just seems odd to me, sir."

Georgiou decided to leave it and change the subject.

"Anyway, Athens forensic are still checking out her apartment in Glyfada, but nothing from them yet. There's another odd thing though. Athens police told me there was nothing really at her home that suggested what she did for a living to be able to live in such an expensive apartment. There were a few academic books apparently, but as you said last night at her room in the Acquagrand, Greek Universities don't pay the sort of salaries to be able to afford that apartment in Glyfada, even to the most prestigious Professors. I'm waiting for the details of the financial check on her from our specialist officers on that at Rhodes Town station. Hopefully, that will tell us more."

The Inspector turned back to add on the board beneath Sophia Orlova's name 'Glyfada – expensive apartment. Her occupation/income source?'

Once again he stood there gazing at it for a minute or so before saying, "So, we now know who our mysterious victim is, but apart from that we know very little about her, what she did for a living in order to be able to afford to live in such an expensive apartment, or even what she was doing in Lindos this time. We know she was here at the end of last summer, and that she may have been an academic, but certainly wouldn't have earned anything like the sort of money needed to live in that apartment in that part of Athens."

As he finished he pointed to a photograph which Georgiou had stuck on the board earlier beneath her name and had written 'Athens Glyfada residence' beneath it.

"Holiday, sir," the Sergeant commented.

"What? Holiday? What?" Papadoulis commented as he spun around to face him.

"A tourist, sir, maybe she was just a tourist and had decided on a holiday here. She was here towards the end of the season last year, we know that. Perhaps she liked it so much she decided to come back for a few days? Athens is less than an hour flight, so …"

"Hmm …," the Inspector let out a disdainful noise, bordering on a grunt, as he shook his head once, then added, "I doubt that. I very much doubt that. Maybe she did like it enough last year, but it seems a bit too much of a coincidence that she knew Alexander was still here this summer."

"Perhaps they kept in contact," Georgiou suggested. "We know he went to Athens at the end of October last year on his way back to London, so maybe that was it. She knew he was here, came to see him for a few days, and they fell out over something."

"Hmm …," Papadoulis let out another low grunt like sound, then added, "Well, if we'd found her phone we might have a better idea on that."

His frustrating tetchy tiredness was back.

He rubbed his chin again thoughtfully for a few seconds before he said, "Although, if we think the killer took her phone because the murderer didn't want us to discover whatever messages or whatever else might be on it that could lead us to the killer it does suggest the murder was premeditated, as we said before. And it wasn't a spur of the moment, panic action by the killer. He, or possibly she I suppose, was calm enough to find and take the phone. Again, that supports what Christof concluded, that our killer is a professional. But, as I've said before, all that we know about David Alexander so far, which admittedly is not a lot, doesn't in any way suggest he fits that profile at all, a writer, or at least an intended one, and possibly a former university lecturer."

Papadoulis walked back over to his desk and slumped down in his chair, expressing his exasperation at their lack of progress as he did so.

"It's a bloody mystery, Sergeant, that's for sure. We have one prime suspect, Alexander, but his profile, what we know of him, hardly fits that of a professional killer."

"And if he did kill her because they argued over something, that suggests he killed her in some sort of fit of rage on his part, sir. Perhaps he'd had too much to drink and tried it on with her, but she wasn't having any and he got angry, thinking she'd led him on. We don't know what happened last October when he stopped off in Athens on his way back to London. Maybe he misread it, especially if she then turns up here to see him again."

"Plausible I suppose, but again, then why take her phone, and a professional killing by Alexander? Even if there were some messages on it from him to her and her replies, unless they were threatening, which I doubt, why after killing her in a fit of rage would he bother to take her phone, as well as anything pointing to where she was staying, like a hotel key card."

He shook his head again once as he commented, "No, it makes no sense, and I don't even think we can assume it was someone who mugged her and robbed her. Not in Lindos for sure, and if they did they left the euros behind in her pocket. And your proposition that Alexander killed her in a fit of rage after they argued doesn't fit either with it possibly being a pre-planned and premeditated murder, nor with it being by a professional, does it, Sergeant?"

The Inspector slumped back in his chair once again and let out a long sigh as he stared across at the by now filling up Incident Board. They'd hit a wall.

He sighed again before saying in exasperation, "We've got a fair bit of information on that board now, but it's not telling us much really. For instance, how the bloody hell does it all fit together?"

From his experience of working with him on previous cases Georgiou knew Papadoulis wasn't expecting an answer, even if he had one, which he didn't at all. However, before he could say anything, even something that actually wouldn't contribute towards answering his Inspector's question in any way, the phone on his desk rang.

"Ok, I see. Yes he's here. Put them through," the Sergeant told the caller from the station front desk.

Meanwhile, Papadoulis barely noticed what his Sergeant was saying, but instead continued to peer across the room from his desk in bafflement at the Incident Board. He only turned his head slightly in the direction of his Sergeant's desk when he heard him say, "Yes, sir, he's here. I'll put him on for you."

When he heard the Sergeant referring to the caller as 'sir' he realised it must be someone important. As Georgiou covered the mouthpiece of the phone with his hand he held it out in the direction of the Inspector, who had got up out of his chair and walked over towards him.

"It's Athens, sir-"

"What do they want? I thought you said they had nothing on the woman or Alexander," he interrupted, the frustrating tetchy tiredness back in his voice.

Georgiou held the phone further in the Inspector's direction. While still covering the mouthpiece he replied, "It's not about them, sir. The front desk said it's the Chief of the Hellenic Police in Athens for you."

Papadoulis took the receiver from his Sergeant and in response to him saying into it, "Inspector Yiannis Papadoulis speaking," a man's very important sounding voice replied,

"Police Lieutenant General, Nikolais Kouris, Chief of the Hellenic Police, calling from Athens."

"Yes, sir, what can I do for you?" Papadoulis asked.

"We've spoken before I think, Inspector, a few years ago on another murder case."

"Yes, we did, sir."

"And now it seems you've got another one, Inspector, in Lindos again."

"Yes, sir, but I hardly think they are connected. It's not as if we have-"

Papadoulis never got to finish. The Chief of Police wasn't really interested in his observations, or it appeared even any details of the current case. The Inspector was beginning to wonder quite why this important police officer had called him about it when he clearly wasn't interested in the detail of it. So why would this particular case interest him, or rather what part of it did?

"No, no, of course not, Inspector. It's not as if you have some sort of killing spree going on there on Rhodes. I expect that was what you were going to say. And that previous one was four or five years ago, I think. Anyway, that's when we spoke previously."

"It was, sir, what I was going to say I mean, not some sort of killing spree, but yes, four years ago. This present one is a woman, British, well British passport holder. Although from witnesses in the hotel she stayed in, as well as in some of the bars and restaurants she visited while here in Lindos, they say she had an Eastern European, or perhaps even a Russian accent. But we have a possible suspect, a man, David-"

Once again he never got to finish.

"Yes, David Alexander, I know. One of your officers contacted the London police about any information or records they had on him and the victim, a Sophia Orlova."

Now the Inspector's curiosity about why he was getting a call from this important police office was going into overdrive and he was becoming a lot more wary, fearing what was coming. He remembered very well the conversation the two policemen had over that case four years before. He didn't have good memories of it. The Chief of Police ordered him to shut it down, resulting in the Rhodes police, more specifically him, not finding the murderer, and he was never given any explanation for that course of action. He obviously suspected it had something to do with London, the London police or higher up. He was simply ordered to do it, shut it down. So he did.

"That's right, sir. My Sergeant contacted them yesterday about anything they had on the victim or our chief suspect, Alexander. He's been staying in Lindos over the last two summers. He's also a British passport holder according to the Border Control records at Rhodes Airport, and he left Lindos the morning after the murder according to a guy who lives in a flat next to his. Although, there's no record of him leaving through the airport, so possibly on one of the ferries to Athens or one of the other islands. We're still trying to trace him. He was seen having dinner with the victim in one of the restaurants in Lindos earlier on the evening she was killed. We've had no luck tracing him so far though but-"

Papadoulis was about to explain that he thought anything the London police had on David Alexander, any information or even any police record, might help track him down. However, the patience of the Chief of Police was rapidly running out. Papadoulis was going on a bit and he didn't need to know any more. He didn't let him finish. What he interrupted him with shocked the Inspector.

"He's dead, Inspector."

It was said in a cold, official, almost 'matter of fact' way.

"What?"

It wasn't that Papadoulis didn't hear him clearly, or even understand what that phrase meant. It was simply that he couldn't believe what he'd just been told.

"Dead," he added, his voice filled with incredulity.

"Yes, Alexander is dead, Inspector. London informed me an hour ago in response to your Sergeant's enquiry yesterday. He was killed in a car crash just outside London yesterday. London said it was a narrow country lane apparently. That's how they described it. An accident as his car went off the wet road in a thunderstorm and into a tree. Sounded pretty messy. The car burst into flames, they said, and there wasn't much left of the poor guy by the time the emergency services got there."

The Inspector was stunned, not just by being told of Alexander's death, but also by what it meant for the case. As he was rapidly turning that question over in his mind the Chief of Police answered it for him though.

"So, the case is obviously closed, Inspector. Your chief suspect, only suspect I think, is dead. We can't arrest and put a dead man on trial can we?"

It was a rhetorical question and the Chief of Police wasn't expecting an answer. He didn't give Papadoulis the chance to offer one anyway.

"Good work though, Inspector. Pity we couldn't catch him and put him on trial, but at least you solved the case."

"I ... erm ... but-"

Papadoulis tried to raise some more questions, including could he talk to the officers in London about it, the Chief of Police's contacts, to get some more information about Alexander. He was so caught off guard by what he'd been told though that he never got the chance.

"Ok, wrap up the usual paperwork and loose ends, Inspector, and you can get back to Rhodes Town and some of the more usual stuff you have to deal with there. Get one of your officers to try and trace any relatives of the victim, this woman Orlova. I think you said she lived in Athens, although she's not Greek. So-"

Now it was the Inspector who interrupted, puzzled.

"I don't think I did, sir, say she lived in Athens."

Papadoulis knew he hadn't and was now wondering how the Chief of Police came upon that information. He obviously assumed it was from London, but how would they know that, unless they knew a lot more about Sophia Orlova than they, and the Chief of Police, were prepared to divulge.

"Oh, sorry Inspector I thought you did."

"I only said that some of the witnesses we've interviewed in some of the bars and restaurants here said she had an Eastern European, or perhaps even a Russian accent, so obviously wasn't Greek, sir."

"Right, right, yes, Inspector, must have heard it from London then. Presumably they got it from some of the checks they did on her for your Sergeant's enquiry to them yesterday about her and Alexander."

He thought it better not to pursue that conversation further. Interrogating the Chief of Police over any of his inconsistencies wasn't exactly a good career move. Although what he was thinking was that it was pretty dam quick and a very extraordinarily short period of time from the day before, when his Sergeant contacted them, for the London police to make enquiries about Sophia Orlova and then inform the Chief of Police about things such as where she actually lived, especially as it wasn't even in the U.K., but in Athens.

His line of thought on that was interrupted though by one more instruction from the Chief of Police.

"Anyway, London will be in touch, later today probably, about arrangements for the release of the woman's body to the British Consulate in Rhodes Town, presumably for shipment back to the U.K. and to any contacts for her relatives there."

Something else that appeared odd to Papadoulis. Why was her body being shipped back to the U.K. when she lived in Athens?

After the Chief of Police ended the call and the Inspector relayed to Georgiou what he'd been told, and instructed to do, that was also the first thing his Sergeant picked up on.

"Assume the London police had found that her relatives live in London, or at least the U.K.," Papadoulis suggested.

"All seems pretty bloody quick though, sir, doesn't it? All that information about her gathered in less than twenty-four hours, and Alexander suddenly dead as well."

The Inspector walked over to stare in silence at the Incident Board and all the information on it for a few seconds. All he could say while once again rubbing the back of his neck was, "Well, Sergeant, if that's what the Chief of the Hellenic Police says is so, who are we to say otherwise?"

His Sergeant wasn't leaving it at that quite so easily, however.

"Alexander could still have been the murderer though, sir, even if it is true he was killed in a car crash yesterday-"

Papadoulis spun around to face him as he interrupted.

"Are you suggesting he wasn't? Suggesting that this is all some sort of conspiracy involving the Hellenic Chief of Police and the London police, or whoever there, Sergeant? That's a pretty serious accusation."

"Err ... no ... no, sir, well maybe, who knows, but that wasn't what I was about to say. It's just that we know Alexander left Lindos early on Tuesday morning according to his neighbour, so he could still have murdered Orlova late on Monday evening, which according to Christof was when she was killed. And if he died in a car crash near London yesterday he must have left Rhodes by ferry on Tuesday, probably to Athens, and then flew to London from there. We only checked the Rhodes airport departures when we tried to trace him and his movements from Tuesday."

"And what, Sergeant?"

The Inspector looked puzzled. He couldn't fathom the logic of whatever Georgiou was trying to say.

"Just that Alexander could still have killed her, Orlova. He could still have been our murderer, was our most likely suspect. Him being dead, killed in a road accident two days later doesn't really change that does it?"

Papadoulis shook his head slightly once before replying, "No, it doesn't, Sergeant. You're right there, but with our chief suspect dead we can hardly charge him with the murder can we?"

The Inspector wasn't wanting or expecting an answer. He wasn't waiting for one as Georgiou sat in silence.

Papadoulis went over to sit at his desk as he told his Sergeant, "And anyway, the Hellenic Chief of Police is telling us that's case closed so-"

"But what if we found other-"

Georgiou interrupted, but he never got to finish what he was about to suggest before Papadoulis shut him down firmly.

"What, other suspects, what if we found other suspects, Sergeant? Is that what you were about to suggest? Do you really think that would be a wise thing for us to do career-wise, carry on investigating a case that the Hellenic Chief of Police has told us is now closed, and that as far as he is concerned Alexander was our killer?"

The Sergeant let out a small sigh before agreeing.

"No, sir, you're right, it wouldn't be a clever thing for us to do. It's just that it's the second time the Chief of Police has shut down one of our murder investigations here. There was that one four years ago, the British guy who was found dead on one of the paths going up from the centre of the village towards the top lane along the back. Ok, it looked like an accident and like the guy slipped on the uneven path and steps up there and cracked his head against the wall, but we both weren't entirely convinced it was an accident were we?"

Papadoulis simply stared across at him without commenting. He knew what he was getting at, and yes he remembered that case well, but he wasn't saying anything.

"London, or the powers that be in London, had a say on that too, and the Chief of Police in Athens told us to shut that case down too as he said it was clearly an accident. Appears a bit of a coincidence, sir," Georgiou added.

Papadoulis sat up in his chair, but he was too weary for any thoughts about vague conspiracy theories. Also, he knew that would be a waste of time, as well as not exactly a clever thing to explore career-wise after the Chief of Police's clear instruction about closing the case.

He puffed out his cheeks slightly before telling his Sergeant, "Perhaps, you're right, and it is too much of a coincidence, although the two cases are not entirely the same. However, if the Chief of Police says the case is closed, then the case is closed, Sergeant. So, the British Consulate in Rhodes will be in touch, probably later today apparently, about arrangements to collect Orlova's body from the Rhodes Town mortuary. I'll leave you to deal with the initial paperwork on the case and I'll look it over tomorrow back at the Rhodes Town station. I've got a few personal things to sort this evening."

As Papadoulis took out his phone he seemed distracted as Georgiou asked, "Family, sir?"

"Err … erm … yes, yes, family stuff."

He typed a message. "You home tonight. I really need some more of that relaxation and stress removal therapy of yours." And clicked send.

PART THREE:

THE PEOPLE

12

The suspect: his visible life

An overall picture of David Alexander's relationships with women during his adult life could easily suggest they were based upon a 'lightness of being', built upon and constructed around that premise. Not always intentionally, at least that's what he often told himself, attempted to convince himself. And, to some extent, there was little doubt that to portray them in that simplified way was a misrepresentation. In fact, he had two personas. In reality there were at least two David Alexander's, two sides to him; the loving, faithful one in some of his relationships, embracing and enjoying, the 'weight' personified within those, and the alternative 'lightness' depicted and demonstrated by the unfaithful part of his personality in his relationships and encounters with women. He was no doubt unaware of it, but those two sides of his personality exemplified what the French writer, Claire Démar, wrote in the 1830s, that, "Fidelity has almost always rested exclusively on fear and the inability to do better or otherwise."

Ironically, Démar was a feminist writer, and wrote that in relation to women and women's life in marriage. However, as a man, fidelity in any of his relationships had always eventually nurtured and produced fear within David Alexander, as well as a curiosity as to whether he could do better than his current relationship at the time and in the women he met. At times, too many times, overcoming that fear and pursuing his curiosity had led him far too easily down the path of infidelity, and 'lightness'. It was that fear that he couldn't do better in his relationships with women, as well as in the type of women he had those relationships with, which he found easiest to ignore and overcome. In turn, that had often led him too easily to explore better relationship possibilities and challenge any prospect of long term fidelity and 'weight'.

Even so he wasn't above justifying to himself that the 'lightness' of his sexual physical unfaithfulness didn't affect, or have any bearing on, nor any meaning for, his emotional faithfulness to whichever woman he was actually in an emotional relationship with at the time. And if, in fact, any woman he was carrying out his sexual physical unfaithfulness with at any particular time shared that same 'light' outlook on life in their encounters then that only enabled him to justify further to himself his detachment of those sexual encounters, and his actions, from his emotional faithfulness to whichever woman he was in that emotional relationship with at that time.

Although, of course, David Alexander's ability to, and desire to, compartmentalise and separate in his mind the 'lightness' of his sexual physical unfaithfulness and the 'weight' of any emotional faithfulness was always very much dependant on the women he was with at any particular time also embracing that same approach to those things when it came to relationships. Difficulties always arose for him when eventually they didn't and the two things crossed over, became more complicated. Such that a woman who was initially contented with the 'lightness' of their sexual physical relationship came to want more, her feelings spilling over into wanting the 'weight' of emotional faithfulness and fidelity between them, even though she'd initially said to him that she didn't.

Conversely, there had been women he'd been with who were, in fact, in terms of their emotions towards him 'heaviness' personified. Women who had given themselves body and soul to him within the 'weight' of emotional faithfulness initially, but who later found when they discovered it – what his character and life was really like - that they rightly couldn't cope with the 'lightness' of his sexual physical unfaithfulness.

In the early summer of 2019 that had mostly been the story of David Alexander's relationships with women to date throughout his adult life. Although, he wasn't always totally indiscriminate and undiscerning when it came to the 'lightness' and physical sexual encounters. He prided himself on turning down some opportunities, particularly the wife of his former university academic boss when she approached him with an offer.

In fact, up until that point his life and relationships, his affairs and ultimate infidelity, could have been offered as a very good example of the German philosopher, Friedrich Nietzsche's concept of eternal return, which stated that time repeats itself in an infinite loop, and that exactly the same events will continue to occur in exactly the same way, over and over again, for eternity. When it came to women, and his relationships with them, in a number of instances throughout his adult life that had been David Alexander's experience– an infinite loop of recurring clashes between the 'weight' of emotional faithfulness and the 'lightness' of sexual physical unfaithfulness. His process of Nietzsche's eternal return in his past relationships with women was fuelled by Démar's argument that, "Fidelity has almost always rested exclusively on fear and the inability to do better or otherwise"; fear of somehow feeling trapped under the 'weight' of a loving relationship, while simultaneously thinking and wondering if he did have an inability to do better, or whether, in fact, there might be what he considered a better woman for him out there somewhere, and consequently initially setting out to explore that possibility through the 'lightness' of a physical sexual encounter with another woman.

There had been a few episodes of 'lightness' since his divorce, even some with a little more 'weight'. When he reflected on those episodes of 'lightness' with women since his divorce he couldn't help thinking it sounded like a catalogue of disasters, disastrous attempts at the 'weight' of a relationship. He thought it would certainly sound just like that to anyone else. However, he was sure there had been some good things within them, even if longevity was not really one of them, except for one particular one if four years constituted longevity, plus another two years after him and that particular woman got back together.

By the time he got to Lindos in early May 2019 for his first long summer stay there, planned to last until October, he'd just turned thirty-nine and been divorced for ten years. Prior to that he was married for eight years, and had three children, two boys and a girl, all teenagers now and living with his ex-wife, except when his eldest son was away in his first year studying Law at Manchester University.

David Alexander was around six feet tall, with light brown shortish hair, and a relatively slim figure. Although not exactly well built he'd managed to stave off the seemingly obligatory paunch, or even larger stomachs and beer bellies so proudly displayed by some British tourists he'd seen on his previous holiday visits to Lindos.

There were not yet any creases of middle age showing on his quite long, thin face, with its striking jaw line. Briefly at one time he'd tried to cultivate the standard academic beard. As a lecturer in Russian Literature it was no doubt very suitable. However, when he thought it made him look more like Rasputin than Chekhov he quickly abandoned that idea. Resembling a mad Russian mystic wasn't really a good look for a university lecturer. Consequently, he was now clean shaven. Initially he thought that maybe during his summer sojourn on that particular Greek island he would try the beard once again as part of the bohemian writer look, if only from laziness of not bothering to shave. He soon realised from experience, however, that beards weren't particularly comfortable at all during the heat of the Rhodian summer, even if some Greek men favoured them, particularly the big, bushy type.

He'd taught Russian literature for thirteen years at Bristol University. In more recent years that had strayed over into also teaching contemporary Russian foreign policy, not least because the two subjects were historically linked. Whenever anyone asked him what he taught though he just told them about the Russian literature, never mentioning the foreign policy stuff. He decided that as a subject of conversation that was a bit of a minefield in the current political climate.

Nearing forty he decided to deal with any approaching mid-life crisis by impulsively quitting his well-paid Senior Lecturer post to do what he had wanted to do for years. Instead of reading and teaching about famous Russian writers such as Tolstoy, Dostoyevsky, Turgenev and others, he would become a practitioner rather than an observer by attempting to write his own great novel. Where better to try and find the peace and unhindered solace than the picturesque village of Lindos on Rhodes. That was the aim he set out with at the beginning of that summer of 2019. He'd been there quite a few times before for one or two week holidays. This time he'd stay for the whole summer, from early May to late October if necessary. From his past holidays there he knew quite a few of the Greek locals, as well as some of the Brit ex-pats living and working in and around the village.

He completely severed his ties with his old life, not only as a University lecturer, but also in the more secret part of his life as a supposed consultant on Russian affairs with the British Security Services. His new life was to be filled with writing and sunshine, accompanied by some, not too many, booze filled nights. It wasn't exactly going to be the bohemian writer's lifestyle of somewhere like Paris. Instead, he'd simply settled for a safe start in Lindos, at least for that first summer, a place he was familiar with amongst people he knew quite well. He rented a functional small flat for the six months right in the centre of the village, just behind a couple of the popular bars, Yannis Bar and Bar404. It was more than adequate for his intention of writing and completing the first draft of his novel through that summer.

Any sort of meeting or relationship with a woman was furthest from his mind, whether one with 'lightness' or with 'weight'. His initial intention was to simply focus and concentrate on his writing. He approached the allocation of his time in Lindos during the long summer in the same way as he had through much of the previous parts of his life; methodically and well planned, whether that had been in his previous family life before his divorce or within his academic life lecturing at the university, or even in his very occasional minor undertakings for MI6. He liked to know as precisely as possibly where the things he was involved in, being asked to do, were headed and what the aim was. That was who he was, what made him tick.

So, ideally when it came to his long summer in Lindos, as long as his writing in the mornings went well he would reward himself with a quick baguette lunch and a cappuccino at Café Melia in the Amphitheatre square just around the corner from his flat, or at Giorgos café bar on his way to the beach, mostly Pallas Beach, for a deserved swim in the clear blue Lindos Bay cooling sea.

He never really discovered why his marriage eventually ended in divorce. It certainly wasn't his choice. It never involved infidelity, by either of them, definitely not on his part, and as far as he knew not on her part. She simply told him she was unhappy and wanted them to separate. He hadn't any idea that was coming. On reflection, the fact that he didn't have a clue she was so unhappy, and needed to say what she did, said it all. After living apart for almost two years she filed for divorce and he didn't contest it.

For a while after his divorce he was well and truly disillusioned when it came to any thoughts of relationships with women. Initially he threw himself into his work, and only after some time had passed did he intentionally or otherwise set out on a path of 'lightness' when it came to any encounters with women. There were eventually a few of those, not entirely successful, or even in some cases remotely so.

The one time since his divorce that he'd abandoned the 'lightness' and embraced, even pursued and enjoyed the 'weight' of emotional fulfilment, turned out to be a disaster, an emotional disaster. He was in a relationship with the woman for four years and perfectly happy, physically and emotionally. So was she, he thought, until she went off for a fling with a French guy for six months. Eventually she did come back to him, wanted to come back and them be together again, and much to his surprise he agreed. However, what followed was almost two years of pain. He always thought he would never be able to handle what had happened between her and the French guy if she did ever want to come back to him. Nevertheless, when she told him she wanted to he changed his mind and convinced himself that he could. It wasn't the same between them though. Not least because actually it was her who found it much more difficult to handle what she'd done. For some unfathomable reason at that point, despite her infidelity she clearly never trusted him. He had absolutely no idea if that was a reflection of her being unable to deal with her own guilt or not. However, by then she was regularly going through his phone and his work diary. He actually had nothing to hide, as he constantly told her. He was being completely faithful, still wanting and trying to embrace the 'weight' of fidelity. Given the 'lightness' of his later string of subsequent relationships that was something some people, including some of his friends male and female, found hard to believe. At least he knew it was the truth.

The madness of the situation, the 'weight' of it, got worse and worse. It bizarrely culminated with her suggestion that he should have sex with her best friend. In a nonchalant way over dinner one evening she suggested it, telling him that would even up their infidelity. What he found equally as amazing was that, according to her, her friend had agreed to it. That knocked him sideways. That was when he realised there was no future between them and ended the relationship.

That whole experience and the way it ended set him off on the path of 'lightness' once again, convinced him cynically in a sour way that was the best and safest option. He had surprised himself in firstly getting back together with the woman, and then, retrospectively in his more light-hearted moments, with his reluctance to take up the offer as her friend was very attractive, very lovely. He reflected that if he'd still been that man of a few years before, simply pursuing sexual physical 'lightness', he would most likely have taken up the offer. By that time though, he'd changed, through having been in a 'weighty' relationship for the most part of six years.

The disillusionment sent him determinedly on a series of 'lighter' encounters with women in the following years. Academic conferences proved to be places where, for one reason or another, he would sometimes end up embarking on those. A year after the end of his relationship with the woman who wanted him to sleep with her best friend he met an Austrian woman from Vienna, Anna, at an autumn conference in the small town of Baden bei Wien, just outside that city. She was twenty-nine and a lecturer in literature, mostly Czech and Austrian, at Vienna University, Her attractive longish face was perfectly framed by her shoulder length dark hair above her slim body. Initially she struck up a conversation with him during a coffee break at the conference on the first morning. Straightaway she seemed interested in what he did, or at least interested enough to have a quite long conversation with him, which she continued at the conference dinner that evening when she seemed determined to sit next to him.

Perhaps the narrow atmospheric streets of the town, defined on either side by beautiful perfect historic examples of the architecture of the earlier Habsburg Empire, were simply conducive to producing some sort of romantic encounter. The buildings definitely added to the romance of the place. In his mind he could easily picture the musical masters Beethoven and Mozart scurrying down the narrow streets while the sounds of magical symphonies were incubating in their heads. Beethoven had a summer house there where he stayed, away from the stifling heat and dust of Vienna. While there he regularly used the mineral baths in the Spa town in an attempt to cure his many ailments. It was whilst there in the summers of 1821, 1823 and 1824 that he composed large sections of his famous Ninth Symphony.

In the park near the hotel where the conference was being held the strikingly coloured falling autumn leaves had already begun to carpet the paths which David and Anna occasionally strolled down together in the chill early evening air. The crisp leaves crunched beneath his shoes and her black leather ankle boots. No doubt influenced by the setting of the place he found himself attracted to her, and seemingly it was mutual. After the conference they kept in touch. Two weeks later he found himself on a flight to Vienna to meet her. It was for a long weekend, much of which they spent wandering the very cold, yet even more atmospheric, narrow streets in that city. Even the occasional snow flurries didn't seem to bother them. They visited Mozart's house and then a classical concert in St. Stephen's Cathedral on Saturday afternoon. Everything was going well, especially when she insisted she took him to Café Central on Saturday evening.

It was a bitterly cold dark Vienna evening by the time she met him at his hotel and they walked to the café. Encouragingly, he thought, she tucked her gloved hand and warm coated arm into his as soon as they left his hotel and made their way down the alleyways. She wore an attractive round fur hat, somewhat reminiscent of a Russian style one. No doubt keeping her head and ears nice and warm against the cold. He hadn't thought to bring one and now was increasingly wishing he had. Fortunately it was only a ten minute walk from his hotel in the trendy Spittelberg part of the city. While they walked through the cold night air she asked if he knew the history of Café Central, telling him when he shook his head slightly that it was where, Sigmund Freud, Trotsky, Lenin, and even Stalin at one point, used to go for coffee and breakfast when they lived in the city.

Café Central was very popular with tourists, as well as with a smattering of Viennese residents. As they entered Anna told him there was nothing that compared to the rich aroma of a Viennese coffee house. She was right and it hit his nostrils as soon as they walked through the swing doors. The interior was old-style traditional Viennese. It had arched ceilings, padded maroon velvet benches around the walls, and a multitude of small round light brown marbled tables with dark wooden straight-backed, also maroon patterned linen covered chairs, most of which were occupied. In the centre of the large room were six beige marble round pillars supporting the various arches in the roof and surrounding a grand piano, at which the pianist was playing a medley of pleasant music from a bygone Viennese age.

They ordered dinner and she insisted they had a bottle of wine, red, only to keep out the cold she told him with a mischievous smile. The dinner and the evening went well, as did the weekend eventually. Just as he was feeling more relaxed with a woman than he'd been for quite a while, and actually beginning to let himself wonder if this was going to turn out to be the start of his rehabilitation and return to a belief in, or acceptance of, the possibility of the 'weight' of emotional faithfulness in his encounters with women she threw him a 'curve ball'.

As they waited for the bill she reached over and squeezed his hand suggesting, "Why don't you come back to my flat tonight. I'm sure it'll be nicer than being alone in your hotel room?"

"I do a nice Viennese breakfast too," she added with a small smile.

Was this her version of the 'lightness'? Was she simply also engaged in what he'd previously decided was the safest, less emotional option when it came to encounters with the opposite sex?"

Anyway, he just nodded as he agreed, and she did, indeed, do a nice Viennese breakfast.

A few weeks later she flew to Bristol for a weekend with him. They spent a couple of months, mostly at weekends, flying back and forth between the two cities. They even spent Christmas at her flat in Vienna together; a very enjoyable, romantic Viennese Christmas.

He started to get confused. What was this developing into? Was any growing seriousness between them making him scared? Or was he, in fact, simply beginning to experience Démar's fear, her basis of fidelity? Did he want the 'weight' and responsibility again, even leaving aside the practicalities of the geographical difference between their two cities and lives? Undeniably he was enjoying the 'lightness' of their relationship, and to hi she was a strikingly beautiful and clever woman, but what was she expecting was the question he found increasingly difficult to remove from his thoughts.

In the end he needn't have worried. It turned out she was quite happy, content, with the 'lightness' of their relationship. When he finally raised it after almost three months and asked where she thought, could see, what was between them going, she shrugged her shoulders as she told him, "Nowhere really, David, nowhere more than this really."

Nonchalant probably wasn't necessarily the best way to describe her response, but it felt like that to him. Of course she added some things, chiefly about the difference in their geographical locations and long term issues around that, particularly in their work situations. However, he guessed that maybe she was in the same place emotionally as he'd been before they met. So, it seemed, turned out, that she didn't want the 'weight' of emotional faithfulness and responsibility either and eventually, after a couple more months, his Viennese visits and 'lightness' evaporated. Maybe he'd escaped emotional pain further down the line was what he told himself, and moved on.

Two months after it finished with Anna, at the beginning of May his friend, Paul, invited him to a dinner dance at the Cavendish Hotel in Piccadilly in London and he met Maria. She was English, with long blonde hair and what could be described as a fuller figure. She was a Personal Assistant in a firm of solicitors based in Lincoln's Inn Fields in London, and was slightly older than Anna at thirty-three. She'd never been married and had no children. He was seated next to her at the table at the dinner by the company that organised it, and they instantly struck up a pleasant conversation. It was the usual where are you from, what do you do for a living, sort of thing, interspersed by him with a few comments that made her laugh, or at least smile. She was easy to talk to and at the end of the evening phone numbers were exchanged, along with tentative suggestions by him about meeting up for a drink sometime, which she appeared enthusiastic about.

So, they did, in fact once meet for a drink and then three times over the next two weeks for dinner. She appeared keen, and when he told her the last time they went for dinner in those first two weeks that he was going to be away for the last two weeks of May on holiday a clear look of disappointment spread over her face. He was actually going to Lindos. It was one of the final times he went there for a short holiday before deciding to go for the whole summer the following year. He'd rented a flat for two weeks in the centre of the village which turned out to be the same flat he rented for six months for the whole of that first summer the following year.

Maria's response to his revelation about his upcoming holiday surprised him. Straightaway she asked, "Can I come and join you for a week? I could do with a holiday and some nice warm Greek sun, and I'm due some leave from work. How big is the flat you're renting?"

"Ermm ... well ... err, yes, I ... err ... I suppose you could, if you wanted to of course," was what he eventually manged to get out of his mouth in some disbelief.

"Good, that's great, I'll check some flights. So, how big is it?"

"What? Oh, flights, yes."

He was still stunned, already trying to figure out what this meant in his grand scale between 'lightness' and 'weight'.

"The flat, how big is it?"

"It's err ... ok ... a lounge, small kitchen, shower room and toilet of course and ... ermm," he hesitated for a moment before adding, "a double bedroom, but there's only one double bed."

She smiled at him and her blue eyes widened as she replied, "Perfect . That's perfect then, David. Isn't it?"

She tilted her head slightly to one side and added, don't you think?"

All he could do was slightly nod his head and say quietly, "Erm ... err, yes, I suppose it is."

So, she joined him in Lindos for the first week of his holiday, and immediately there were no awkward moments about where she was going to sleep, even though he did point out to her as soon as she arrived that the sofa in the lounge opened out to a bed, Another smile spread across her lips and she kissed him before adding, "We won't be needing that."

And they didn't. He spent a very good week with her on Lindos Pallas Beach, in the clear blue sea in the bay, and at plenty of the restaurants and bars in the village, as well, of course, in the double bed. He even told her one evening over dinner in the Village House Restaurant that he was seriously considering giving up his job as a lecturer and coming to Lindos for the whole summer the following year to write his 'grand novel', even renting the same flat. That was when she told him she thought that was a great idea and it meant she could come out and visit him as much as she wanted, maybe even take a month or so off work.

Once again that set some alarm bells ringing in his head, not least because he had another, different, secret life that he definitely couldn't tell her about, particularly when at times he might be required to do certain things within that life, even occasionally in Lindos or that were connected to his time on Rhodes. As well though the alarm bells were ringing in his head again because she was obviously getting more serious over what was developing between them. That scared him. Was this moving from the 'lightness' of physical sexual enjoyment towards the 'weight' of expected emotional faithfulness as far as she was concerned? Unlike Anna, it increasingly appeared that was what Maria wanted, but he certainly wasn't at all sure now that was what he wanted.

He tried to persuade himself of it, however. Maybe he should try again. Try once more and embrace the 'weight' of emotional fidelity and responsibility. He could do worse, was the rather crude way he thought of it at times. Perhaps he should embrace Démar's fear of the inability to do better, accept fidelity and that he wasn't going to find any woman better than Maria. She was, indeed, a very lovely woman, who obviously liked him a lot. He even tried to discuss it with an English guy he knew that was working as a DJ in Lindos for the summer, and had been there for a couple of summers. When he met her during her week's holiday in Lindos with David the guy told him he thought Maria was lovely, perfect for David. However, when David tried to explain his 'lightness' and 'weight' dilemma to him, not in quite that way, he burst out laughing, then told him he thought David had some kind of illness, was "sick" was the way he jokingly put it before adding, "You're crazy."

In the end David couldn't find it in himself to abandon the 'lightness' of his outlook in his encounters with women. That would mean too much 'weight', too much responsibility. The thought of another period of fidelity was too much for him. He simply couldn't convince himself of Démar's fear of his inability to do even better. Consequently, he put off seeing her a couple of times and then eventually plucked up the courage to tell her he thought they should stop seeing each other. He used the geographical distance excuse Anna had used about him being in Bristol and her in London, and what that meant for their work. She wasn't happy, but eventually gave up on him.

There was one more encounter with a woman before he came to Lindos for that whole summer of 2019. He met

Christine in the late summer of 2018 at a friend's party in Bristol. She had an apartment in Clifton Village, a very nice part of the city, and again was in her early thirties, divorced with no kids. He thought she was also some sort of P.A., although he was never really sure and each time he pressed her on it she always seemed to avoid giving him too much detail. She was tall and slim. What she did tell him was that she exercised regularly, did an hour in the gym in the local fitness club every morning. When he later recalled their brief encounter and time spent together what always jumped to the front of his mind was that he regularly had to stifle a laugh, or at least a smile, whenever she referred to them as having, "had a moment." It was as if she couldn't actually bring herself to say they'd had sex, which they had quite a few times over the period of a month. Aside from the amusement her comment gave him, he took it as an indication that she was also contented with the 'lightness' of their relationship, and wasn't remotely interested in moving it on to the next "weighty" level. Perhaps he wasn't her only lover was what ran through his brain a few times. At the time she was his only lover. But strangely he couldn't cope with it, not knowing. He confronted her about it. She never outright denied his suspicion and he took that to mean she was seeing other men, other lovers. So, he couldn't cope with that and it was him who stopped their relationship, which even he had to admit to himself was unusual, as there was clearly no possibility of it developing into a faithful weighty one, or any possibility of her wanting that. She clearly was just enjoying the 'lightness' of their sexual encounters, and that was all she wanted, which usually he did too.

    That experience, on top of the ones over the previous few years, was probably the point at which David Alexander decided to give up the chasing and the dating game; both the 'lightness' or even any possibility of wanting any development towards the 'weight', and instead concentrate on his academic work life. Unfortunately though, that was soon also to be bedevilled with turmoil and craziness, the craziness of academics and their vindictive underhand ways, or at least of some of them whom he worked with. In fact, that, together with the disasters of his dating and relationships experiences led him to eventually decide to take a pay off from his university post and make plans to go to Lindos for the summer to write his great novel. He'd been saying that was what he wanted to do for the past five years at least. Now circumstances had contrived to push him to actually do it.

Consequently, he was going to be in Lindos for the whole summer of 2019. The plan, the aim, was to get on with his writing. That definitely didn't include any relationships with women. At least that is what he intended, until a British woman working as a waitress in Lindos crossed his path, as well as an unexpected surprising encounter with a female acquaintance from a past academic conference in Moscow, each eventually epitomising in their own way his 'weight' and 'lightness' dilemma.

13

The suspect: his invisible secret life

There was another, darker, secret side to David Alexander which obviously very few people knew about, certainly not the women he either had the 'lightness' of physical sexual encounters with or even the couple with whom he'd had more 'weighty' emotionally faithful relations. Although, one of those had been his ex-wife, and that was actually some time before the secret part of his life started and developed. In official terms, alongside and as part of his academic life, he was a consultant on Russian affairs to the British Government Foreign and Commonwealth Office. In effect, though, it was to the British Security Services. For obvious reasons he was a very closed person with all the women in terms of that other side of his life,

In his university employment position he'd written and published articles on Russian Foreign Policy in academic journals, particularly emphasising that to understand it required acknowledging it was rooted in Russian history; the history of the Russian State. Russian and Soviet leaders throughout history, as well as the Russian people generally, believed for security reasons it was necessary to always have some kind of buffer-zone between the borders of Russia and western states. That belief was founded on invasions of Russia throughout time, going back through Hitler and as far back as Napoleon's ultimately unsuccessful invasion in 1812. The buffer-zone foreign policy was also influenced by, and based on, documented historical memory of the invasion by twenty-three insurgent foreign armies after the 1917 revolution, fighting against the new Bolshevik government in Russia during the civil war between 1918 and 1922, including armies from the United States, Britain, France, Japan and Czechoslovakia.

He was approached by a fellow academic at a conference at Birmingham University Centre for Russian and East European Studies in 2014 who asked quite casually if he, "would, be interested at all in doing some consultancy work for the British government, the Foreign Office?" He was a little flattered, and didn't really take it to be a very serious suggestion at all. With a slight shrug of the shoulders he replied, "Sure, why not."

When he heard no more about it for a month he assumed it was just what he initially thought it to be, a casual enquiry from a fellow academic who was simply trying to impress him through his supposed connections. It was the sort of thing some academics did just to make themselves sound more important than they really were, maybe even sound cleverer than they really were.

However, just over four weeks later he got a call on a Friday morning from a very official sounding guy who told him he was a special adviser on Russian affairs in the Foreign Office. He said that David had been recommended to him, and the Foreign Office, by the academic he'd met at the Birmingham University conference.

"Oh, yes, I'd forgotten about that," was his initial response. "Something to do with some consultancy work, wasn't it?"

"Yes, yes, something like that, Mr. Alexander, David, may I call you David? We thought you might be able to help us with a few things."

The guy's voice was very formal, a very straight down the line Oxbridge civil servant bureaucrat type of thing.

"Sure, David's fine. Russia wasn't it? A few things on Russia, foreign policy and the like?"

"Hmm ... yes, yes, sort of, but-"

Now the guy's voice didn't sound quite so calm and reserved. David was being a little too direct about the subject on the phone, plus he didn't let him finish, which appeared to actually fluster the guy somewhat.

"Well, I'm not sure what I could help you with, but-"

Now it was David who didn't get to finish what he was saying. The guy's patience had clearly run out.

"Look, David, just come and see us. Let's meet and we will see how much, and in what ways, you could help us. After the weekend, shall we say Monday at two at the Foreign Office in King Charles Street?"

"Err ... Monday at two ... yes I can do that, but who-"

Again he didn't get to finish. He didn't even know the guy's name or department and was about to ask, but before he could he was instructed, "Just tell the staff on reception who you are. They'll know to expect you and someone will bring you to my office. Oh, and by the way, bring your passport please. Just security and identification purposes, you know."

David didn't "know", but before he could ask anything more the guy rang off.

The mystery of that first phone call proved to be nothing compared to what followed.

When he arrived at the Foreign Office reception on that Monday afternoon, and informed them who he was, they were, indeed, expecting him. He was told someone would come to fetch him, to take a seat in the lobby in the meantime, and was offered a coffee. He took a seat, but declined the coffee. Within five minutes a quite soberly dressed woman in a dark blue business suit, who he reckoned to be in her early fifties, appeared and took him to the lift and up to the third floor with its long corridor and a number of very heavy looking dark wooden doors on either side. Eventually she knocked on one, opened the door and led him in. As she did so she introduced him to the two men in very smart, dark waist-coated suits sat in the high backed velvet armchairs at the far side of the large room. However, seemingly deliberately she never introduced them, or even what their position was in the Foreign Office. He asked straightaway, but they ignored his question, simply asked to see his passport, and then told him after he produced it and handed it to one of them that they thought he could be very helpful to them.

One of those conversations ensued over the next fifteen minutes where at the end of it he still wasn't really sure what they thought he could help them with. At the end one of the men phoned the same soberly dressed woman, who then arrived in the room to escort him back down to reception for him to leave. In the lift she informed him that she would email him a claim form so he could be reimbursed for his train fare. As he left the building he definitely still didn't have a clue as to what it was all about. As they finished the meeting and both shook his hand, one of the men simply told him, "We'll be in touch soon." He didn't really think they would or even why they would.

By the following Friday morning though, he got another call from the same guy as previously, asking him to come to London again on Monday. However, it wasn't to be to the Foreign Office this time, but to the building at 85 Albert Embankment at eleven. Through his research on Russian Foreign policy, and the Russian Security Services, as well as not least some of the James Bond movies he loved to watch, he knew straightaway that building was known as the SIS Building. More commonly it was called the MI6 Building and was the headquarters of the British Secret Intelligence Service, hence SIS Building. He wasn't sure whether to be intrigued or wary and concerned. Without thinking though, or even being given time to think about it by the guy on the phone, for some reason he just agreed. He didn't even get to ask this time who he should ask for at the reception as he was quickly told the same procedure as before at the Foreign Office would occur when he arrived. He would be expected, and would be taken to the relevant office for the meeting. However, when he asked if he should again bring his passport he was simply told, "No, that wouldn't be necessary now."

When he finally learned at that second meeting what they wanted him to do, even if only spasmodically, plus where that meeting took place, he assumed the delay of a month between the initial approach at the Birmingham University conference about consultancy work and the first meeting at the Foreign Office, was obviously because they were conducting security and background checks on him. He was clearly being vetted.

When they actually got around to spelling out clearly just what they wanted him to do it all initially seemed pretty low level stuff to him. The way it was put to him was that they simply wanted him to approach some academics, Russians and others from the former Eastern bloc countries or from the former Soviet States whose governments were still sympathetic to Russia and the Putin regime, at, as they put it, "The odd academic conference. Just listen mostly and see if they let any information slip that you think might be useful to us about what the Russians are up to."

That didn't feel very demanding. At least it did all seem pretty innocent and low level, not very demanding, until they added in an almost matter of fact way at the end of their explanation that of course he would be required to sign the Official Secrets Act. However, they reassured him that was simply a necessary bureaucratic formality due to the fact he would officially be on a consultancy contract to the Foreign Office, for which, they added immediately, he'd be, "Paid well, pretty damn well compared to an academic's salary, old chap."

All in all it appeared harmless enough to him and nothing remotely dangerous or difficult; nothing more than having to suffer the company of the usual mostly boring academics at often mundane conferences. He did actually wonder if MI6 perhaps had a whole network of academics operating for them in the same way they wanted him to. No doubt the Russians had something similar going on. There was always a lot of often meaningless gossip at academic conferences, especially over conference dinners and a few drinks in hotel bars. Most of it was just that though, gossip, and academics loosely speculating, often after too much alcohol. Anyway, he'd always thought from experience many times that academics were the worst gossips; the worst at spreading rumours and speculation which often simply had no foundation or substance. At one time he'd even been a victim of that in his own university faculty and department, rumours with no substance whatsoever.

Consequently, when he thought it over he decided it came down to the fact that he wasn't actually being asked to do, or required to do, anything more than he already did; make small talk and listen into conversations at occasional academic conferences. So, he agreed, and at first, for the first couple of years, it was fine and hardly a difficult thing to do. Money for nothing he told himself. He went to three conferences during those two years, including one in Budapest and one in Brussels. He picked up only a couple of very minor bits of information at those about the Russian government, both of which he thought were really inconsequential. The other one, which was actually the first one in the autumn of 2014 in Moscow, entailed him doing a little more, although nothing he thought was that dangerous, if at all. He was instructed to simply at the conference discreetly verbally pass the secret contact details of an MI6 operative in Moscow to a Russian woman academic, Alexandra Ivanova. She was a Russian Foreign Policy specialist who wished to defect MI6 had been informed, bringing with her plenty of information she was in possession of on what the Russians were up to in terms of the real aims of their international policy. The contact details were the protected 'burner' phone number of the MI6 operative. David was instructed that under no circumstances was he to write the number down, merely to memorise it and pass it on to her verbally.

She did eventually defect, bringing a range of Russian Foreign Policy information with her. MI6 gave her what they refer to as a 'Legend'; a new life, an appearance makeover, an apartment in Athens, and a new personal history, including a new name, Sophia Orlova.

Apart from that one thing at the first conference there was nothing of any importance he was asked to do, and virtually nothing of any real substance that he picked up at the other two. At that point he thought MI6 and his contact there – a guy who was introduced as his 'handler' when David first met him back at the SIS Building – would give up on him, thinking that he wasn't going to be a source of much, if any, useful information. He was wrong though.

Instead they stepped up the demands on him, not in terms of his time or even the number of academic conferences they wanted him to attend, but where they wanted him to go, and in what capacity. The biggest change came when they'd heard from their operative in Havana that the Cuban Ministry of Education was seeking to arrange lecturer exchange programmes with European universities. Since 1999 the Cuban government had successfully implemented a program specifically to attract students from less privileged backgrounds from a number of countries, including Britain, to study medicine in Cuba. Over the years since 1999 that also developed into providing state subsidized higher education to foreign nationals under a range of other specific programs. The programs provided for full scholarships, including accommodation, mainly at Havana University. As a result, except for during some periods of political difficulties between the governments, on the whole over the period of almost twenty years Cuba maintained quite close co-operation on education with the United Kingdom, as well as with other nations in the European Union. To such an extent that as far back as 2002 the Minister for Education in the Welsh Assembly Government and representatives of the Universities of Swansea and Glamorgan in Wales visited Cuba to create provisions for future liaisons over educational projects between officials in Britain and Cuba.

So, MI6 wanted David to push for his university to become involved in the proposed lecturer exchange programme between E.U universities and Cuban ones, which they'd been informed of by their Havana operative. The plan was then for him to go on an exchange to Havana within the programme once it was up and running. Basically, MI6 saw it as a useful cover for a way to get another person on the ground in the Cuban capital who could gather and feed any useful information back to them on the Cuban government, including its foreign relations.

He was again initially reluctant. This seemed much more dangerous than simply overhearing conversations at academic conferences. However, after some pressure from his handler and a higher up MI6 official he eventually agreed to at least raise it with the International Office in his university, mainly because they assured him it would only be for three months and if he actually never came across any useful information that would be fine. Because of that assurance he started to again think that what they wanted him to do would be harmless, simple and straightforward, probably amounting to nothing, or almost nothing.

When he did raise it with the International Office they were immediately very enthusiastic, not least because it would mean some funds coming to the University from the Cuban government, as well as a lot more from the European Union. It was in the summer of 2016, just after the Brexit vote, and as the U.K. was thought to be going to leave within a few years his university was keen to get something set up in the programme quickly before that happened, and thereby secure the E.U funding. Consequently, they did, and he went to Havana University within the programme for three months in the early spring of 2017. Ostensibly he was there to teach a course on Russian literature of the nineteenth and twentieth century, but in reality, of course, he was also there to covertly continue his work for MI6. That turned out to be not quite so occasional or harmless there though.

For the first month everything was fine and easy going for him. He instantly fell in love with the city and not just because of the university or the students. The university was fine, and the students were enthusiastic enough over having a lecturer from England and a course in English. It was the city itself he fell in love with. Everything he'd heard about Havana turned out to be accurate. It was vibrant every night, exciting. Habana Vieja, the Old Town, was full of life with dancing and music in the many bars as well as on the streets. It seemed every bar and every street had a story. No wonder writers like Hemingway loved it there and stayed for many years. The whole place had a terrific atmosphere. You had to be there to experience it, and enjoy it, and of course, most of the time the weather was nice, constant sunshine and warm. Havana was different from anywhere he'd been, something else. It was a strange sort of cocktail mixture of a hangover from the nineteen-fifties and some of the more modern stuff of the late seventies and early eighties.

Every day, and especially every night, had that special sort of feel and he quickly came across some very interesting characters. He couldn't help thinking it was all very odd though. It was so obvious that there were plenty of shady characters around, not least spooks, spies, operatives to give them their 'code' label. No doubt based in every foreign embassy – Russian, French, Canadian, and from virtually every former Soviet East European bloc country you could name, as well as the British, like him from MI6, even though he never looked upon himself as a spy. And there were the Americans of course, who'd re-emerged since the re-opening of the US Embassy in 2015. He'd walk into a popular tourist bar or a hotel bar like in the Hotel Inglaterra right in the centre of Havana by the Capitol building, and there they'd all be, the supposed embassy bureaucrats, drinking their early evening Margheritas in faded bar furnishing surroundings that had seen better days and the fading twilight outside. What soon became clear to him and was the weirdest thing in it all was that basically they all really knew one another, or at least who they were and what they actually did. Not what their false job titles were, but what they actually did for their countries. They were all there, drinking in the same bars at the same time, literally watching each other watching each other. He thought it really was like being in a Grahame Greene novel from the nineteen-fifties like 'Our Man in Havana'. It was bizarre, but he quickly became used to it and at the same time it felt quite comfortable, even pleasant, and not a bad place to be for that first month, Havana. It wasn't even as though he had to do much, except teach his course. In addition, there was never anything interesting or useful for MI6 to overhear in any of the bars, such as in the Hotel Inglaterra or in Floridita. The foreign embassy operatives appeared far too experienced, comfortable in their surroundings and enjoying their life in Havana, to give anything sensitive away.

Things seemed to be going ok, no stress and no dramas. He hadn't actually come across anything useful to report to his 'Havana handler' at the British Embassy. Even his apartment, provided by the Embassy, was much better than he'd anticipated, with quite modern furnishings and appliances. Not that he used the kitchen one very often. Most of the time he would eat out as the restaurants were so cheap. It was very central though, in one of the better looking streets just behind the Capitol Building across from the Parque Central, and very close to the Prado of the Paseo de Marti with its tree lined central pedestrian area full of stalls with a multitude of interesting goods, as well as benches on which to sit and people watch.

In some of the more popular bars, like Floridita, Hemingway's favourite for a Margherita, there were plenty of women tourists, Canadian, British, East European, and Russian of course. For the first month, however, he was determined not to even get into any 'lightness' sexual encounters, deciding that was not a good idea. He should just concentrate on his university work and anything that came up through the British Security Services.

But then at the start of the second month he met a woman, Yurima. She told him that in English the equivalent was Vanessa. He met her when introduced to her by a Cuban colleague from the university at a drinks reception at the British Embassy to celebrate the continuing and developing Higher Education links between Britain and Cuba. She was originally from Camaguey, a city just over five hundred kilometres from Havana towards the south-east of the island. She worked in the Ministry of Education in Havana in a department she told him translated in English as something like the 'International Co-operation department', or near enough, and that was why she got invited to the reception.

She had very attractive bushy dark black long curly hair, although it was tied in a loose pony tail for the reception. Her vivid green dress fully displayed her shapely body, and complemented perfectly her slightly dark skin, something typical for some of the Cuban population. After they were introduced she seemed genuinely interested to talk with him. When he told her he was at the university in Havana on the lecturer exchange programme she became even more interested, telling him that she hadn't met any other lecturers from England on that so far. He was very wary of telling her too much about himself and stuck to talking about his university academic work. Immediately after asking if she went to Havana University he somewhat undiplomatically asked how old she was. She let out a small laugh, showing off her bright perfect white teeth and told him, "Thirty-two, but I didn't go to the university in Havana. I went to Camaguey University. Not as good as Havana, but nearer home and my family."

He'd actually managed to talk to very few people when after almost an hour she suggested they went on somewhere for some food and maybe more drinks. He shrugged his shoulders slightly as he readily agreed, "Why not?"

"What about the Ambos Mundos Hotel roof bar? We can take a taxi. It'll only be fifteen minutes to the Old Town and the hotel and they do great lobster pasta, as well as a good mojito, one of Hemingway's favourites. He lived in a room in the Hotel for ten years in the nineteen-thirties and wrote three of his novels there."

He knew that, but simply shrugged again and nodded in agreement before agreeing again, "Well, it's your city, so I should go by your recommendation." Then he added with a smile, "But I think Hemingway had many favourites when it came to alcohol."

She smiled at him again, this time mischievously, as she told him, "Well, David, technically it's not. I'm from Camaguey, remember."

She was right though. The lobster pasta was excellent, and so were the two mojitos they had. Almost a couple of hours later as he was about to put her in a taxi she said pointedly, "We must exchange numbers. I really would like to see you again."

So, they did, and then she kissed him on the cheek goodnight and disappeared into the Havana night in her taxi.

For the best part of the next two days he kept thinking about her. Should he call her? She hadn't called him yet. But was it wise to get involved with a woman, a Cuban woman, even one as lovely as Yurima, even if it was only probably likely to be another 'lightness' encounter in his life? And what would his Havana handler make of it? Indeed, would it be dangerous? He'd warned David as soon as he arrived in Havana to be careful, to always be wary of casual conversations in bars and cafes. Sometimes Cuban Security Services operatives, particularly female ones, would target male foreigners who they believed had some connection with the British Embassy and deliberately sit next to them at a bar or in a café to start up what appeared to be an innocent everyday conversation. That could lead to them being over friendly and propositioning him one night, seeking to put him in a compromising situation.

Despite that this was the old David again. He couldn't resist, and when he called her two nights after they met she sounded pleased and told him she was, "Very happy he called."

After that they met regularly a couple of times a week over the next four weeks for dinners and drinks. One evening after dinner at the end of the second week she asked what his flat was like. A slight smile crept across her lips as she added, "Can I see it? I must admit I'm curious to see what sort of flat the university provides for visiting lecturers. See how good it is, or bad even?"

He hesitated, but before he could answer she said with heavy emphasis in a much softer tone of voice, "I mean tonight, David."

He knew instantly what she meant, and it wasn't just her wanting to see his flat and how good or bad it was.

So, she saw it, and not just for an hour or so that evening. The bright warm Havana sun was rising in the clear blue sky when she called a taxi and left.

Consequently, although he'd initially been so determined to avoid one, another episode of the "lightness" in his relationships began and they started seeing each other and sleeping together three or four times a week. She seemed very happy to be with him. They spent quite a few early evenings strolling along the Malecon hand-in-hand watching the bright red ball of fire that was the fading sun dying slowly across Havana Bay while small groups of Havana residents, mostly young, were talking together, or drinking and a few played guitars.

All the while, of course, he could justify to himself it was ok what he was doing with her, what he was drifting into, through the knowledge that in just over five weeks he would leave. There was no possibility, therefore, of this developing from 'lightness' to the 'weight' of a relationship between them.

As they lay in his bed early one Tuesday morning she asked if he'd seen any of the island apart from Havana. When he said he hadn't she suggested they go away out of the city for the coming weekend.

"I have a car," she told him. "We could drive somewhere to the coast. It would be a nice change to get out of the city. Maybe even get a swim in the sea from a nice beach."

"Ok, sounds like a good idea. What sort of car though?"

She laughed.

"Don't worry, David. It's not a Lada, or even one of those prettied up classic old American cars for the tourists that you see everywhere in Havana. It's a Dacia and just two years old."

That did worry him a little. How did a bureaucrat at the Cuban Ministry of Education manage to afford a quite new foreign car. He knew there was quite a high level of purchase tax on foreign cars. So, it wouldn't have been cheap and he didn't think her position in the Ministry was very well paid or a high-up one.

"Where are you thinking of taking me then on this mystery Cuban weekend of yours?"

"Cienfuegos, La Perla del Sur, the Pearl of the South in English. It's on a bay on the south coast. It's a beautiful small city, known for its colonial-era buildings. The buildings and the whole city have a very French influence. There are some nice beaches nearby, and it has a nice harbour. The Bahia de Cochinos, Bay of Pigs in English is not far away, but I don't think we'll pay that a visit. You know, where the failed attempt by the United States and Cuban exiles in April 1961 to overthrow Castro's Revolution Government took place?"

"I do, but no I don't think that's worth time out of our weekend. Sounds like a nice place though, Cienfuegos. So, yes, let's go. How far is it?"

"About two hundred and forty kilometres, so should take around three-and-a-half to four hours. We should leave on Friday lunchtime, about one, if that's ok with you? I'll pick you up from your flat."

"Yep, that's fine. I've got no classes on Fridays so at one will be good. I'll bring my swim shorts. Can't wait."

She smiled again. It was a bright happy smile and her eyes were sparkling. She kissed him, then told him she had to shower and go to her place to change and then into the Ministry for work.

The weekend was great, as was Cienfuegos. It was everything she told him it was. The whole atmosphere of the place was, indeed, somehow very French, or at least French colonial. And she was more than great, in every aspect, such that on both mornings, Saturday and Sunday he found it difficult to want to get out of bed, or let her out of bed.

However, she insisted that he had to see the city, or at least the centre of it as it was designated a UNESCO World Heritage Site for its stunning architecture. Also, she told him she was determined that they get to one of the beaches nearby and, "I'm determined to get you into the Caribbean Sea. I want to see those sexy swim shorts of yours."

With that weekend in Cienfuegos things moved on quite a bit between them. He wasn't thinking at all anymore about when he would be leaving, what would happen then, or any danger of him being compromised by the Cuban Security Services. He was happy. He wasn't even thinking about any concerns he might have over drifting into the 'weight' of any relationship.

After their Cienfuegos weekend there was another drinks reception on the Wednesday evening connected to the Cuban/EU Higher Education Co-operation Programme. This one was at the French Embassy. David's handler from the British Embassy was there, as was Yurima. At one point, a Cuban Professor, a Science Professor she knew, approached her while she was talking to David and appeared keen to be introduced to him. So, she did, and they exchanged pleasantries and meaningless small talk for a very few minutes before the Professor moved away. After just over an hour Yurima was keen for them to leave once again. However, just as they were making their way to the doors of the large reception room David's handler side-tracked him and said he needed a quick word in private. They went off to a quiet corner of the room while Yurima waited by the doors. The handler told David he was to call the Science Professor tomorrow afternoon and arrange to meet him later in the week, but not at the university. As he told him that he discreetly placed a small piece of paper into the palm of David's hand, telling him, "This is his private mobile number." When David asked why the handler said he'd call and explain tomorrow morning, but to just do it after they'd spoken, and tell the Professor that he wanted to meet to talk to him about developing the Co-operation Programme.

"Do we?" David asked.

"No, but that's all you need to know for now. He'll be expecting your call. He'll know what it's really about. He's been forewarned. It's his idea. It's what he wants, and definitely what we want. He's got, knows, a lot of information about the links between the Cuban government and the Russians, particularly on weapons technology development, as well as cyber science. His title at Havana University may be Science Professor, but his role entails a lot more than that in terms of links with, and work for, the Cuban Government and the Russians."

David was stunned and more than a little open mouthed.

"Look, I've already said more than I should to you here. I'll explain everything tomorrow," the handler added.

What he said next stunned and concerned David even more though.

"And don't mention this to anyone, especially not Yurima Flores. We know very well you two are close, but we're not a hundred percent sure about her yet, whether she can be trusted."

Despite his growing concern and anxiety to know more, particularly anything that related to Yurima, David just nodded slightly, and said quietly, "Ok."

He was obviously very curious and concerned that he was slowly being dragged into something involving the British Security Services which appeared to be a lot more dangerous than what he'd done so far in Havana, which actually was very little to date.

As soon as they got outside she suggested they go to Floridita in the Old Town for a Margarita and asked, "What was that about with the guy from your Embassy? Problems?"

"No, no, just something the Embassy wants to talk to me about connected to the Programme, the Co-operation Programme. Extending it, I think, and about who I thought could come here next from the U.K.. If I knew anyone, could recommend them, from my university or another one."

"Are you leaving so soon then?" she asked, with a frown across her forehead.

"No, not soon. Why would I want to leave here soon, and you?"

He smiled, put his arm around her waist and squeezed her gently to reassure her and divert her away from any talk of him leaving.

They went to Floridita and then, as was now usually the case, she came back to his apartment to stay the night.

As soon as she left at just before nine the next morning he called his handler, as instructed. What he was told to do didn't actually sound quite so dangerous or difficult as he anticipated it might be the night before.

"Call and arrange to meet briefly for coffee or a drink, somewhere open like the ground floor terrace of the Inglaterra so that it doesn't look anything secretive, and discreetly pass him a paper with my other number on it, the one you were told not to use unless it was an emergency. As I said before, he'll be expecting your call in the next day or so. I'll do the rest after he calls," the handler told him.

"Is that all, all you want me to do?"

"Yes, that's it, David. He'll know what to do. As I said, he's expecting it."

David let out a small sigh of relief before saying, "Ok."

He thought that was it and the handler would ring off, but instead he added, "But remember, nothing at all to Yurima Flores about this."

He repeated, "We know you two have become close and are seeing a lot of each other, but for her own safety as much as anything, don't involve her in any way or tell her anything."

"Her own safety," what the hell did that mean he wondered? And that was the second time the handler had said to him, "We know you two have become close." Who was that "We"? The British Security Services presumably. Was he, or Yurima, or both of them, being watched? Now he was becoming concerned again. Before he could ask anything more though, this time his handler actually did ring off.

David called the Cuban Professor later that Thursday afternoon and arranged to meet him for a drink late in the afternoon of the next day at the ground floor terrace of the Hotel Inglaterra looking out over Parque Central, as his had handler suggested. The Professor told him he remembered him from the French Embassy reception and that he was happy to meet him to talk about the Co-operation Programme, but that David didn't have to explain anything more for now. With that he ended their short call.

When he arrived David was already sitting at a table at the rear of the terrace looking out over the square. He started the conversation innocently by asking David how much he was enjoying the university and Havana. There followed a few minutes of small talk between them while they ordered a coffee each. After the coffee arrived the Professor asked if David had something for him and could he pass the sugar. David discreetly placed a folded small piece of paper with his handler's emergency number on it under the sugar bowl and slid it over the table to him. He placed a cube of sugar in his coffee and equally discreetly picked up the folded paper from beneath the bowl. They drank their coffees, carried on with some more small talk about Havana University and then the guy stood up and said, "Goodbye." He never even attempted to offer David a handshake, presumably determined not to draw any attention to them.

After that David stayed, and feeling relieved ordered a bottle of Cuban Bucanero beer to sit there relaxed in the late Havana Friday afternoon sunshine watching the world go by ahead of him in the square. And that was it so it seemed. No trouble or bother at all. He could get back to thinking about how he was going to spend another pleasant weekend in Havana with Yurima. It all turned out to be a lot more than simply no bother or trouble, however.

He did spend another lovely Havana weekend with her. They slept in on Saturday morning then went for brunch at Café O'Reilly in the Old Town. She said she was determined to take him somewhere new, and he definitely hadn't been there before. Curious about the Café's name she told him it was, in fact, named after Second Corporal Alexander O'Reilly, an Irish marshal of the Spanish army who was sent to Cuba by King Carlos III to oversee the defensive situation after the British occupation of 1763. For his services to the Spanish Crown O'Reilly was made a Spanish Count and honoured with two historic streets named after him, one in Cadiz and the other in Havana, where the café was located.

"Wow! Brunch and a history lesson," he told her with a smile. The food was good and the coffee excellent. It felt like a perfect Saturday as they strolled together afterwards in the hot

Havana sunshine and ended up in the Plaza de la Catedral sat at a table outside one of the cafes there for a cooling mid-afternoon cold beer The concerns he had, as well as any stress, over what he'd been asked to do in contacting and meeting the Cuban Professor melted away in the sunshine and with Yurima's company. That had disappeared from his thoughts completely and all was right and pleasant in his world once again.

It didn't last, however. Early Monday afternoon his handler called and simply said, "Our package is being delivered. It's on its way, left very early yesterday morning."

David thought he knew what that meant but couldn't resist trying to check.

"So, he's-"

He never got to finish.

"Yes, David, but that's enough on here. Just do your work at the University as usual for the next few days. I expect you'll be busy with that, so it would be best if you don't have time for any overnight visitors."

He knew who that referred to, Yurima, but he still couldn't resist asking more, or at least trying to ask, even though he thought he was doing it in a very clever subtle way.

"How? Where's the package being delivered to?"

He never got an answer. The line just went dead.

He resisted contacting Yurima during the rest of Monday, not even ringing or texting her. They had got into the habit of at least texting once a day when they weren't meeting that day. By Tuesday evening, however, he hadn't had anything from her, no call and not even a text. As he got into his bed that evening he was feeling a little anxious. Despite what his handler had told him to do he decided he'd text her the next morning and suggest they go somewhere for dinner that evening. When he sent the text at just after ten the next morning from his office in the university he got a two word message on his phone screen saying 'NOT DELIVERED'. He was confused. His confusion quickly turned to concern when he immediately tried to ring her mobile and he got a voice message which, from his limited Spanish, he understood as 'number unobtainable'.

He tried hard to let his rational side convince him that perhaps she'd simply lost her phone, or there was something wrong with it, some technical fault. The Cuban mobile network wasn't the most reliable. Many Cubans didn't actually have access to a mobile phone, and he'd often seen even the minority who did in long queues in Havana waiting to buy the equivalent of 'pay as you go' credit phone cards. But Yurima Flores wasn't one of 'many Cubans'. She had a quite good position at a Cuban Government Ministry and access to the best type of mobile phone available in Cuba, at least the best available to Government officials in her position. He'd seen it a number of times, like when she'd taken photos of them on their weekend in Cienfuegos.

His rational side lost out to the concerned and negative part of his character. So, he called his handler and told him what had happened, how he was concerned about her. His handler wasn't exactly pleased.

"I told you to lay low, David, concentrate on your university work, and not contact her or see her."

There was clear cold anger in his voice as he added, "It's very dangerous for you at the moment, as well as for her."

"Because of the Prof-"

David's question was cut short by an even angrier voice of the handler.

"David, shut up now. Just do as you're bloody told. You're making it worse for all of us by asking too many questions. Go and do what you're fucking paid to do in the university. Go and just be a University lecturer for a few days, and don't even think about Yurima Flores, let alone contact her."

The handler rang off and very reluctantly David did what he said for two more days, during which time he still didn't hear from her. He went into the university, did his lectures and saw his students during his consultation time. No matter how much he tried though, he couldn't get her out of his head and wondering why he hadn't heard from her.

Eventually it was too much and he couldn't resist trying to contact her in any way he could. He decided to call the Ministry of Education. He asked the receptionist if she spoke English. When she confirmed she did in perfect English he asked to be put through to Yurima Flores in the International Co-operation department. The receptionist never said a word, but just put him through. Suddenly he became very nervous. What if she hadn't called simply because she no longer wanted to see him, wanted it to finish between them. That would be awkward, as well as embarrassing. He had no idea why that might be the case though, what he'd possibly done to make her think that, want that.

All those thoughts were racing through his brain while he heard the phone connection to her department ringing for what felt like a very long minute. Eventually a man's voice answered in Spanish. David asked if he spoke English and the guy replied, "Of course, what can I do for you?"

"Good, is Yurima Flores available at all? Can I speak with her, please?"

David's level of concern rose rapidly for two reasons with the guy's reply.

"Yurima Flores doesn't work here any longer, Mr. Alexander."

"What? Err ... are you sure?"

"I am the head of the department. So, I think I know who works here."

"But she worked there last week. I saw her at the weekend and she never said anything about leaving, about another position."

"We know you did, Mr. Alexander, but maybe she simply didn't want you to know she was leaving or where she was going to work?"

"Well ... I ... err."

David was completely disorientated. He hadn't expected this at all, and his mind was buzzing with questions, not least how did the guy know his name? He didn't give it to the receptionist.

Perhaps, after all, this was Yurima's way of dealing with the fact that she wanted to stop seeing him? But he couldn't believe or accept that, so he tried one more question.

"Where has she gone to?"

"Sorry, sir?"

"Yurima Flores, where has she gone to work, another department in the Ministry?"

The guy replied quite coldly, "Camaguey. You know where that-"

"Yes, yes, I know where that is, in the south-east, quite a long way from Havana. But-"

David never got the rest of what he was about to say out of his mouth. The guy simply said, "Good," followed by a brusque, "Now, goodbye, Mr. Alexander."

He was more confused than ever now, and somewhat distraught. Why would she do that? Just leave without telling him, without even contacting him, without even a goodbye. To say he was upset was an understatement. And why was her mobile phone number unavailable?

He became a lot more upset, however, when his handler called him the following afternoon, Friday.

"Your overnight visitor-" he began.

"Yes, yes, where is-"

"Dead, David. She's dead."

There was a silence.

"David, David, you still there?"

Eventually he stammered, "But ... but ... you sure ... how, where?"

"Somewhere on the south coast apparently, a boating accident on Tuesday at Cienfuegos. That's what our contacts tell us the Cubans are saying."

"But that's where we-"

"For the weekend, yes I know, David."

"But why, and why there? Why was she there again and didn't tell me? It doesn't make sense. Nothing does. I called her department yesterday and a guy, he said he was the head of her department, he told me she'd left. Quit her job and gone to Camaguey."

"You did what! For fuck's sake, David. Why did you do something stupid like that? I told you it was dangerous, for you and her at the moment, although she was probably already dead by then."

"The guy knew my name, called me by it, without me even giving it to him or the telephone receptionist."

"Christ! Where are you now?"

"In my flat."

"Right, stay there. Don't go out, don't answer the door to anyone unless it's me."

"What? That's a bit melodramatic isn't it?"

"Melodramatic? Right, stay there, I'll be with you in fifteen minutes. I'll call you when I'm outside and you can let me in. Don't answer the door to anyone else or take any other calls."

Almost spot on the fifteen minutes the handler called and David let him in. His anger hadn't subsided in that time.

"Do you have any idea what sort of fire you're playing with here?"

He weighed into David as soon as he closed the door to his flat.

This is way past you just trying to pick up or overhear some gossip at Embassy receptions. It's no bloody coincidence that you did a job for us with the Cuban Professor, a simple thing you were asked, told, to do, and a matter of a couple of days after he defects a woman you were very friendly with is killed, and the head of her Ministry department is calling you by name when you hadn't told him it, So-"

"Killed? You said it was an accident."

"Don't be so bloody naïve, David. They no doubt assumed it was her who passed you the information on the Professor, what he wanted. She introduced you to each other at the French Embassy reception. No doubt the Cuban Security Services had someone there and to them it probably looked like she introduced you deliberately. And they definitely would have known you and her were spending a lot of time together, that she was staying over at your flat."

David was getting more and more distraught.

"You saying I got her killed? It was my fault?"

"No, just circumstances, she knew what she was doing, getting over friendly with a foreigner always could be difficult, even dangerous, given where she worked. Don't blame yourself. I know I'm angry, but I'm angry because you don't seem to really appreciate the danger she was in, and that you are now in."

"Oh, come on, really, that's-"

The handler didn't let him finish. He'd had enough.

"What? Melodramatic? Well you're out of here tomorrow. You're no use to us now. The Cuban Security Services clearly think they know why you're here. It's much too dangerous now to keep you here. The Embassy will make some excuse to the university; a family thing back home or something similar. You'll be on a plane to London tomorrow afternoon. Get your stuff packed. Don't worry about any personal academic things you have at the university. We'll send a car and a guy to go with you to pick them up."

David slumped in his chair.

"Wow! You really sure that needs to happen. Surely-"

"This is not a discussion any longer, David. I'm telling you, you're leaving. If you want I'll get my boss in MI6 in London to tell you formerly, but he'll be a lot more brutal in telling you you're leaving even than I've been."

The handler made a call and then told David, "A car and one of our guys will be here for you in half-an-hour to take you to the university to get your stuff. He'll stay with you there and then bring you and your stuff back here. Don't attempt to talk to anyone else there, even any students unlikely to be around on a Friday afternoon. Then stay in tonight, don't answer the door or your phone to anyone except me. I'll call you later with the flight details for tomorrow after our people at the Embassy have sorted it. A car will pick you up with the same guy who goes to the university with you today and take you to the airport. I'll text you the time later."

David just sat, slumped, nodded and said quietly, "Ok."

"Oh," the handler added, "and a couple of days after you get back, Monday probably, you'll be required to go in for a debrief. You know where. Someone will call you Sunday evening."

Reflecting on it all on his Saturday afternoon flight to London, his whole Havana experience, it all felt pretty cold, especially the way his relationship with Yurima ended; tragic for her and cold and callous the way his handler and MI6 dealt with it. It felt like more than just another bad ending to a relationship than he was actually beginning to think might somehow, although he didn't know how, develop into one of 'weight' based on fidelity and responsibility.

He did the fairly routine de-brief on the Monday afternoon at the same SIS building in London in which he'd initially been recruited. The guy who debriefed him didn't appear to be anywhere near as angry as his handler had been over what happened. David went back to take up his previous position at the university in Bristol and heard nothing from MI6 for almost two years. But he knew that, as someone had once told him, or maybe he just read it somewhere, once they have you they don't let go.

Sure enough he had a call from London and the SIS building in March 2019. Could he pop into the SIS building and see them. They had a job for him, nothing dangerous, very simple and straight forward, and pretty much the same as he was doing for them before he went to Havana, listening to gossip, only this time not academics gossiping and not at an academic conference.

A couple of days later he was once again shown into the same very large grand looking room – it could hardly be called an office – as he had his first interview in five years before, to be met this time by only one of the smart, dark waist-coat suited men sat in one of the high backed velvet armchairs at the far side of the room

"We heard you've junked the academic life, old boy. Had enough, left your university, doing the Greek island thing and going to Rhodes for the summer to write the great novel."

He wasn't at all surprised by now by how they knew so much about his life, his plans. He couldn't be bothered asking any more so he simply replied, "Yes, that's right."

"Lindos isn't it? Nice little place."

He was growing wary. All this small talk about his life was making him uneasy. He didn't answer. They obviously knew he was going there.

"Very handy coincidence that, old chap, you going there."

"Is it now?"

He knew that what was coming was something they wanted him to do there.

"Yes, yes, you see we had a bit of an unfortunate, well very unfortunate really, mishap there, in Lindos, a few years ago, lost one of our assets there, one of our best men. Of course, he wasn't based there. We got a tip off there was a former IRA operative, a woman, staying in the village, something to do with tracing her family history. Seems her mother worked there as a tour rep for two summers back in the seventies, got herself pregnant by some Greek chappie, but then left and never declared on the IRA woman's birth certificate who the father was."

The guy got up from the armchair and went over to stare out of one of the very large windows.

"Interesting don't you think?" he eventually continued while still peering out of the window as David sat in silence.

"Anyway, we'd been looking for this woman IRA ex-operative for a few years. She did some serious damage to the Service. Infiltrated it at one point on the recommendation of one of our best people, also a woman as it happens, a friend of hers from university, although not that much of a friend obviously as it turned out as she killed her. Pushed her under a tube train at Oxford Circus."

He turned around to face David and with a slight frown said, "All a bit embarrassing really. So, when we heard she was in Lindos doing that tracing her family stuff we sent one of our best people out there to deal with her. Trouble was it was the other way round and she dispatched him, even made it look like an accident. Made it look like he cracked his head on a wall and on some rough steps in one of the back alleys in the village. The local police bought it, of course, and again all a bit embarrassing for us so we just shut it down, played along with the accident story. As far as we were concerned it was water under the bridge. Always very messy revenge killing, so we pulled it, the operation."

"So, what's this got to do with me going to Lindos for the summer," David finally asked?

"We've still got some contacts on the island, not operatives, just a couple of people who drop us little bits and pieces of info they think might be of interest. Two weeks ago one of them fed us a rumour circulating in the village that there had been someone in Lindos who had seen the killing, the supposed accident, a witness to the killing of our asset. Well, that would be more than embarrassing for the Service if it got out back here and, of course, if it was to become general knowledge in Lindos. We'd be a laughing stock in that place full of clowns across the river."

"Parliament?" David asked, although he knew that was what the guy meant.

"Not good for the reputation of the Service at all. There are some over there in Westminster who would just love to cut us down, and that sort of embarrassment would be just the sort of excuse they'd love for them to do that."

He sat back down in the armchair and added, in a much lighter tone, "Well, when I heard you were going on your little summer sojourn there I thought what better man to check out some of that gossip, see if there's any substance to it?"

"Erm ... I don't really know many people-"

David never got to finish. The guy's tone changed considerably.

"Look it's not much, just listen to gossip and see if there's anything to it, this rumour of a witness, and let us know. We'll do the rest, if anything needs doing."

"Well, I'd prefer-"

Again David never got to finish.

"After your bloody Havana cock-up you need to just do this for us. You do understand that don't you?"

He did. He nodded, and said, "Ok, I'll see what I can find out, if there is anything."

Six weeks later he was on a plane on his way to his new life of a full summer in hot, sunny, relaxing Lindos. He'd do what MI6 wanted. Live in the village, engage in the life of the village and listen for any gossip about what MI6 were concerned about. It didn't seem that onerous. Plus, after Yurima, and what happened to her in Havana, he was determined to never again allow himself to drift into, or even consider the possibility of, the 'weight' type of relationship situation.

At least, that was the case until towards the end of that summer of 2019, and into the following one of 2020, when the lives of three people, including David Alexander's, collided in a dramatic fashion in the little tourist village. The circumstances around that caused him to question and challenge his whole belief in the viability and future desirability of the 'lightness' in his relationships. It led him to consider more seriously the alternative and possibility of the 'weight' of fidelity in them once again, and in terms of one in particular. That would entail him making a clear choice in Lindos within the circumstances he found himself in by September 2020; a choice of continuing to be a pawn operating for the interests of the British Security Services, or alternatively, pursuing the 'weight' of a loving, emotionally faithful relationship.

14

The other woman

Alice Palmer decided at the start of the summer of 2016 to give up her job in the city she was from, Sheffield, and take the plunge to come to, "live the dream," as she liked to describe it, by living and working in Lindos. When she met David Alexander it was her fourth summer season. Unlike most of the Brit workers in the village she stayed on through the intervening winters.

Alice was in her mid-thirties. Her fairly slim figure was no doubt maintained through working as a waitress in a Lindos restaurant, requiring her to be continuously climbing back and forth up and down the staircases to its two rooftop terraces every evening to serve the customers. She was married at twenty-three. That lasted for a relatively brief five years. Now she was divorced. She was medium height; around five foot six in her flat waitress shoes or the practical flat sandals most of the women workers wore around the village when not working. When she allowed it to, her long thick dark black hair would reach down to the middle of her back. At work though, she always wore it up, either in a pony-tail or piled up and pinned on top of her head. That was how she was wearing it the night David first met her when she served him in the restaurant, pinned on the top of her head, fully highlighting the best qualities of her attractive thin face and slender neck, as well as her deep brown eyes.

She was a complex character, as David quickly discovered soon after he met her on that first night of his long Lindos summer of 2019 when she served him. Her easy charm and friendly nature when she spoke with customers in the restaurant suggested a soaring, sparkling self-confidence. However, at other times outside of that environment and those work surroundings she displayed lots of self-doubt, bordering on self-deprecation. That could easily spill over to manifest itself in self-defensive aggression at times. Quite soon after they met David realised that, in fact, she was much smarter than she thought, or at least chose to believe. He quickly learned from experience though that it was never easy to convince her of that.

He also soon encountered a number of things about her character of many sides and many personalities. There was her bravado that could border on aggression. It quickly became apparent that often was a shield she used to cover and disguise her lack of confidence. It was almost a reflex response. Her external confidence merely masked her inner self-doubt. She had her ups, "living the dream", and she had her downs, times when she was down, flat, and not bubbly at all. Even though she was living in such a beautiful place as Lindos, in reality it wasn't all up times and, "living the dream." Although even her down times still found a way to surface within the attractive glow of her personality. At least, that's how it increasingly felt to David Alexander through that summer of 2019.

She was always a busy character, seemingly restlessly so, and not content unless she was doing something. Actually relaxing nagged away constantly at her conscience. Even in her down periods there was something about her that attracted him. She had a style, an irresistible style of her own which increasingly appealed to him through that summer, and drew him to her. However, Alice Palmer never really let her guard down, never really actually let anyone in, not in completely. It was as if there was a part of her that could never be really fully reached. A part of her that throughout that whole summer she would never let David, or anyone else, into.

If she remotely suspected he was getting too close at times she would shut down, and her aggressive bravado would surface, sometimes with a level of contempt in her voice. Occasionally that even developed into an argument between them over almost nothing. She wouldn't back down an inch. Instead, she would almost automatically respond with an answer that defied an argument or facilitated any further response. Initially, he thought it was all simply sheer arrogance, until he reconciled it to being her self-defence mechanism; a reflex reaction from a lack of self-confidence deep within her.

He was only partly correct about that, however. When it came to men and any possible relationship her self-defence mechanism was simply a symptom of the root cause, her past experience with one man in particular, her ex-husband.

"Done that, got the t-shirt, no more thanks," she told David late into one night while they were drinking together and a wedding reception was still continuing on a nearby restaurant's rooftop. Basically, she was very guarded about revealing anything about herself and her past to anyone, particularly when it came to men and relationships. When it came to those things she wasn't an easy person to get anything out of. After quite a few drinks on another long night in response to his question whether she had any family back in the U.K. she did actually reveal that she had no children, or any brothers and sisters, as well as that her parents were both still alive and lived in Hallam in Sheffield. But that was the limit to what she disclosed about herself and her past.

That part of her character, not exactly secretive like David Alexander's, but certainly a closed book, resulted from, and was produced by, the experience of how her marriage ended. It left a scar and bred a distrust of men in general. Her divorce had been messy.

She actually met her ex-husband, Colin, in Lindos while on holiday with some women friends in 2006. A year later they married, and returned to Lindos three times after for holidays. During that time she worked as a computer data processor and programmer for a large engineering company in Sheffield, while he worked as a manager of a car rental company. The pay was good for both of them, so they had no problem getting a mortgage to buy a small house on the edge of the city. Alice fell in love with Lindos that first summer she came on holiday with her women friends, the same summer she fell in love with Colin as they kept in touch after the holiday. He lived in Wakefield at the time they met, while she lived on the northern edge of Sheffield. So, meeting up after the holiday wasn't a problem. When that quickly developed into spending every weekend together, either at his place or hers - both rented flats – a seemingly natural progression at the time took place. They moved in together and married soon after.

At that point it appeared Alice Palmer's life was fully planned out ahead of her. That is until by chance she discovered that he'd been having an affair for a year with her best friend. She found out about it soon after he'd told her he was at a national conference in Birmingham for a week for his work. A couple of days after he supposedly got back from that she was going to put a work suit of hers into the dry cleaners. They had a two for one offer. To take advantage of that she thought it was a good idea to put the suit he'd taken to the conference in with hers. When she checked the pockets of his jacket for any rubbish before taking it to the cleaners she found a receipt for a double room in a hotel in Manchester for the week that he was supposed to be at the conference in Birmingham. She had been suspicious of some of his actions for a few weeks, including his increasingly late work nights. Consequently, she took a chance and rang the hotel telling them she was the woman who had stayed there the previous week with him and required a duplicate of the bill. The hotel receptionist responded with, "Oh, yes, Miss Simmons, if you give me your email I-"

She rang off. Carol Simmons was her best friend. She'd been one of the women on the Lindos holiday with Alice when she met Colin. She'd even used her real name for the hotel booking, or rather Alice's husband had. She was shocked and stunned. When she confronted him he eventually admitted they'd been having an affair for the past year, ever since Carol's own divorce. That was the end of her marriage and of her friendship with Carol. She lost a husband and her best friend. Alice took some small satisfaction from confronting Carol physically. The result of which was a nasty looking black eye from just the one blow. Real friendship, as well as any meaningful relationship, didn't come easily to Alice after that.

As Carol and Alice's ex-husband found out Alice Palmer was not someone to mess with, physically on Carol's part and financially as far as Colin was concerned. In the messy divorce Alice's solicitor managed to secure her the largest part of the equity in their house. In fact, her divorce settlement was considerably enhanced when her solicitor discovered that her ex-husband had owned another rather large house for five years besides the one that he owned with Alice. He rented it out through an agent. Alice had no idea about that whatsoever. That gave her some more satisfaction, together with the damage she inflicted on the major part of his wardrobe, viciously taking scissors to his clothes the night she discovered his affair.

That whole experience left a mark on her that she ensured she wasn't going to shake off easily. It made her a much harder person, generally devoid of showing much emotion. She wasn't going to let herself fall into that trap again easily, if at all. Trusting any man again in the way she'd trusted Colin was alien to her by the time she arrived to live in Lindos. She was determined that wasn't going to happen again. She relented a couple of times before she came to Lindos and went on dates with men her work friends had recommended, and were determined to fix her up with. However, she never felt comfortable. It never felt right. It wasn't that they were unattractive. She simply couldn't get past the trust issue. She wasn't even interested in, or engaging in, the 'lightness' of any sexual encounters, let alone the 'weight' of any sort of relationship again based on fidelity.

So, there were certainly a couple, or even more than a couple, Alice Palmer's. She was different characters in different surroundings, and in different circumstances. The Alice who was the waitress working in the Lindos restaurant was friendly and chatty with the customers, the tourists. She was very good at that, and not only in the restaurant, but also when she encountered any of them after work in the late bars or the clubs in the village. Then there was the aggressive, self-preserving, and simultaneously defensive Alice. That Alice occasionally surfaced when she encountered other Brit ex-pats in Lindos, as well as David Alexander at times through that summer of 2019. Often there didn't appear to be any reason or explanation for the contrast in her character, or indeed, the timing of it. Equally though, the chatty, friendly Alice could also unexpectedly suddenly re-emerge. When that happened with him, and she was much friendlier, he put the difference down to something developing between them. Although he couldn't work out at all if it was just the 'lightness' of a possible future sexual relationship she might want or the first signs of the 'weight' of something deeper developing between them. He didn't really know what he wanted it to be anyway, having been adamant before he came to Lindos at the start of that summer of 2019 that he didn't want anything resembling the 'weight' of responsibility and fidelity.

So, by the time Alice Palmer arrived in Lindos in early May of her first summer living and working there permanently in 2016 she hadn't experienced the 'weight' of anything that could even remotely be referred to as a relationship since her divorce, let alone even the 'lightness' of any regular sexual encounters. After she arrived though, it didn't take her long to slip effortlessly into the rhythm of the restaurant and bar workers' summer lives and routines. That meant not just working alongside many of them, but also socialising with them after work in the late bars and clubs in the village. She got to go drinking with many of them after work at one or two in the morning. Not that she would call any of them close friends. Instead, there were merely plenty of acquaintances; tourists she met through her work in the restaurant, the other Brit ex-pat workers or local Greeks and Albanian workers in the village.

The one possible exception was Dianne Arnold. They struck up a sort of a friendship almost immediately after Alice arrived in Lindos. The two women, if not best friends, at least were drinking partners after work on regular occasions. Usually they would meet up after work at one or two in the morning for a late drink in Jack Constantino's Courtyard Bar, or in the bottom bar at Lindos By Night. Eventually, around three, they'd move on for a few more in the clubs, Glow or Arches, sometimes with other summer season workers. Three, sometimes four times a week, that would be their usual routine. More than a few summer nights drifted by in a blur for the pair of them.

Like Alice, Dianne worked in another of the restaurants in the village. She was a tall woman in her early forties and was from Manchester originally. Her well-groomed shoulder length light brown hair framed her long attractive face perfectly. When she wasn't wearing the required restaurant dark t-shirt with its logo and a knee length black skirt, outside work she paraded an impressive wardrobe. She was always immaculately dressed after work in the bars and clubs, whether in a blouse and skirt or a smart dress. Alice introduced David to her in Glow one night during that summer.

Also like Alice, Dianne had been a regular Lindos one or two week holiday visitor over many years from her teens and had decided to come and live and work in the village for the summer six years previously. She enjoyed that summer of 2013 so much that she decided to stay permanently and now lived there all year round. She'd never been married. However, in Lindos she was never short of male admirers, whether they were tourists staying in the village for one or two weeks, Brit ex-pat men who lived there, or Greek local men.

After she met Dianne, Alice Palmer quickly became a soul of the dark night in the little tourist village, just like many of the summer season restaurant and bar workers. She, and her world, only came alive long after the sun had disappeared from the Lindos sky and the stars began to twinkle above alongside the clear moon. She usually worked from early evening to one or one-thirty. Then she'd regularly go and party in the bars and the clubs, usually with Dianne, often until five or six in the morning. Sometimes on Fridays and Saturday in the middle of the summer that would be even later in the open air Arches Plus club down by the Main Beach or in the Amphitheatre club on the hill just outside the village, literally until the sun came up. Then it would be pizza or gyros, bed, and sleep under the air-conditioning until one, or two in the afternoon, sometimes later, followed by some more food, a shower, and back to work by six or six-thirty. She only very rarely managed to visit the beach or swim in the clear blue warm sea. 'Living the dream' didn't really include much living in the sun or days of lazing on the beach for Alice. Like many of the other summer season bar and restaurant workers the nocturnal structure and routine to her life began from mid-May and eventually exhaustingly petered out towards the end of October as the season ran down. By then she was completely knackered, not to mention a serious assault on her liver from the summer's alcohol consumption.

That was the way of life for many of the Lindos summer season bar and restaurant workers. It always started with excitement and enthusiasm for a new season in May and early

June. You could feel the expectant atmosphere of the coming summer in the village, especially amongst the bar and restaurant owners and their staff. Their energy began to drain and slowly slip away during the mid-summer July and August soaring temperatures, with the accompanying spiralling humidity. Relief from the heat and humidity arrived with the cooler, more manageable September temperatures, but by late September and early October the workers displayed total weariness. Despite that the majority of them loved it. Many of them returned summer after summer. It was like it was some sort of harmful drug that they simply couldn't resist, were addicted to. The ones that finally kicked the habit largely did so because they met someone, usually in Lindos, and either stayed together in the village for all time, or returned home to live with them. Quite a few Brit ex-pat women who came to work in Lindos for the summer met Greeks, stayed, married and had their families in the Lindos paradise, as they referred to it. Alice was determined that she wasn't going to be one of those though. That definitely wasn't for Alice Palmer. She'd been married, and not to a Greek. As she told David one time, "Done that, got the t-shirt, no more thanks."

Alice had done the 'weight' of fidelity and responsibility with her marriage, ending up with an unfaithful husband. Of course, just as in most villages, there were rumours, and the village of Lindos was never short of them, particularly amongst the Brit ex-pats. Consequently, there certainly were a few of them about her 'lighter' sexual encounters with men, Brit ex-pat workers as well as Greek and Albanian workers, although nothing about her and those with tourists. Her decision at the start of the summer of 2016 to come to live and work in the village had seemingly been accompanied with a conscious decision to at the very most only pursue the 'lightness' of any temporary sexual encounters if that, but to avoid anything with the possible likelihood of the 'weight' of what could be termed a relationship. Truthfully, however, despite the rumours, it appeared there had been hardly even any 'light' sexual encounters during her previous three summers in Lindos.

Over the months of that summer, and the many late nights and early mornings she spent in various bars and the clubs with

David, it was obvious they were growing closer, but that never grew to even the 'lightness' of any sexual encounter between them. One night in July he had taken the plunge after a few drinks and asked her, "What they were, what did she think was between them?"

"Friends, just friends, very good friends," was the blunt unemotional response he got at that time.

But as that summer of 2019 wore on through the blinding heat and humidity of August he thought he perceived small indications in what she occasionally said to him that she was allowing her determination to avoid any meaningful relationship with him slip somewhat. It was never anything major, not a major statement of her intent, but just little comments about, "them," rather than just her. When she used, "us," as well in some of her comments rather than just, "I" was she starting to think of them as a couple now, or was that just him over analysing things? And did he really want an, "us," anyway? That sounded like far too much responsibility and 'weight'.

However, the greatest indication of the way her feelings about him might be changing came with what she told him one day early in September when they went to Rhodes Town. It was a clear sign she trusted him, and as more than a friend, even more than as a very good friend. The problem was it presented her more than "a very good friend" with a huge dilemma.

One night while they were out drinking late he suggested they have dinner together one evening. They hadn't done that yet. However, she pointed out that it was impossible for her to get an evening off from the restaurant in the season, even in early September. So, instead he suggested going for a day in Rhodes Town, to see the historical part of the Old Town, and have some lunch. He pointed out he'd never been and she told him she'd only been once, in the first summer she worked in Lindos. Eventually she agreed, telling him she'd hire a car for the day rather than rely on the buses. That way she'd be certain of getting back on time to start her evening shift in the restaurant.

As they drove to Rhodes Town she certainly seemed a lot more relaxed than he'd seen her before. She'd opted for plain white shorts, along with a loose fitting white short sleeved shirt outside her shorts given the anticipated heat in Rhodes Town. Also to counter the heat she'd tied her long thick dark black hair up in a ponytail. The neck of her shirt was left deliberately open to counter the heat, far enough down just barely reveal the start of her cleavage. Her white trainers were sensible for walking the cobbled and flagstone streets and alleys of Rhodes Old Town. For David it was also shorts, dark blue, black trainers and a light blue t-shirt. Once they began to walk in the town he wished he'd also chosen a loose fitting short sleeved shirt in the heat, rather than the t-shirt.

When they'd almost reached Rhodes Town she asked, "So, why not stay in England to write? I know it's obviously nicer here, but does that really help with writing? Isn't it too easy to be distracted and go off to the beach, or go out drinking half the night and lose part of the next day?"

He laughed, which drew a frown from her and a quizzical "What? What's funny?"

"Go out drinking half the night and lose part of the next day, Alice? I think you've played your part in that, and if only it had been half the night. A lot of the times it was till daybreak."

She stared straight ahead through the car windscreen for a few seconds in silence, then let out a small chuckle before she told him, "Well, yes, maybe, but it does take two you know. And you can't blame me for every night."

"Well, the more you travel the more ideas you hear, the more things you see and are exposed to. Sometimes you can use them, somehow. Not all of them though of course, but some, in your, my, writing. You become more open to ideas, as well as the exchange of stories and thoughts the more you travel."

She chuckled once again. "Maybe, but I still think it's because you prefer the sun here, and the late night drinking."

She briefly glanced sideways at him, quickly studying him. He could feel her eyes penetrating. He turned his head towards her and smiled. This was a much more relaxed Alice Palmer. Maybe it was the effect of getting her out of Lindos, even if only for half a day, but he liked it, liked this Alice a lot. Things were going well.

As they found a place to park near the Old Town wall she turned into Alice Palmer tour guide, impressing him with her knowledge.

"You know that the most famous image of Rhodes is the bronze statue, the Colossus, one of the Seven Wonders of the World, built to commemorate the Rhodian triumph after the siege of Dimitrious the Besieger in 305 BC. Apparently, it took twelve years to complete. The most popular image of the thirty-one metre tall statue, the one used all around the world, is one straddled across the entrance of the harbour with ships passing beneath it, but it is more probable that it stood on dry land somewhere close to where the Palace of the Grand Master is now. Wherever it stood though, it didn't stand there long because it fell in the earthquake of 266 BC."

He obviously wasn't aware of the debate over where it actually stood, and was even more impressed as she continued.

"Did you know that it was built by someone from Lindos, David? He was known as Chares of Lindos apparently. Well, it was designed by him at least. I doubt that he actually built it hand by hand, so to speak."

Alice Palmer's hidden depths, is what he was thinking as she added more.

"We should obviously go and see the Palace of the Grand Master, as well as the Street of the Knights. It was all constructed and inhabited by the Knights of St. John between the fourteenth and sixteenth century, after the Crusaders were defeated and driven out of Jerusalem and the Holy Land. Interesting, don't you think? I do like a bit of history. It fascinates me. It's the most beautiful and interesting part of the Old Town for me, the most important street of the medieval town. The street has been completely restored or preserved beautifully, and is lined by the buildings where the holy warriors spent their time in prayer or military practice. It stretches up a slight hill to the Grand Master's Palace at the top"

After they'd parked they made their way through the crowds of tourists, including those from the two cruise ships in the harbour, to the bottom of the Street of the Knights and Alice continued her tour guide information.

"Apparently the Knights were divided into seven languages according to their birthplace, including English, French, German, and Italian. Each of them was responsible for a specific section of the fortifications and the street has a Palace or Inn for each language."

That drew a sideways look at her from him.

"What? What are you looking at me like that for?" she asked.

"Nothing, it's good, it's like having my own personal guide," he replied, with a bit of a patronising grin.

"I told you I like a bit of history, and I've been here before remember? Also, I did some reading up on it online last winter here. It was one way to get through the endless boredom and the multiple coffees in the Red Rose Bar, and use their Wi-Fi of course. Which was just as well, as besides the Ice Bar up at Krana it was the only bar open."

They made their way slowly up the cobbled slight slope of the Street of the Knights. The sandstone coloured high walls of the imposing medieval buildings on either side reflected the bright sunlight, only occasionally offering them some intermittent shade. The mixture of light and shade added to the atmospheric historical mood the street conveyed, as well as to his enjoyment of her company of course.

She was much more relaxed than he'd seen her be all summer. He hoped it was because she was spending time with him, and not just because she was away from Lindos and thoughts of work. Alice Palmer was never slow in telling people what she didn't like, saying what she thought of anything or them. It appeared though that she liked this day, or at least half-day, out in Rhodes Town with David Alexander.

However, her relaxed frame of mind was disturbed just over halfway up the street. She slipped on the shiny cobbles, no doubt worn that way by the thousands of tourists walking over them. She grabbed his arm to prevent falling completely.

"You okay," he asked.

"Yep, I'm fine, just a slippery cobblestone. No problem."

"I guess some of the old streets and alleys here can be just as slippery in places as some of those in Lindos, what with all the thousands of tourists traipsing over them over the years. I heard that only a few summers ago in Lindos a guy slipped and cracked his head open. You must have been here that summer," he asked?

She seemed vague and hesitant as she answered. He simply put it down to the slight shock of her slip.

"Err … yes … yes, I would have been if it was in one of the previous three summers. I never heard about it though. Not that I would expect to really, or if I did, I probably wouldn't have taken much notice, which is probably why I don't recall it, especially if it was my first summer working in Lindos."

They carried on in silence for a few more yards as she continued to hold on to his arm. Then she told him, "I think I need some coffee now."

"It doesn't look like the Knights of St. John got round to building a café in this street," he replied jokingly.

"Maybe somewhere at the top by the Palace of the Grand Master. We're nearly there, David."

What she added next surprised him.

"I've got something important I want to tell you now. I'll do it over coffee though. I need that first."

She didn't need to wait until they reached the top of the street for her coffee. Three-quarters of the way up it, at the entrance to a small archway, there was a little sign off to the left with an arrow and 'Café' written on it. Through the archway they found a pleasant small courtyard with a nice looking café. It was busy. All except one of the dozen tables in the shady courtyard were occupied by what looked like tourists. It was surrounded on three sides by the old medieval stone high walls, giving plenty of shade from the hot sun.

As soon as they sat down at the table he started to ask her what she wanted to tell him that was so important. He couldn't wait. But she made him while they ordered a couple of cappuccinos and some water.

"Why do you write? What made you start?" she began.

He was more than a little perplexed. Had she changed her mind about telling him whatever was so important?

"Is that it? I don't follow you. How is that so important?"

She reached across the table to squeeze his hand reassuringly.

"No, no, it isn't that. I'll tell you in a minute, after the waitress brings the drinks. Honestly I will. I just don't want to get halfway through telling you and get interrupted by the waitress with our drinks, and have her overhearing what I'm saying."

He nodded, telling her, "Okay."

"But I do want to know the answer to my questions. I'm interested. So why do you write?"

"Well," he reached up to rub his chin for a moment and then continued. "I guess a writer writes because they believe they have something to say, I suppose a story to tell. I know that once you start you can't stop. Anyway that's the way I feel. You must write, have to write, and keep on doing it, despite the loneliness at times, despite the piles of rejection letters, or sometimes just rejection paper slips or email in response to the synopsis of the story you want to write which you've submitted to loads of agents and publishers."

"You have a story to tell then?" she asked.

"I hope so. Although a lot of the agents and publishers I sent the synopsis to didn't think so. Luckily one does, a publisher I mean, and they put me in touch with an agent they use."

"And that's led you to do what you're doing in Lindos this summer?"

"Trying to, but I've been a little distracted, Alice."

He grinned across the table at her and added, "But if writers do not write their soul will starve."

"That's a bit deep. Is that what you believe?"

He let out a very slight deep chortle. "Maybe, but I can't claim it for myself. Wish I could. It's from James Joyce, I think."

"Irish wasn't he?" she asked.

"Yes."

"Hmm ... they are everywhere ..."

Odd thing to say, he thought. Her voice tailed off as the waitress appeared with their cappuccinos and two small bottles of water. He put one spoonful of sugar in his cappuccino and took a sip. There was a low murmur of conversations in various languages from the other tables around them.

"You do know he'd dead, Alice, Joyce" he said sarcastically, followed by a slight grin across at her. "But much as I am always happy to talk about my writing, are you going to say now what is so important that you need to tell me?"

She put her cup down and leaned forward across the table slightly.

In a low voice she told him, "That guy you said slipped and banged his head and died in Lindos, it was three summers ago. Only he didn't, he didn't slip, David. It wasn't an accident."

His eyes widened as he asked, although not in the same low tone of voice, "How do you know that?"

She looked around them to check if anyone had heard him, then told him, "Lower your voice. This is serious. I don't want anyone in this café to hear."

He stared across the table at her as she momentarily sat back, visibly took a deep breath, and then leaned forward again to answer his question and continue. She was almost whispering.

"I saw it happen that night. It wasn't an accident. It was murder. The police decided it was an accident. That's what I heard in the village they thought it was. But I saw it, so I knew it wasn't."

"What happened, what did you see? Did you see the murderer?" he asked quietly.

"It was a woman. I was going along the back alley, just a bit along from Jack Constantino's Courtyard Bar, and I heard a bit of what sounded like a stifled scream coming from the alley just ahead of me, the one to the left going down towards the centre of the village. It was dark, always is up there at that time of night. I stopped walking and tentatively peeked around the corner down the alley. As I said it was dark, but I saw the outline of a man attacking a woman. He had his arm around her neck from behind her. They both had their back to where I was hiding. At first I thought he was some sort of sex attacker, but that's not the sort of thing that happens in Lindos though."

David stared across the table with an incredulous look on his face and a half open mouth. She thought the incredulous look across his face was because of what she was telling him. It was, but not for the reason she thought.

Alice stopped for a few seconds to take a quick sip from her bottle of water. Her throat was dry from the nervousness over what she was telling him.

"The woman managed to fight him off and he lost his footing and fell backwards onto the rough path. That was when I saw that he'd had a gun. It dropped out of his hand as his head hit the ground with some force. He was moaning a lot and, from what I could make out in the dark, his head was cut, on the back I think. I thought that might be it, and that the woman would simply run away. But she didn't, David, not at all. He was obviously dazed. She picked up the gun, pointed it at his temple and told him to get up. She said something to him. I couldn't really catch it all, couldn't hear all that she said, make it out, but I heard him call her, "An Irish bitch." I was frozen, unable to move. I didn't know what to do. So, I just shrunk back into the darkness around the corner. Then I heard him groan again and when I peeked around the corner again he was doubled over on his knees and she was beating him furiously around the back of his head with the handle of the gun. As she did so she was saying something. I couldn't hear properly from where I was, but it was something about this being a message for someone. I thought at one point I heard her say, 'bastards', and 'MI6', but I couldn't be sure. I did make out that she had what I thought was an Irish accent though."

"Blimey!" What did you do then? Did you go to the police later?"

"I waited. I still didn't know what to do. I was sure the man was dead. As I said before, it's very dark up there at that time. I was praying that the woman would go on down the alley towards the centre of the village, and that she wouldn't decide the best way to get away was to come up to the top alley."

"You were lucky she didn't."

"But she did, though you're right, I was lucky. She must have taken a minute or so to check there was no blood on her clothes before she left the body, and to set it up like it was an accident. I heard a couple of thuds, like bone hitting something hard, the wall I guess from what I heard a couple of days later in the village about blood on a wall. She must have somehow manoeuvred his dead body and cracked the back of his head against the wall to make it look like he'd fallen and hit it there. When I heard those thuds I decided I had to get away, or at least find a better place to hide. I crept ten yards or so back along the top alley towards Jack's to an even darker doorway and hid there, hoping that if she did come up to the top alley she wouldn't come along in that direction, but go the other way. Literally a few seconds after I made it to there I heard her footsteps going off along the top alley, thankfully in the opposite direction."

He knew she obviously didn't go to the police from what MI6 had told him at the SIS Building in London before he came to Lindos, but he still asked, "So, that's when you went to the police? But why did they still think it was an accident after you told them what you saw?"

"No, I didn't."

She looked sheepish as she told him that and then looked across at him out of the top of her deep dark brown eyes with her head slightly bowed.

"Of course I heard in the village over the next few days the police were investigating, but I didn't want to get involved. I couldn't afford to, David."

An incredulous look fixed across his face once again. His dilemma was about to get even trickier.

"Why on earth not?"

"It's complicated. I didn't want to get involved with the police here then, in Lindos I mean. As I said, I couldn't afford to."

He was shaking his head slowly from side to side. Then he told her, "But that's crazy, Alice. It makes no sense. Why, why couldn't you 'afford to'? For god's sake what do you mean by that?"

He was still whispering, but there was an undeniable insistence and agitation in his voice. Almost by accident he'd done what MI6 wanted him to do, found their mystery witness, but he had idea why she didn't go to the Lindos police at the time. As a police witness she would hardly, could hardly, have been in danger from MI6 back then, not like he knew she was now. He couldn't tell her that though, or explain why, or why

143

he knew she was. Just when he was starting to think everything was going so well between them as well.

"Look, David, after a few days everything calmed down in the village. I found out, and I know it was only village gossip, but I heard the police had investigated and finally concluded it was an accident, unfortunate, but an accident. That's what everyone in the village took it as it seems. And that's obviously what you've heard since. So, what would have been the point of me going to the police about what I saw and just causing myself problems?"

Now the firmness was fully evident in her voice, even though she too was still whispering.

This was turning out to be one of the most eventful cappuccinos he'd ever had.

"But a man was murdered," he told her even more forcibly. "I'm sorry, Alice, but I just don't understand why you couldn't go to the police, 'couldn't afford to', as you put it. What could possibly be so important, more important to you, than a man's murder? It doesn't make sense. What problems could going to the police and telling them what you saw have possibly caused you?"

"Okay, okay, David, I'll bloody tell you, but you have to promise me not to repeat any of this to anyone, what I've already told you, and what I'm about to tell you. Not anyone."

She was glaring across the table at him now with a fixed stare and steeliness in her eyes as she said that.

He wasn't sure at all he could do that, agree not to tell anyone. This was about a murder. Okay, it was three years ago, but if any of this somehow came out he'd certainly be facing serious charges about withholding evidence, as would she. Besides which, if she was right about hearing the woman refer to MI6, he knew he'd be facing a much more serious situation with MI6 than simply withholding evidence from the Rhodes Police in a murder case. He would be withholding information about the identification of a witness who'd seen one of their operatives murdered. That was precisely what they'd instructed him to find out about during his summer in Lindos, and now he'd come across it seemingly purely by accident. His dilemma was that the witness was the woman sat across the table from him, a woman he'd spent a lot of time with that summer and had grown to like a lot, a lot more than as 'just good friends'. He knew he couldn't tell Alice any of that at the moment though, if ever, despite the fact that by divulging that secret to him she obviously trusted him and seemingly had some feelings for him too.

For him, the irony in all this was that he hadn't given much importance or credibility to the rumour there had been a witness to the killing of the MI6 operative. He assumed it was just that, rumour and gossip in a small tourist village. Plus, he wasn't exactly keen to do what they wanted in Lindos and get back embroiled with MI6 anyway after what happened in Havana. So, that was another reason not to take the gossip about a witness seriously. In relation to them, MI6, now though there was this little thing called the Official Secrets Act he'd signed, which could bring real problems for him, as well as possibly her, after what she'd just told him and if he also told her all he knew.

His head was spinning with all the issues and permutations, consequences for them both from what he'd just heard from her. However, there was another element to all those, and his dilemma, that she was about to add.

While all those concerns were running through his brain she took another sip of her cappuccino. Then she fixed another intense stare across the table at him, accompanied by a pained frown, and told him simply in an even lower whisper an even more startling revelation.

"I stabbed a guy."

"What?" he blurted back at her. This time he raised his voice.

"David," she glared across at him once more, as she reminded him to keep his voice down simply by indicating that through placing the index finger of her right hand onto her lips.

Their relaxing trip to Rhodes was rapidly becoming increasingly eventful, and extremely stressful, he thought. He'd definitely never had a discussion over a cappuccino like this before.

He was shaking his head again. Then he stopped abruptly. He'd gathered his senses a little as he asked back almost in a whisper, "Here? In Lindos, I mean?"

Her head was bowed and she was looking out of the top of her eyes across the table at him again. "No, of course not, back in Sheffield."

"Oh, that's okay then."

He had a sarcastic half-grin on his lips as he finished telling her that, and was once more shaking his head.

She wasn't exactly impressed by his sarcasm. Despite still almost whispering she sounded agitated now. "It's not sodding funny, David. It was in his leg with a bloody fork, and he bloody deserved it."

"What? A fork?"

He was thinking this was getting more and more bizarre. They were sitting in a beautiful pleasant courtyard café in one of the most famous places from the medieval world on a hot sunny September day and he was hearing about a bizarre set of events from the woman opposite him whom he liked a lot, really a lot.

He'd thought and decided as the summer went on that Alice Palmer had quite a few sides to her character, to her personality, but these things she'd told him that afternoon were way beyond anything he'd imagined or seen from her in relation to her character. A murder in Lindos she'd witnessed, but not reported, and now the fact that back in the U.K. she'd stabbed someone, and in the leg with a fork. Bizarre! He recalled that about a month or more ago he was convinced Alice Palmer was not a person to let anyone in, open up to them about how she felt or about herself in general. Now he was beginning to really understand why. Now he was getting the full on opposite of her not letting anyone in, and it was the turbo charged version.

In so many different ways he wasn't sure if that was good or bad, even though some of it was actually directly about what MI6 had instructed him, to find out.

She was merely staring across the table at him in silence for a moment or two whilst biting her bottom lip slightly. The look across her face told him she was not best pleased with his reactions.

He took a deep breath, tilted his head slightly to one side, and told her while trying to sound more serious and sympathetic, "Okay, Alice, tell me what happened with the guy and the fork, and why that stopped you going to the police in Lindos to report what you saw. I can't make out how it's connected, I'm intrigued."

She sat back, took another sip of her cappuccino, and started to explain.

"I was working as a waitress in a restaurant in Sheffield part-time three nights a week, mostly over weekends. At the end of the summer of 2015 I decided I was going to come to Lindos for the whole of the summer the following year. So, I wanted to get some extra money on top of what I was getting in my regular job to have enough to quit that and do what I planned. I thought I could get some work in the village too, in a restaurant or a bar, but I wanted some money behind me as insurance in case it took a while to find a job in Lindos."

He sat in silence looking across at her, wondering what she was about to tell him.

"It was all going well, and with tips and what they were paying me I was managing to save quite a bit. Basically, I was saving everything I got from the restaurant waitressing job. The run up to Christmas was particularly busy with quite a few party groups from local businesses, the tips from those were always great. Christmas coming and parties makes people generous, I guess, especially when they've had a few drinks. In fact, by then I'd already saved more than enough, or at least I worked out it was more than enough for what I wanted to do the following summer. So much so that I thought about giving up the restaurant job then. Wish I had now…."

Her voice tailed off and she reached for the final sip of her cappuccino. As she placed her cup back on the saucer on the table she glanced over at him before she continued. She was wondering just what his overall reaction would be to all this, what was going through his mind?

"Anyway, I didn't, didn't give it up. On the last Saturday night before Christmas we had a group in the restaurant of a dozen people from a local office, all on one table. There were five women and seven guys. There were two of us serving them, me and another much younger waitress, Sarah. She was nineteen, a student, who also only worked weekends to get some money to help her at Sheffield Uni. Some of the group were getting quite pissed, especially a couple of the guys, who looked like they were about my age. The five women all looked a lot younger, early twenties I reckon. Secretaries and general admin staff perhaps? But clearly not any of the men's wives, if they were married, or girlfriends I suppose. That was obvious as the evening wore on and they got through their meal, as well as quite a few bottles of wine and Prosecco. There was a lot of groping of the women going on, and then as we were serving them their desserts the guy who was clearly the most pissed put his arm around Sarah's waist and tried to pull her onto his lap. She let out a loud, 'No,' and pulled away. Obviously she was upset, so I told him quite calmly, 'Please don't do that, sir.' I found Sarah in the kitchen a bit shaken and talking to the boss. I explained to him what had happened and he asked me if I could just finish serving the group for the rest of the evening by myself. I told him, 'Sure, no problem'. We'd almost done serving them anyway. A couple of the more pissed guys had been making some quite crude remarks to me and Sarah throughout the evening. It looked like they'd had more than a few drinks prior to arriving at the restaurant. But we just laughed the remarks off. I can give as good as I get, as you have no doubt seen by now. So, a few crude remarks were no skin off my nose."

At least that last remark brought a temporary small smile to her face as he nodded slightly in agreement.

"Instead of backing off though the guy who was the most pissed, the one who'd put his arm around Sarah's waist, got arsier when I was serving the last of the desserts to the rest of the group. He started taking the piss, trying to be cocky, and going on about me, 'Only being a bloody waitress,' and how I should, 'Know my place.' I took a deep breath and told myself to ignore him. A couple of the women on the table told him to, 'Pipe down,' and to, 'behave'. That only seemed to make him more angry and obnoxious. Then as I leaned over to pick up one of the finished empty desert plates from the table in front of the woman next to him he grabbed my arse and made an oink, oink sound, like a pig. I didn't wait to ask him what he meant by that. I saw red, grabbed the fork from the desert plate I was holding and stabbed him with it in the thigh as hard as I could."

David's eyes widened in disbelief at what he'd just heard, although he was also desperately trying to stifle a laugh. Meanwhile opposite him the woman who only a few weeks before he thought couldn't open up and let anyone in to really know her was chuckling to herself quite loudly. Her shoulders were vibrating with the force of it. From that David knew it would be ok for him to at least let a broad smile break out across his face.

"He squealed like a bloody skewered pig. Well, he did between screaming obscenities at me and telling me I was 'a fucking bitch'," she added between her chuckles. "There was blood everywhere, as you can imagine."

She reached for her small bottle of water and took a drink as he asked, "So, what happened then?"

She replaced the cap on her bottle and told him, "The police got called and I got charged with assault. They said it could have been with a deadly weapon, but they weren't sure a desert fork was one."

She let out another small laugh as she finished telling him that.

He asked, "And?"

"After Christmas it went to court and I pleaded guilty. My solicitor said I didn't really have much option. There were plenty of witnesses. Although the solicitor said the court would take some of the provocation into account to some extent, plus what the guy had done to Sarah. Also, if I pleaded guilty I was likely to only get put on probation because of that and because it was my first offence."

She added, in a quite matter of fact fashion, "I lost my job at the restaurant, of course." She was tilting her head to one side slightly and grinning again as she told him, "Not exactly good for business for a restaurant, I suppose, having a waitress stab one of the customers."

Sarcastically she added, "I didn't even get a tip from that group."

"No, I guess not, not exactly a good advertisement for the restaurant service, Alice. Although it sounds like the guy was a complete prat and had it coming to him."

What he was actually thinking as he told her that was that Alice Palmer was clearly not a woman to mess with. Hidden depths indeed.

"Yep, he was, believe me, a total prat, and I definitely don't regret what I did. As for losing the job, as I said earlier I was thinking of giving it up before Christmas because I already had enough for my planned Lindos summer. I probably only hung on for the expected bigger tips in the run up to Christmas. That didn't happen though after that night."

She took another swig from her bottle of water. As she did so she noticed he was frowning, but it wasn't for the reason she thought. It wasn't actually because of what she'd just told him. There was another reason. He was bemused.

Now it was his turn to lean forward slightly across the table and whisper, "But I still don't see what all that has got to do with you not telling the police here what you saw in Lindos that night when the woman killed the guy? I don't understand what the connection is?"

She hesitated for a few seconds and bit her bottom lip again. There was a firm, intense edge to her voice as she told him, "Look, David, I was on probation. I wasn't supposed to leave the bloody country was I? That was part of the terms of my probation. Therefore, I could hardly turn up at Lindos police station and tell the Greek police what I saw. I was afraid that somehow they'd contact the police in the U.K. to check up on me, even if only for background to see if I was a credible witness. And don't forget I heard one of them, the guy who was killed or the woman who did it, mention MI6. I'm sure if I'd told the Greek police in Lindos that they'd have contacted the police and who knows what others back in the U.K. On top of that, it was my first summer here, 2016, when I saw the murder and because of my concern over the probation thing I didn't apply for or have the necessary foreign workers' tax papers and the rest of the documentation that I should have had, and needed to have, to work here anyway. That would have been the first thing they'd ask. I've got them now, got them last summer.

Don't ask how. So, going to the police was impossible after what happened in the restaurant back home."

He nodded. "Hmm ... right, oh yes, I can see that now."

He was nodding and agreeing with her logic, but some entirely different questions and issues were racing through his mind now about Alice Palmer, as well as just what he should do with the information he'd just heard from her about the murder. He definitely knew she was right about the Greek police and MI6 though.

Was it possible that her aggressive nature which sometimes surfaced in her voice also did so in her actions? In a temper she'd stabbed a guy after all, albeit only with a desert fork. How did he feel about that? This was a whole new conundrum he now faced over how he felt about her. There was him thinking that maybe the important thing she'd said she wanted to tell him, needed to tell him, was about the two of them and their possible relationship. This was very far from that. However, she hadn't finished. There was more.

"But then I saw her again, the woman, the killer, two nights later with a guy in Jack's. I went in for a late drink after work as usual and there she was. I know it was dark in the back alley that night of the murder, and I couldn't be completely sure it was the same woman, but I think it could have been, probably was. I overheard her and the guy talking in the bar. She had an Irish accent, but he was English. From what I heard in the alley I think the guy she murdered was also English."

David's mouth was gaping wide open yet again. When she finished he asked, "Do you think that if it was her there was any chance she recognised you in Jack's?"

"I don't think so. I can't be sure, but I don't think she could have seen me that night in the alley. I'm pretty sure she couldn't have."

She hesitated, before adding, "I hope not anyway. It was dark and when I saw her do what she did she had her back to me. I was ten yards or more away, peeking around the corner in the gloom. I don't know though. I couldn't, can't be sure. I must admit I was a bit worried for a week or so after in case she'd seen me and would come after me. But after that night in Jack's, and over the next couple of nights, I never saw her around in the village again, or for the rest of that summer. I did ask Jack about her a few nights after I saw her in his place with the guy. I tried to sound as casual as possible about it while I was chatting with him late on. Just dropped it into the conversation about overhearing her speaking and that I thought she sounded Irish. He said she'd been here trying to trace her birth father apparently, who she thought was Greek, but never knew who he was. He said her mother worked in Lindos for a couple of summers in the seventies, so Jack arranged for her to meet his mother and grandmother a couple of times to hear from them about those times. He confirmed she was Irish, and said she'd been here earlier that summer in 2016 with some friends, her first time in Lindos. Anyway, she wasn't exactly a regular Lindos visitor, but I must admit I worry occasionally that she did see me and might just turn up here again at some point if she thought, had any idea that for some reason I might suddenly decide to go to the police."

"That was over three years ago, Alice." He tried to reassure her and reached across the table to take hold of her hand as he did so. "Surely if she'd seen you that night she would have done something about it at the time, or even, if she recognised you, soon after she saw you that night in Jack's?"

"I know you're right, and she would surely have done something about it by now, but I do still worry that ..."

Her voice tailed off and a worried look spread over her face.

"Worry that what? What is it?" he asked.

She put one of her index fingers onto her lips, shook her head slightly from side to side slowly, and then told him abruptly, "Let's pay the bill and get out of here."

The relaxed appearance she'd radiated earlier when they arrived in Rhodes Town had drained out of her. Tension had returned, fully evident in her voice and across her face.

"But what, what is-"

He tried again, but this time she interrupted him.

"I'll tell you outside," she whispered.

She didn't even wait for the waitress to appear, but just left the money on the table with the bill she'd given them when she brought their drinks. Then she stood up and told him, "Let's go," tucking her arm tightly into his.

Once again he was bemused. There was obviously never a dull moment with Alice Palmer. Was it a good sign that she took his arm, or was it just that something had obviously spooked her? Something had definitely suddenly made her very twitchy.

They quickly made their way out of the café and the alley in total silence, him wondering exactly what was going on. He couldn't wait any longer. As they walked arm in arm further up the slight slope of the cobbled Street of the Knights towards the Palace of the Grand Master he started to say, "So, what is-"

Once again though she stopped him, this time putting her index finger to his lips as they kept walking. They were almost at the top of the street and near the Palace when she spotted another small alley off to their left. While still grasping her arm in his she told him, "In here, quick."

She guided him ten yards or so down the narrow deserted alley, then stopped, removed her arm from his and pushed him against the wall. She stared up into his eyes intently. For the briefest of moments it crossed his mind that she was going to kiss him. Far from it.

"Didn't you hear it?" she asked.

"Hear what?"

"The accent."

"What? What accent?"

He was thinking that this was getting more and more bizarre. So much for a lovely relaxing sunny September afternoon in Rhodes Town together.

Alice was now very agitated and obviously visibly nervous. He'd never seen her like this before. He repeated his question, hoping it would calm her down.

"What accent? What are you talking about, Alice?"

He was getting agitated too, at her strange, unexplained behaviour.

"The woman sat two tables over from us in the café with her back to us, with the guy. Her accent was Irish."

He tried to desperately, but he just couldn't stifle an incredulous slight laugh. It didn't help her disposition at all. She scowled at him. She definitely wasn't happy at his reaction at all. She almost barked out at him, "The woman, David, the woman that I saw in the alley in Lindos, the killer, was-"

But he didn't let her finish. He knew precisely where she was going with what she was about to say. He interrupted,

"Jesus, Alice, yes, the killer was Irish and there was a woman customer in the café who was also Irish. So what? There must be hundreds, if not thousands, of Irish tourists on Rhodes. So what makes you think that was the woman? Did you recognise her? Could you have recognised her? You said you only saw the woman in the alley that night from the back, and you only just saw the woman in the café a few minutes ago from the back. Perhaps you're being a little bit paranoid don't you think?"

As he finished telling her that he wrapped his arms around her shoulders and drew her in close to him. Then he brushed one side of her hair off of her face, pulled her in even closer so that she was pressed right up against him with the wall behind. It was all a bit blurry and just seeming to happen between them. Maybe fear does that to some people. It certainly seemed to do that to her, remove all her defences and release her inhibitions, all her doubts. They shared a long soft, he hoped reassuring, kiss.

As their lips parted she told him, "Sorry, I didn't really get a good look at that Irish woman in the café just now. I was in too much of a hurry to leave. I panicked. So, I couldn't even say for certain either that she was the same woman I saw in Jack's bar two nights after I saw the murder. I know, I was just being-"

Now it was his index finger that was placed on her lips to stop her speaking. Her eyes were sparkling with a concoction of fear and pleasure as he told her, "Stop it. Let's forget all about all that; what you saw, what you did back in that restaurant in Sheffield. We all have secrets, Alice. Some are easier to live with than others though."

Her face displayed a quizzical look.

"Really? What are yours then?" she asked immediately as she drew her body away slightly from the ring of his arms around her shoulders.

He never answered her question directly. He still wasn't sure how much he could tell her. He was still going over it in his mind. Instead he suggested, "Let's go and see the Palace. Then we'll find a nice secluded table outside a restaurant and perhaps I'll tell you all about it over lunch. The telling needs wine."

It was her turn to be confused now. What could his secret possibly be that it needed a, "secluded table and wine?"

A few minutes later they made their way into the Palace.

The Palace of the Grandmaster is the single most impressive site on Rhodes, if not all of the Dodecanese Islands. It was originally built on the foundations of the Ancient Temple of the Sun God, Helios. In medieval times the Palace was the residence of the Governor of Rhodes and the administrative centre. It's enormous, with one hundred and fifty-eight rooms, although only twenty-four were open to visitors. Consequently, their tour wasn't going to take anywhere near as long as it would have if all one hundred and fifty-eight had been open. On the first floor they viewed the official rooms, as well as the private quarters of the Grand Master. On the ground floor Alice insisted they visit the Grand Reception Hall, the impressive ballroom, as well as the elegant music room. She'd been before. She began to appear more at ease once again, and was clearly enjoying being his unofficial tour guide, insisting they see the Medusa mosaic. Finally, she took great pleasure in informing him that the Palace belonged to the Greek State now, although at times in the past it had served as a holiday residence for the King of Italy, Victor Emmanuel the Third, as well as for Mussolini.

"See, told you I liked history," she commented again, accompanied by one of her lovely, more relaxed smiles.

They didn't really linger in any part of the Palace and were only just over an hour going around. It was already gone two by the time they entered it after their traumas earlier, well to be exact, Alice's revelations and traumas. They wanted to have a nice long lunch, even if it was a late one, before heading back to Lindos in good time for her work.

A couple of times as they were going around the Palace she reached for and squeezed his hand, telling him the first time, "Thank you for bringing me, suggesting this, persuading me." There was what appeared to him to be a deep caring look in her eyes. The new Alice Palmer had re-surfaced, hopefully the real one.

After they left the Palace they made their way back down the Street of the Knights and found a busy, nice tree-shaded restaurant in Great Alexander Square. Once the waiter had delivered their menus David told her, "I'd love to share a nice bottle of cold white wine with lunch, but you've got to drive us back to Lindos and got to work later, so I guess it'll have to be a glass each."

She looked across at him and agreed, "Very sensible. Good job one of us is."

They did just that and ordered a glass each, with some Calamari and salad for him and Moussaka, also with a small salad, for her.

While they waited for their food she looked across the table into his eyes and asked, "Come on then, David, I've told you mine, so what are these secrets of yours? You said earlier we all have secrets. Everyone has, has things they keep just to themselves, things about themselves, and their past and present that only they know."

She tilted her head slightly to one side and raised her eyebrows as she finished.

"I did, yes, and I suppose that's true, we do all have secrets of some sort. Is mine a secret though? Of sorts, I suppose. We simply don't always admit it however, even to ourselves. Most people do that. Keep it, them, their secrets about themselves, firmly locked up deep inside. You said you had, about the woman and the murder, and stabbing that guy in the restaurant back home. I suppose I do to. We're no different from everyone else in that respect, you and me, even if we think we are, convince ourselves that we-"

The look on her face across the table had now turned to frustration. Alice Palmer wasn't the most patient of people at the best of times. David's frustrating prevarication was pushing that to her limit. His prevarication was really a consequence of him hesitating and trying to decide if telling her his 'secret' was a wise thing to do or not. Eventually she'd had enough and interrupted.

"David, for god's sake spare me the philosophy in this lovely place and Rhodes sunshine. There have been a lot better philosophers even than you who lived in this place hundreds, no thousands of years ago. So, just bloody tell me."

"Okay, okay," he took a deep breath and started to tell her. "You said earlier that you thought you heard the Irish woman who murdered that guy in Lindos mention MI6 in the alley that night and-"

"So, what about it? I could have been wrong, but I thought I did. What's that got to do with your secrets?"

She interrupted him again.

"Just let me finish, Alice. It's nothing bad, really it isn't, just a coincidence related to MI6, and not actually connected obviously, but I thought I should tell you after what you shared with me. And anyway, if the guy was from MI6 they'll almost certainly know, or at least assume, it wasn't an accident. They'll know who the murderer was too, most likely have a pretty good idea anyway. You said he had a gun, and it seems pretty certain to me that he'd have been sent here by MI6 to look for her. It seems obvious that she was most likely someone who had crossed them in some way, MI6, and they were looking for her, and then got a tip off she was here-"

"Tip off by who? Someone in Lindos?" She interrupted again.

"Maybe, or someone on Rhodes, an informant. They have them all over the place. Could even have been someone, an MI6 informant, in the Greek Border Police, at the airport perhaps, who knew they were looking for her and picked up her arriving on the island through the airport."

"But how do you-"

Now it was him not letting her finish. He knew she was going to ask how he knew so much about MI6. He was about to tell her, but was still pondering just how much to tell her about that. Instead, he changed the direction of their conversation slightly first.

"Anyway, MI6 will have dealt with her, the Irish woman, by now as it was three years ago."

"Dealt with her?"

"Yes, disposed of her, killed her I expect. So I really wouldn't worry about overhearing a female Irish accent, on Rhodes or anywhere. I'd bet the woman's dead."

She was shocked. Not just by what he'd said about the woman being, "dealt with," but that he appeared to know so much about MI6. Was that the full extent of his 'secret', or was he simply just trying to reassure her.

"You think so?"

She rubbed the back of her neck firmly with her left hand as though she was feeling tension building up there as she asked that, seeking more reassurance.

Before he could answer she added, "But what's all that got to do with your secrets?" she asked again, growing impatient. "And how would you know all that about MI6?"

"I'm not entirely sure I should tell you, whether I'm allowed to. I've not signed the Official Secrets Act or anything, but …"

That wasn't exactly the truth, of course. He was hesitating again. Across the table her frustration was surfacing rapidly, and mention of the Official Secrets Act was definitely making her nervous over what he was about to tell her. What the bloody hell could be so difficult to just tell her. After all, eventually she'd just found it easy enough to tell him that she'd seen a murder and that she'd stabbed a guy with a sodding fork.

"But what, David? Unless you think you're going to be arrested and carted off for treason just bloody tell me, and then we can forget all about it and get on with our nice lunch. And you better be quick about it, the waiter will be back with our food soon hopefully."

He nodded slightly before telling her, "Okay." Then he hesitated for a few seconds again, and took a deep breath, before he blurted out, "As I said, it's just a coincidence, related to MI6 too. They tried to recruit me, MI6. They tried to recruit me because of my Russian academic expertise, Russian foreign policy stuff."

"As a spy?" she exclaimed as her eyes widened and her forehead creased in surprise.

Now it was his turn to tell her to keep her voice down.

Alice was left hanging in frustrating curiosity at that point as the waiter appeared with their food and glasses of wine.

"No, no, not really recruit me in that way, not permanently," he told her quietly after the waiter left. "They simply wanted me to help them with something at an academic conference I was going to in Moscow."

She leaned forward across the table to ask, "What was it?"

"They wanted me to give a Russian academic at the conference a number of one of their people in Moscow she could contact. I guessed that they wanted her to defect, leave Russia, come to the U.K. and share any of the secrets she had access to about Russia's foreign policy intentions. In academic circles internationally she was known as a very clever woman. Officially she was simply a Professor at Moscow University, and an academic expert on Russian foreign policy in the Far East, especially China, Japan, Vietnam, and North and South Korea. I knew that, of course, but I reckoned there was more to her, shall we say, activities, than that. I had no way of knowing, and really didn't want to. I assumed that as MI6 wanted me to give her that contact number at the conference she must have had some connection with the Russian Secret Service, probably the GRU, Russia's Main Intelligence Directorate, the foreign military intelligence agency. Although it could equally have been, or as well as, the SVR, Russia's Foreign Intelligence Service, and the FSB, Russia's Federal Security Service. Who knows? They are all descendants, if that's the way to put it, of the former Soviet KGB. Presumably they, the Russian Security Services, used her academic knowledge on certain projects they had in play, which would have meant she had access to a lot of information on those, as well as Russian foreign policy intentions in general, and MI6 obviously wanted that."

"Foreign policy intentions about what? I'm interested, and curious, David."

"Oh no, no, I definitely don't think I should tell you anything more on that."

His voice got a lot more strident. "You really don't need to know. Not that I really know much more to be honest. A lot of what I've just told you about MI6, about her, and her possible defection was, is, just me speculating. As I said, I didn't know, and didn't want to. Call it an educated guess, and there's not really much more to tell. I just wanted to tell you that, to show you we all have secrets."

"So, you didn't do anything else for them, MI6, and you don't work for them now?"

"No, of course not, that's all."

He was being economical with the truth again and not being entirely honest, but he certainly wasn't going to reveal anything more about what he'd done for MI6, particularly anything related to his time in Havana.

"That's all they wanted me to do, so I did it. It seemed simple and straightforward enough. Put them in touch with the Russian woman, or to be exact pass on verbally the number she could use to contact one of their people in Moscow. It entailed only having the briefest of conversations with her at the conference, largely about academic stuff, while telling her the number. The contact details message had to be verbal, nothing could be written down. That was their instructions, MI6. I've heard nothing from them since, thankfully, and would prefer not to. I assume they know I've left the university in England now though and am here on Rhodes. So, I don't expect to hear from them again."

Once again, he was being economical with the truth.

"I don't even know what happened to her, whether she actually defected or not. As I said before, I never signed the Official Secrets Act or anything like that, but I'm not sure I should even have told you all that I have, but anyway, I thought, wanted to-"

"What happened after, after you did that?" she interrupted.

"As I said, no idea. I didn't want to get any more involved. That was the deal when they asked me to do what they wanted me to do at the conference and contact the woman."

What Alice asked him next stunned him. She leaned forward across the table, stared intensely into his eyes and asked, "And did you sleep with her? Did what they wanted you to do mean you needed to sleep with her?"

He shook his head vigorously.

"What? No, of course not. I know that's how people think spies operate, from the movies, but it wasn't like that, and as I said I wasn't a spy anyway. I'm no James Bond, Alice."

He smiled as he said that last bit and then added, "We just had a very brief conversation over coffee during one mid-morning break at the conference consisting of some academic stuff as cover and then me telling her the phone number as discreetly as possible."

She placed a piece of her Moussaka in her mouth and then after swallowing it leaned forward across the table again to ask, "Was she attractive though? How old?"

He was thinking this definitely wasn't supposed to go like this at all. It was supposed to demonstrate to her that he was prepared to share one of his secrets with her, as she'd done. However, it looked like spikey Alice was back and a jealous side of her character was rapidly surfacing. To some extent he should have been flattered by the jealousy, and seen it as a good sign perhaps, but he didn't see it like that at all at this point. Just when he thought he was making headway with her it now felt like they were going backwards again.

"What? Are you deliberately being stupid, Alice?"

She didn't react angrily at him suggesting she was being stupid. She just ignored what he'd said and repeated the same questions.

"So, was she, was she attractive? How old was she?"

"Bloody hell, Alice."

He was raising his voice once again. That provoked her to slightly wave one of her hands up and down in front of him across the table, signalling to lower his voice.

Almost in a whisper, but with anger ringing in his voice, he told her, "She was around my age at the time, mid-thirties I'd guess, and yes, she was attractive, in a typical European Russian sort of way. But I had one conversation with her at the conference, quite a brief one during a mid-morning break for coffee. I was told by MI6 that she knew someone was going to contact her from the British Secret Services, so she was expecting it and the contact number I was relaying to her. It all had to look innocent, like two academics chatting while waiting for their coffee. It took no more than a minute. There were agents from the Russian Secret Service watching everyone in the conference, as well as outside it. And again, no I didn't shag her. No way. I didn't want to. That's not why I was there. I was actually there for the bloody academic conference. Contacting her for MI6 was not the real main reason I was there, and actually it only arose when they approached me after I'd already arranged to go."

He tried to lighten the mood a little as he finished by telling her with a smile, "I think you watch far too many James Bond movies, Alice."

She allowed herself the slightest of slow smiles, but she wasn't finished asking her questions.

"What was her name?"

He laughed slightly.

"I can't tell you that."

He added firmly, "No way. That really would be a dodgy thing to do. I'm not saying I don't trust you, but if anything did come out about it somehow, and her, I'd immediately be under suspicion and be in deep trouble with MI6, and so would you. Besides which, if she did defect, they, MI6, would have furnished her with what's called a 'legend', a new identity and a whole new personal history around that identity. So, her name now wouldn't be the same anyway as it was back then at the conference and I've got no idea what it would be now. I don't know and I don't want to know."

She nodded, signifying she understood that, then added, "I see, but I'm curious, you do seem to know a lot about them, MI6, David, what they do, all that stuff about, what was it, a 'legend'. So, when was it?"

"Err … erm …"

He was genuinely trying to remember, work that out, although he definitely wasn't about to answer her comment about him knowing so much about MI6.

"It must have been spring five years ago, early April, 2014 perhaps. That's when most of the academic conferences take place, in the Easter break."

"Quite a while ago then? And you haven't seen her since, or know what happened to her?"

"No, I told you, after that day over the coffee break I never even spoke to her again at the conference. Apart from anything else that would have really aroused the Russian Security Services' suspicions. That would have been dangerous for her, as well as for me. As I said before, I assume she was going to defect, get out of Russia, and that she had some information useful to MI6. The Russian Secret Service is known to recruit academics. They become their sort of useful eyes and ears in their universities, and in the academic world internationally. To be fair, so do the British Secret Services and many others worldwide, especially the Americans. But I didn't know, and I really didn't want to know if that's what happened to her. That was the deal I did with them and they haven't bothered me since, thank god."

Once again he wasn't being completely honest. He couldn't be. That would be risky for him, as well as for her.

"To be honest it was all a bit hairy, a bit dangerous I suppose, Alice, although, of course, not as hairy as your secret sounds."

As he told her that he reached across the table to give one of her hands what he hoped she would take as a reassuring squeeze.

She smiled back across at him and then took another bite of her moussaka. She finished that mouthful, bowed her head slightly, looked sheepishly across at him out of the top of her eyes once more, and told him, "I'm sorry, David. I told you before it's very difficult for me to trust anyone because of what I saw that night in Lindos, as well as because of what my shit of an ex-husband did by cheating on me with my best friend. It's a really big thing for me to share all that with you, trust you. Sorry I reacted the way I did."

He smiled across at her.

It seemed he'd weathered any difficulties with her over what he'd told her he'd done for MI6, and what appeared her jealousy over the Russian woman academic,

The way she'd trusted him in telling him her secrets over the murder she saw in Lindos in 2016, as well as over the incident in the restaurant in Sheffield, gave him cause for optimism. He thought it showed she was warming towards him, and perhaps wanted to be more than just "very good friends."

Set against all that positivity though, was the huge dilemma she'd inadvertently presented him with by trusting him in revealing she was witness to the murder in Lindos in 2016, and by chance that meant she was the elusive witness he was instructed to find for MI6.

15

The other woman: signals of 'weight' or merely 'lightness'?

When, soon after, Alice Palmer reflected on their time in Rhodes Town she wondered whether what she'd told him, her 'secrets', would give off the wrong impression about how she felt about him. Additionally, there was her reaction of obvious suspicion and jealousy to what he'd told her about the Russian woman academic, particularly her blunt question about had he slept with her that she'd put to him quite forcibly a couple of times. What sort of signal had that sent to him? Would he think her feelings were moving towards something more serious between them, rather than 'just friends, good friends'? Was that what she was actually thinking; seeking to overcome her almost automatic self-defensive mechanism of the last five years or so when it came to anything resembling a possible relationship? She turned those things over in her mind quite a few times over the next few days, constantly wondering if what was between them, their relationship, was now moving more towards something resembling Kundera's 'weight' of responsibility and ultimately fidelity, not that she would describe it in those terms, of course. She knew it was a friendship, a 'good friendship', and at that time it hadn't even yet moved on to anything more, and she wasn't at all sure she wanted it to.

Whatever it was, whatever her intention was through any signals she'd given him, nothing initially changed between them. In her mind she wrestled with what she actually wanted to happen with him while their late nights and early mornings drinking and talking continued, and if anything increased.

However, one night in September she got very drunk. Or more accurately, by almost early morning as the darkness of the night was beginning to be challenged by the rising sun and the first small glimmer of daylight it brought while they sat talking on one of the benches in the small courtyard outside the Arches Club in the centre of the village. Eventually she told him she felt sick, obviously the effect of too many vodka and cokes mixed with a number of tequila shots she'd appeared determined they had earlier. He'd declined some of those, instead sticking to a few bottles of Greek beer. He got her some water and then walked her back the short distance down the alleyways to her flat and bed. She never threw up, but then to his surprise she asked him to stay and sleep with her. He wasn't entirely sure what she meant by that, to just stay with her because she felt so sick or because she wanted them to have sex? Either way he politely declined, believing it wasn't a good move to sleep with her for either reason when she was so drunk. He helped her into her bed and left a bowl and a bottle of water beside it, then left.

The next day, as her hangover eventually wore off and she began to remember bits of what had happened she was actually impressed by him doing the honourable thing in putting her to bed and leaving, even though she'd asked him to stay. It clearly gained him some brownie points. After she finished work the next night, while they were drinking together once again, she told him she liked that about him. She said she reckoned it definitely wasn't the way some of the other Brit ex-pat men in the village would have behaved.

When what subsequently happened between them a couple of weeks after their Rhodes Town trip she still had no idea why it did, or whether that was all she wanted between them or more. Neither did he. It seemed apparent to Alice he shared her indecision and confusion over that, not least because he agreed with what she told him after the second, and final time that summer, that they slept together.

Nevertheless, after a long, often hot and humid Lindos summer of enjoying each other's company drinking and talking late into the nights and early mornings, the 'dance' between them finally ended with them enjoying sex with each other on the night that clicked over the dying of the cooler September summer days into the start of October.

It started out as just another regular Lindos Monday night. Monday nights were usually busy in the village, even as September ended and October began. For those people leaving for home early in the morning on one of the changeover days, Wednesdays, Monday night was their last real chance to have a good long night in the bars, and maybe one of the clubs.

She texted David as she finished work at one asking, as usual, where he was. Instead of the Courtyard Bar, he was up at Lindos By Night chatting with one of the young Greeks who worked up there on some nights, Angelos. They both knew him well. Instead of going straight to meet him after David replied though, she went back to her flat to shower and change out of her work clothes. Even though it was approaching two o'clock, and almost at the end of a long and tiring season, she still looked stunning and fresh, when she arrived at Lindos By Night, deliberately so. She'd changed into a simple short black sleeveless dress with a loose wide red leather belt. Her appearance, along with her broad smile in David's direction, caused Angelos to raise his eyebrows towards David. It was the young Greek's turn to smile as she reached to put her left arm on David's shoulder and kiss him quickly on the lips. David's pleasant surprise reaction was clearly in evidence all over his face as Angelos asked, "Vodka and coke, Alice?"

"Sure, just the one and then let's go to Glow, David. It sounded busy as I just came by."

Her whole mood, and attitude to what was between them, seemed to have been transformed for some unknown reason, and in a positive way.

After they got their drinks inside Glow they went outside to sit in the small courtyard to talk, as they'd done quite a few times that summer. However, this time not for very long, nowhere near as long as they had in the past. Within seconds of them sitting down on the wooden sofa-like bench with its plump soft cushions she placed her vodka and coke down on the table ahead of them, twisted her body to face him, and then placed her left hand on the side of his cheek to kiss him fully on the lips firmly.

As she pulled back from that there was a distinct show of obvious pleasure and affection in her eyes and across her face. This time she wasn't drunk at all. There was a vibrant, excited look in her eyes and a rich, distinct, smile across her lips. He seized the moment, gently took her upper arm and tugged her back into him for them to kiss again. This time it was a long lingering kiss as he removed his left hand from her arm and ran his fingers through her hair. As their lips parted once again her eyes opened wide and flicked up to stare into his. There was obvious affection between them, signified by mutual small grins of satisfaction. All of the frustration and tension of their long Lindos summer 'dance' evaporated. After a long minute staring into each other's eyes she broke the silence.

"Make a suggestion, David," she told him softly, her brown eyes fixed on his, almost pleading for him to make the right suggestion. The one she'd now finally decided she wanted to hear.

"Oh, well, err ..." he stuttered.

Why was he getting tongue-tied now for god's sake? For some crazy reason he was looking bemused. His mind was a muddle of tangled thoughts over the surprise at what was finally happening. Was this what he wanted? What would it mean between them though? To her he appeared incapable of fully understanding what she meant. She didn't wait. Instead she helped him. She knew exactly what she'd decided she wanted. For that particular night at least she'd completely abandoned struggling over what sex between them might mean, what it might lead to, or even any expectation of what it might or might not lead to.

"Your place, let's go to your place now."

Her voice was strong, determined and committed.

This time he didn't hesitate. Just as it had in hers, for that night at least the fog in his mind cleared, his confusion over what it might or might not mean between them in the future, disappeared.

She didn't wait for his reply. She took his hand and stood up, telling him simply with a smile, "Come on."

As they left the courtyard she released her hand from his and instead tucked her arm into his, giving him a reassuring small squeeze of it as she did. Arm in arm they walked along the short alley and down the steps outside one end of the Courtyard Bar, then on through the almost deserted main alleyway of the centre of the village towards his flat. It was approaching three o'clock. Most of the late night tourists were in the clubs by then, along with some of the summer season workers and the locals. The very few people they came across were those outside Nikos place waiting for their pizza or sat on the small low walls around the square munching on the slices they already had. Above them the clear night sky with its array of bright stars and the striking moon over the Acropolis seemed to be guiding them towards his flat as she clung even more tightly to his arm.

As he reached into his pocket for the key to the door of the courtyard and his flat inside she removed her arm from within his and reached up behind his head to draw him into her for another lingering soft kiss. As she finished she said softly, "Well, yes, ok, I guess I do like you as more than just a good friend."

Before he could respond she placed the index finger of her right hand on his lips and added, "Don't, don't say anything. Just take it for what it is, David."

It was a simple remark, but she knew the intensity in her voice would have an effect on him. Maybe that was what she intended, even though she wasn't completely sure what it really meant, or more accurately what she wanted it to mean. It was the first time she'd actually gone as far as telling him how she felt about him with some passion and feeling in it, rather than the sanitised, lacking feeling, "Friends, very good friends."

Nevertheless, at that time they were both actually still not sure quite what they wanted what they were about to do to mean in the future. Was it the simple 'lightness' of a sexual encounter - an 'erotic friendship' – the phrase used by the main male character in Kundera's novel, 'The Unbearable Lightness of Being'? Or did either of them, or possibly both of them, want more; the 'weight' of responsibility and fidelity between them?

They never got time to think that through, and anyway it certainly wasn't the appropriate time. Minutes later she was pulling her dress over her head by the side of his bed to reveal her black bra and pants, while he was also tugging his polo shirt over his head, kicking off his deck shoes and unfastening his shorts.

She lay back on the bed, unfastened her bra and removed her pants, then beckoned him on to her. He'd waited a long time to see her like this, and in his bed, or at least on top of it. He thought it would never happen, but now it was. This was definitely not the time to consider anything between them going forward. He took a very brief moment to dwell on how good her body was, how good it looked. After their long 'dance' of the summer there could have been some awkwardness, but there was none, none whatsoever.

They enjoyed each other's bodies, and joint satisfaction for over an hour. Then finally they just laid beside each another in silence for a few minutes. Her eyes flickered closed for a few seconds. Drowsiness and the lateness of the night, or more accurately the approaching early morning, as well as from their exertions and her earlier long hours working in the restaurant, started to overtake her. She fought against it. She didn't want to just drift straight off to sleep. Now, more than ever, more than ever before, she felt she needed to talk to him, but drowsiness and sleep overwhelmed her.

The season was drawing to a close in a few short weeks. Alice was going to stay for the winter, as she'd done previously, and then work again through the following summer season. He had to go back to England though, for the winter at least. He couldn't avoid it or even put it off for a few weeks. He had meetings with his agent and possible publishers. And anyway, she didn't appear at all sure if she wanted him to stay, or even to come back the following summer. She wasn't giving him any indication of either of those options, even in the few days after they'd slept together. She seemed determined not to. They did sleep together a second time, but he never raised it then. He figured she would if she wanted to. But then she cooled off a lot towards him. Her text messages for their after work meetings and drinking almost stopped, and she never replied to his, not even with a reason for not meeting up later.

Consequently, their late night meetings and drinking sessions became less and less frequent, mostly only happening by chance if she came into the bar that he happened to be having a late drink in. She gave nothing away to him, nothing about how she felt, or about what had happened between them. It seemed she simply ignored it, erased it from her memory. She'd told him, quite pointedly, after that second time they'd slept together that sex between them would only be till the end of the season. She'd been quite adamant in stating that, and in ensuring that he agreed and understood. However, her subsequent actions, or lack of, in terms of any interaction between them whatsoever demonstrated a clear loss of any intent at all on her part, even in that regard. There was no indication at all from her that sex between them would happen again, let alone only be till the end of the season.

His confusion returned. He was back where he started, and even more bewildered. The elation of finally getting to bed with her rapidly drained out of him. In the end he tried to be relaxed about it, although he couldn't help being not just confused, but also a little angry.

When their paths did cross in one of the bars late one night during the week following the second time they'd slept together he couldn't help noticing what looked like a sadness to her, a sadness in her eyes. Perhaps it was merely tiredness, the effect of the long season, but her spark had definitely gone. He was back to not really understand Alice Palmer, quite what she wanted between them, but then, did she really understand him, what he wanted?

However, that dilemma for him, what their finally sleeping together actually meant was soon clouded even further by what he was told a few days later. He was informed of one other particular 'light' sexual encounter of Alice's, and by someone who he reckoned was a pretty reliable source, Dianne Arnold. It seemed that at least one of the rumours in the village about Alice was true.

Late one night in Glow Dianne told him that Alice said she'd slept with a Brit ex-pat in the village earlier that summer in late May, Simon Chapel. Over the summer David had come across him a couple of times in bars and instantly concluded he was a complete arsehole, not a very pleasant character at all. Even though Dianne added that Alice said she regretted it, and that it had only been the once, David found it difficult to get his head around it.

Dianne's revelation threw him back into a mind-set of being very wary of anything resembling the 'weight' of fidelity and responsibility at that time with Alice, or any woman for that matter. He never confronted her about it. From what Dianne told him, and from the way Alice cooled off on anything between them soon after the second time they had sex, he merely concluded that she wasn't interested in anything more than the 'lightness' of sexual encounters in Lindos.

However, Dianne's revelation led him to soon do something he would ultimately come to regret; seek again for himself what he thought was simply the 'lightness' of another meaningless sexual encounter.

Just like David, Alice Palmer was clearly deeply scarred by a past relationship disaster; in her case in her marriage. They were two emotionally damaged people.

16

The victim, and the British and Russian Security Services

Alexandra Ivanova, or Sophia Orlova, as she was known in the late summer of 2019 five years after she defected, was an attractive woman in a particular way. Her face portrayed all the characteristics of the classical elegance of many women members of the Russian aristocracy of the nineteenth century, although she obviously wasn't one. Indeed, she could easily have been one of Tolstoy's heroines such as Anna Karenina. Slim and tall, almost six foot, even in flat sandals, she'd kept her figure well in her late thirties. She spoke good English, which had obviously been polished in her academic career having previously learned it as a second language at school in Russia. She was born in Lipetsk and lived there until going off to Moscow State University in 1981 at eighteen to start her undergraduate degree. It was a city almost three hundred miles south-east of Moscow, located on the banks of the Voronezh river in the Don Basin.

To a large extent the history of the city, particularly at the time of Peter the Great, as well as in the second half of the nineteenth century, influenced her choice of, and interest in, the subject of her Ph.D.; Contemporary Russian Foreign Policy and its roots in nineteenth century Russia. The foundation of the modern city of Lipetsk dated back to 1703. It was at that time that Peter the Great ordered the construction of a cast iron factory there for making artillery shells, mainly because of the nearby iron ore deposits

In the second half of the nineteenth century, during the period 1861–1864, the city had links to the Russian clandestine revolutionary organization Land and Liberty (Zemlya i volya), sometimes translated as Land and Freedom Eventually that was re-established as a political party in the period 1876–1879. It was a central organ of the Narodnik movement, a movement of the Russian Empire intelligentsia in the 1860s and 1870s, some of whom became involved in revolutionary agitation against the Tsarist regime. Their ideology was a form of agrarian socialism. The inspirers of Land and Liberty were the famous Russian writers, Alexander Herzen and Nikolay Chernyshevsky, and their goal was the preparation of a peasant revolution against the Tsarist Regime.

Those days of any peasant revolution against a Tsarist Regime had long gone of course, been overtaken by history and events. But Alexandra Ivanova was particularly fond of Chernyshevsky's writings, especially his novel 'What Is To Be Done' first published in 1863. It was subtitled 'Tales About New People', and it became the bible for women in Russia in the second half of the nineteenth-century, when they flocked to the cities to find work, independence and, hopefully, happiness. Throughout the 1860s and 1870s women of all classes in Russia left their families to look for work and education in the cities. The heroine of the novel is Vera Pavlovna, who can no more deny her need for love than her need for work. In Chernyshevsky's novel her attempts to find satisfying sexual relationships and to organise new collective ways of working were an inspiration to all those unmarried daughters who, like her, were thrown out into the world, expected either to find a rich husband or support themselves. Pavlovna's dreams and aims of work and freedom, love and pleasure, also had an enormous influence on later revolutionaries in Russia such as Alexandria Kollontai and Lenin.

When it was first published Chernyshevsky's hopeful, sensual novel was hailed as an example of how fiction can change people's lives. Although not part of her studies, when she initially read it in her first year at university it certainly had a profound effect on her. It changed Alexandra Ivanova's outlook on life, particularly when she returned to re-read it years later. In the years between, while pursuing her academic studies and eventually her academic career, plus her subsequent connections with the Russian Security Services, she had subdued her views about Pavlovna's beliefs depicted in the novel. The change within her, the resurgence of the impact on her of Chernyshevsky's novel and the beliefs within it, came through her growing disillusionment with the Russian regime under Vladimir Putin.

She was at junior school when Mikhail Gorbachev tried to introduce his reforms in the nineteen-eighties that were subsequently crushed with the collapse and disintegration of the Soviet Union in 1991. Even so, when she was older at university she believed she could see some similarities to Chernyshevsky's ideas, especially in relation to women in Russia under Gorbachev. She saw them as equivalent to some of Chernyshevsky's 'new people'.

Perhaps in some part her liking for Chernyshevsky's novel, and his heroine Pavlovna's search for work, independence, love and happiness, along with that of all women in Russia, was due to Alexandra Ivanova's relationship with her father, which wasn't good at all.

He was often very cruel to her in childhood. She had no siblings, so was an only child. Her father wanted a son, and she obviously wasn't that. From an early age her father demanded she had to be a prime student; only being the best would be good enough. Consequently, he drove her on to go to university, demanding that she go to Moscow State University. He was a staunch Communist Party man, what was referred to as 'hard line', and a former KGB officer. Stalin was his hero, and he never hid that. In that respect, his politics differed significantly from Alexandra's by the time she was at university. He didn't like Gorbachev at all, and his attempted reforms.

Her love of Chernyshevsky's novel, along with her father's cruelty, produced within her a wariness of men in general. Although not at all times and towards all men, as a result she despised some men at times; some of whom she thought of as the 'Stalinist dinosaurs' in the Russian Security Services, or some of her academic colleagues, or definitely at times the men she had to engage with on projects for the Security Services.

Even so, despite that she soon understood that she could use them professionally for her own benefit.

As her father demanded, she got a place at and went to Moscow State University to study for her undergraduate degree initially. Also as he'd demanded, she was a top student; a keen learner, conscientious and devoted to her studies. As a result she was soon identified by one of her Professors, who had his own links to them, as a potential candidate for recruitment to the Russian Security Services and of use to them internationally once she had completed her undergraduate and postgraduate degrees. There was never any doubt that she would obtain a first class result in her undergraduate degree, and the same Professor made sure he strongly encouraged her, and supported her, in going on to study for a Doctorate in International Relations and Russian Foreign Policy. Her Ph.D. was actually in Contemporary Russian Foreign Policy and its roots in nineteenth-century Russia, set within theories on International Relations. She completed it in almost record time of just over two years, and the awarding of it was virtually automatic. Everyone who knew her academically at the university knew it would never be in doubt. Neither would her subsequent initial appointment as a lecturer at Moscow State University and her rapid rise through the academic ranks there, eventually to the position of Professor of International Relations. Within her rise in academia she took very little persuading, if any, to accept recruitment as an asset to the Russian Security Services, to be called upon by them from time to time for specific operations, usually involving information gathering from foreign nationals within the academic world. Initially, she was recruited to the GRU, Russia's Main Intelligence Directorate, the foreign military intelligence agency. However, by the time she reached the position of Professor at the university she was regularly also being contacted by, and had links with, the SVR, Russia's Foreign Intelligence Service, as well as even the FSB, Russia's Federal Security Service.

Irrespective of her identity, in both her previous life as Alexandra Ivanova and in her new one as Sophia Orlova she was a very cold hearted individual. A regular comment about her from her contacts within the Russian Security Service was that she was cold enough to produce a Siberian permafrost. Calculating and ruthless were other words her superior officers often used to describe her. Those characteristics had been ingrained within her by the experiences of her life when she was young, very young; ingrained in her by her father. They were maintained, and added to, by her training in the Russian Security Services, although in truth that side of her character didn't need much more training at all. She was completely receptive to it, almost expected it and what it was aimed to do. All of her calculating ruthlessness was contained within one key overriding element in her character, that of self-interest and self-preservation. She learned, and had been trained to learn, that her concern in both her professional and personal life should be what was good and best for the Russian State. Even above that, however, what was good and best for her was always her prime concern in both her professional and personal life, if necessary in certain situations, above the interests of the Russian State.

Her Russian Security Service training, not least the constant suspicion and lack of trust it produced within her, left her with very little appetite or desire to pursue any meaningful relationships with either men or women. Nevertheless, there had been the 'lightness' of a couple of sexual encounters while she was a student at Moscow State University, as well as a few more after she joined the Russian Security Services. What ones there were then were merely part of any information gathering operation in which she was involved for them, whether within her academic life and contacts or wider within her personal life. To some extent those could be very loosely categorised as Kundera's 'lightness' of sexual encounters, although they hardly qualified as anything resembling an 'erotic friendship', far from it in fact. For Alexandra Ivanova they were simply part of the job, and she expected and accepted having to do that at times. She was very good at it. She used them, the sexual encounters and the men's desires, to her advantage very well in order to get whatever information she was seeking. She certainly had no scruples whatsoever about that. It was just something she did which she accepted was necessary at times.

When necessary she maintained that attitude in her new persona as Sophia Orlova after she defected.

In both her professional and personal lives, whether in her old or new identities, she deliberately avoided any possibility of the 'weight' of fidelity with men or anything that could be termed a relationship and responsibility. She was very focused and clear about that in her mind. She had a way of ensuring straightaway that they understood that, particularly when it came to any sexual encounter. She employed something from Kundera's 'Unbearable Lightness of Being', which she'd enjoyed reading. She would tell the men that she believed the only relationship which could make both partners happy was one in which sentimentality had no place and neither partner made any claim on the life and freedom of the other. In fact, it was her equivalent of 'erotic friendship'. That belief of hers, along with her occasional activities for the Russian Security Services, meant that she should exclude all love from her life. She relied on that belief, and found it useful, especially when focusing on any particular target for the Security Services. In addition, telling them precisely initially that she thought sentimentality had no place in a relationship had the effect she required of preventing the men she was with, the targets, thinking anything could go too far in terms of an on-going relationship between them. There weren't actually that many of them, but those that were turned out most of the time to be one night sexual encounters. That was exactly what she wanted them to think, and what she wanted as long as she got the information she required on that one night. Her 'sentimentality has no place in a relationship' belief revelation usually meant they dropped their guard a little, felt secure with her, especially with her also being an academic like them, and they then sometimes told her even more than they should have. There was never any doubt she was clever. Her actions regularly confirmed what some in the Russian Security Services said about her being ruthless and calculating.

The focus of the rule by which she lived her life - what was best for her and her self-preservation - appeared to change early in 2014 with what seemed her complete disillusionment with the Russian regime under Vladimir Putin. There was a series of changes within Russia and the regime, not least Putin's growing authoritarianism and what she believed was a rapidly accelerating slide to Stalinism and the terror that had brought previously. The final 'straw that broke the camel's back' for her – what made her take the step to change her life in the way she did – was Russia's Tsarist like annexation of Crimea in March of that year of 2014, and further on-going threats to neighbouring Ukraine and its independence. She could see a long, drawn out war eventually looming, and Russians, including herself, suffering increasing hardship. She decided she had to do something for her self-preservation.

As discreetly and subtly as possible she made it known to an academic colleague in the university that she thought she could trust, and who she believed had some connections in the British Embassy in Moscow, that she was very unhappy with the Putin regime, especially over the escalating Crimea situation. That was a dangerous thing to do at any time, and even more so in the prevailing growing climate of fear in Russia. It was also especially dangerous because of her links with the Security Services. They had informants everywhere, particularly within the academic community. A couple of times during the week after she made her feelings known to her colleague she even thought that she was being followed home to her flat from the university. The atmosphere in Moscow, as well as in the university amongst the academics, wasn't good at all. Suspicion and mistrust was everywhere.

She heard nothing for over a week and was starting to think that what she'd heard about her colleague's connections in the British Embassy were simply idle gossip and rumours. At the end of the second week she was scheduled to give a talk on 'Global International Relations since the collapse of the Soviet Union' at an academic conference over that weekend in Moscow. It was an international event, with academics attending from all over the world, and had been scheduled for over a year. In the light of the situation over Russia and Crimea she was surprised when she learned it was going ahead, and many international academic would still be attending.

She gave her talk on the Saturday, in the afternoon of the second day of the three day conference. It seemed to go down well, was well received. She pointedly avoided any reference to Russia and Crimea. Even when, in questions after she finished her presentation an Italian academic asked her if she thought Russia's current foreign policy resembled in any way that of under Stalin in the nineteen-forties and fifties she avoided a direct answer, simply replying to the audience in general that, "The foreign policy of all countries has links back to their history and roots in many parts and times in their past, for example Italy's, as well as Britain's, or more accurately, should that be England's in respect to our Scottish and Irish colleagues here today." The last bit of her reply at least drew a few more light hearted small laughs.

Her talk had been in the first conference session after lunch on that second day and was followed by a short coffee break. As they broke for coffee immediately after her talk her impression was that she'd navigated a possibly difficult and awkward scenario in terms of any reference to the Crimea situation well, particularly with her answer to the Italian's question. She felt relived, and pretty pleased with herself.

However, while she was standing at one of the small, high round tables having her coffee no one at all joined her to talk about her presentation, particularly none of the Russian academics or even any from her own university. She was beginning to think that odd and starting to panic a little. Had she been completely wrong about her colleague whom she thought had links to the British Embassy? What if she had been and what she told him discreetly about her disillusionment with the Putin regime, and over the Crimea situation, he'd simply passed on to the Russian Security Services? Had word about that got out amongst the Russian academic community? Was that why no one wanted to be seen in conversation with her over the coffee break? She knew that the Security Services would undoubtedly have a couple, or possibly more, of their people watching everyone at the conference, Russians and foreigners, and reporting back. Anyone seen talking with her would come under suspicion too if her disillusionment with the regime had been exposed and reported back to the Security Services, who's people at the conference could equally have been some of the staff serving the coffee and overhearing conversations, as much as individual Russian academics.

She'd almost finished her coffee and started to surreptitiously scan the room, wondering who might be from the Security Services. She had no idea what she was looking for though. Intelligence agents, even Russian ones, didn't have a standard uniform. Some of the Russians, as well as most of the Eastern Europeans, were wearing the more academic traditional dark suit and tie. Even what few Russian and East European women there were had similar outfits of dark business suits, with skirts and no ties of course. Quite a few of the rest of the men and women though had more casual wear, some with jackets, but quite a few without, like the Italian who asked the question and a couple of guys he was talking with. From what she could hear from distance, they appeared to be French, or at least talking in a mixture of French and Italian.

She sighed slightly over her futile, and somewhat panicky, stupid attempt to even think she would be able to pick out any Russian Security Services people from what they were wearing. As she took the last bit of her coffee, emptied the cup and placed it back on the saucer on the high table an English voice from behind her said, "I really enjoyed your talk. Thank you, very informative."

She turned around to face a tall man with light brown shortish hair and a slim figure contained inside a jacket that couldn't be described as either light or dark blue, but was somewhere between the two, which partially covered an open neck pristine white shirt above beige chinos. From his accent he was obviously English.

"Thank you," was all she could respond, somewhat nervously as she was sure there would now be someone watching the two of them.

"Yes, very informative, and I liked the way you handled that difficult question from the Italian. Must have been awkward, but you were very diplomatic."

She had no idea who he was, other than obviously an English academic, and was growing increasingly nervous by the second over who might be watching them, particularly as no one else had bothered to engage her in conversation.

He quickly picked up how uncomfortable she was and in any case had no intention of prolonging their conversation. He was equally aware of how dangerous it was for her.

Up to that point he'd spoken in a normal level of voice, intent on anyone nearby actually being relatively easily able to overhear his comments and their conversation of a general nature about her talk and presentation.

He lowered his voice considerably, ensured that he didn't make any forward movement whatsoever to lean in to her and make it look like he was telling her something he didn't want overheard, and then simply almost whispered, "You need 8495222333."

He raised his voice back to the normal level so he could now be overheard as he added, "Yes, I hope you can find it. I think that academic source reference will be useful to add to your presentation if you are going to turn it into an academic journal article for publication. I'm not sure you need to cite it precisely though."

"Yes, thank you that will be very helpful. I think they are starting the next conference session now," she told him curtly, and then added, "I need to go to the toilet first though. You go in."

He knew what she meant, that they shouldn't be seen together any longer than was necessary. She still had no idea who he was. Basically, she didn't want to, and it was clear he didn't want to introduce himself. It was safer for both of them that way. She'd memorised the number well though. It was clearly a contact phone number for her, most likely of a 'burner' phone, a disposable cell phone with a prepaid service. And she took his comment about not needing to cite the supposed academic source reference to be about the number, and that she should dispose of it immediately after she'd called it.

She was obviously wrong in having doubts about her academic colleague whom she'd spoken to briefly about her disillusionment with the Putin regime. He clearly did have links to the British Embassy in Moscow.

For the rest of the afternoon session at the conference she went over and over in her mind what she thought would be best for her now. She thought she had been clear about that before she spoke to her academic colleague about her disillusionment over a week previously. As she tried to listen to the afternoon session talk and concentrate on it she attempted to weigh up the benefits and problems from what she was considering doing. By the time the conference ended for the day she'd decided. There would be no going back on what she intended to do, what she thought she had decided to do a few short weeks before.

That evening she took the metro from her apartment for three stops, heading for a street near one of the university faculty buildings in the city centre on Mokhovaya Street, near the Arbat and, ironically, almost alongside the Kremlin. As she'd left that faculty building a few weeks before after a university academic meeting and headed for the Arbatskaya metro station she'd noticed one of the very few remaining public street pay phone booths in the city. She no doubt noticed it because of their rarity. Not that she ever envisaged having to use it, and indeed, as she spotted it she actually wondered who would possibly ever use it in these days of everyone's mobile phones? Now she was hoping it was still there and in working order. There was no way she was going to use her mobile phone to make the call she'd decided she wanted to make.

It was still there and when she lifted the receiver and put it to her ear there was a dialling tone. She dialled the 'burner' phone number. It rang for a good minute, so much so that she almost hung up. Just as she was about to a man's voice answered with a simple questioning, "Yes?"

Even though he only said the one word she guessed from that he sounded English. She could definitely tell he wasn't Russian, and was relieved, thinking at least it wasn't a trap.

She was about to say who she was but never got the chance. The guy said firmly, "Listen and remember."

Again, she never got the chance to respond as he added, equally firmly, "You are invited to a three day E.U. sponsored academic conference on E.U. foreign policy over the weekend of the 11th of April in Brussels. You will receive an email from the conference organisers with the formal invitation tomorrow, for you to present to your university in Moscow. You-"

She started to interrupt, "But what if they-"

"What if they will not let you go? Don't worry they will. Why wouldn't they? If they query it you can just tell them you will be able gather some useful information for your contacts in Moscow from some of the academics from the E.U. states who will be there. You know, and your faculty head at your university will probably also know, who you mean by 'your contacts in Moscow'. It may take them a day or two to check up the line with their Russian Security Services contacts, but they'll let you go eventually. Why wouldn't they? The Security Services will look upon it as an opportunity for you to do some investigating for them and information gathering."

"But then what, in Brussels, what-"

She knew she probably shouldn't ask that at this stage, but it didn't really matter. He wasn't going to tell her anything more at that point. He'd already been on the line too long as far as he was concerned.

"Just go, that will be sorted out when you get there. Don't worry, you'll be advised soon after you arrive. Oh, and make sure you go into the conference tomorrow. Don't do anything odd or stupid, like not attending the final day. Don't do anything odd that might draw attention to yourself. Goodbye. Safe journey."

The line went dead. She knew she shouldn't, but she lingered in the phone booth for almost half-a-minute after she replaced the receiver, trying to think through what was happening to her. Was she having doubts? Was she doing the right thing?

She went home and decided to sleep on it. She couldn't do anything straightaway that evening anyway. Whatever she decided, she knew she should go into the final day of the conference the next morning, and act as though everything was normal. When she woke the next morning and checked her email before going into the conference the email with the formal Brussels conference invitation was there. The conference was in the French speaking part of the Free University of Brussels.

Whether it was that which completely had the effect or not, for some reason it seemed to clear her head and her thoughts.

She'd definitely concluded that what was best for her then was to defect to the U.K. She went into the conference, acted completely normally and simply deliberately engaged in general academic conversations with various groups of other academics.

On the Monday morning she went into her faculty at the university and presented the Brussels conference invitation firstly to her Head of Department, who told her he didn't think there would be any problem with her going, but that he would have to check with the relevant faculty and university people, technically his bosses She took that to mean probably also with the Russian Security Services.

She spent a nervous two days, but in the late afternoon of the second day her Head of Department called her to say everything was ok and that there was an email on its way to her from the, "relevant officials", including the Human Resources Department and the Dean of the Faculty, formally giving her permission to attend. She took the phrase "relevant officials" to mean the Security Services. Her Head of Department, as well as the Dean of the Faculty, would not have necessarily been aware of it, and they'd never given her any indication that they were, but she was very aware that the various sections of the Russian Security Services would know her, and of the occasional bits of information gathering work from foreign academics and others which she'd done for them in the past.

Her Head of Department finished the call by telling her, "The International Section in Human Resources will be in touch in the next couple of days with your flight tickets and Brussels hotel booking confirmation. Enjoy the conference. I look forward to some feedback when you get back."

Her relief at it all seeming to appear so smooth and straightforward was only slightly disturbed by his comment about feedback after she got back. She wasn't coming back of course, but it just seemed a bit of an odd thing for him to say. He'd never asked to be briefed after she'd returned from any other international conferences outside Russia. Was he just trying to subtly warn her to make sure she returned? Or maybe she was simply being paranoid and he was actually just really interested in what he thought she might learn academically about EU foreign policy? Nevertheless, he never got his debrief as she never returned to the university or even Moscow.

As soon as she checked in at the hotel in Brussels and got into her room on the Friday evening before the start of the conference the following morning the phone in the room rang. When she answered a male voice, this time with a seeming rather upper-class English accent, said, "Memorise this and use it now, not from the room or the hotel, 0032456789012."

With that he rang off.

She immediately left the room and asked the hotel receptionist if there was a public phone booth nearby. He told her there was one just about a hundred metres to the right outside the hotel, but that she would need what he called a telecard, and then explained it was a phone card, which she could buy at the tobacconist opposite the hotel. She went to the tobacconist, bought the card, then found the public phone booth and called the number.

She never got to say one word, not even hello, before this time a woman's voice, again with an English accent, told her succinctly, "Leave the conference when they break for lunch tomorrow. Go to the Brussels-Midi/Zuid Station and get a ticket for the 14.52 Eurostar to London. More information will be on the train."

The line went dead. But what did, "More information will be on the train," mean was what she was thinking?

Nevertheless, she did as instructed. She left the conference as soon as it broke for lunch at one o'clock, quickly went back to her hotel nearby to pick up her laptop bag, along with her small weekend bag which she'd packed the previous night after she'd made the call from the street public pay phone. Then she made her way by taxi to Brussels-Midi/Zuid Station. It was only a ten minute or so taxi ride from the hotel.

It was only just after one-thirty when she reached the station and bought a ticket for the 14.52 Eurostar to London St. Pancras International station. She had an anxious hour and twenty minutes or so to wait before she could board the train, hoping meanwhile that other Russian academics at the conference wouldn't notice her absence as she suspected there might be one amongst them, or maybe more than one, who had links to the

Russian Security Services. Also, as she bought her Eurostar ticket with her Russian Visa credit card all sorts of crazy thoughts were rushing through her brain. What if the Security Services were watching her, had been watching her all along, including at the conference that morning, and had tracked her credit cards, identifying her purchase of the ticket? She took a deep breath and tried to calm down. Trying to be more rational she convinced herself she was panicking unnecessarily. Even if they were tracking her cards, there was no way they would have picked up her ticket purchase so quickly surely. She decided she would pass the time by trying to eat something at one of the station cafes for lunch to calm her nerves, a baguette perhaps with a coffee.

At twenty-past-two she saw on the departures board that the 14.52 Eurostar was ready for boarding and made her way to the manual passport control booth to present her Russian passport before boarding the train. She was desperately trying not to show how nervous she was, thinking her Russian passport might provoke an issue, although logically she couldn't really think why it should. Plenty of Russians must travel between Brussels and London on Eurostar. She needn't have worried. There was no problem. A few minutes later she was placing her small weekend bag and her laptop bag on the overhead rack before taking her seat by the window. Now she was at last starting to relax, although beginning to wonder again precisely what the comment of, "More information will be on the train" meant. She didn't have to wait long to find out.

As soon as the train pulled out of the station a grey-haired guy in a dark suit clutching a folded newspaper immediately sat down in the aisle seat next to her. There were just the two seats, with the backs of the seats in front ahead of them. After a minute or so, much to her surprise, he asked if she'd like to read his Times newspaper? Then without waiting for her to reply he carefully passed it to her, telling her there was some interesting news on Crimea inside on page four. After she took it he got up straightaway and left her, only pausing very briefly to say quietly, "I'm sure someone will be glad to help you at St. Pancras International if you haven't been to London before."

After he left she carefully discreetly opened the newspaper at page four to find a British passport inside in the name of Sophia Orlova, with the photograph of her and a new date of birth. The place of birth shown was London. She quickly placed it in her handbag.

The rest of her journey was uneventful. No one spoke to her, with the exception of the Ticket Inspector, and the train arrived at St. Pancras International on time an hour and fifty-five minutes later at three forty-five U.K. time. There was no Border Control, so no passport check, which was just as well as she was unsure which one she should show. There was only the Customs Inspection area which she strolled through trying to look as relaxed as possible.

As soon as she emerged onto the main station concourse a woman in a dark business suit, who appeared to be in her early forties, approached her and simply said, "Follow me please." She took her outside the station to a black car with a man in the driver's seat. After the two women got into the back the car drove off.

They drove for almost an hour and took her to what the woman referred to as a "Safe House," where she would be comfortable and safe, and would stay there for a couple of weeks, or perhaps three, while she was, what she referred to as, "debriefed and security checked." The woman also told her that they would provide her with some clothes while she stayed there as she only had what she'd taken to Brussels in her weekend bag. The woman added, "A woman colleague of mine will check your sizes with you after we arrive."

In fact, she stayed there for almost a month while she told two others as much as she knew about Russia's Foreign Policy intentions, as well as various other bits of what she thought might be useful information for them to know. She actually didn't think most of what she was able to tell them was all that important, but they seemed pleased with it and interested. It was a man and a woman, who also stayed at the house the whole time, but at no time fully introduced themselves, just their first names, which she guessed were false anyway

But then the interrogation stopped, as abruptly as it had started. Another guy, obviously in a more senior position, turned up at the Safe House to meet her and informed her she would not be staying in London or even the U.K. She would be given what he referred to as a 'Legend', a new identity, Sophia Orlova, as per her new British Passport, along with a new invented personal history. This included where she went to school and university, her family details and background, and how she came to have a British Passport when from her accent she was obviously brought up in the early part of her life in Russia. Her new passport showed her actual real date of birth, but her place of birth as London. According to the 'Legend' she was able to apply for and obtain a British Passport because she was actually born in London, being the daughter of a Russian businessman who was based in London with his wife at the time of Sophia's birth. The 'Legend' included her employment history, mostly that she had been employed in London as well as in other European countries, including Greece, as an interpreter.

It was all fiction of course, or at least the vast majority of it. She was told that for the next two weeks she would be expected to learn it, rehearse it, and be tested on it by two MI6 officers at the Safe House. Plus, mostly for her own safety there was one other thing that they required her to do that wasn't fiction, change her appearance a little. That entailed changing the colour and style of her hair, dyeing it from dark brown and cut to shoulder length to blonde and cut very short.

She didn't have a problem with that, and could understand why it was necessary. However, she started to ask, "But what about the-"

"Your new British Passport? Yes, we'll take care of that," the guy started to tell her. "The one you were given on the Eurostar was only temporary, just in case you were stopped and asked for identification on the train or in the Customs Inspection area at St. Pancras. We will need that back and will provide you with another one with all the same personal details, date and place of birth, plus of course a few border control entry and exit stamps within it from places you've supposed to have visited over the years. It'll have a different photo of you in it of course taken after you've had your hair cut and dyed. Don't look so worried. We have very good people who can do that for you. The woman is very professional."

As he got up to head for the door and leave he added, "She will come to do that for you tomorrow morning, as well as help you select some more clothes online for your whole new wardrobe, which she will collect and bring to you in a new set of luggage for your travels."

"My travels. Where am I going?"

"Oh, yes, sorry, I almost forgot that part. Don't worry. I'm sure you'll like it. Athens, we've got you a very nice apartment in one of the better parts of Athens, my dear, Glyfada. Very nice, and quite expensive property. You'll be given a very nice lump sum amount of cash, very nice indeed, deposited in a Swiss Bank account in your new name, plus a very tidy sum deposited regularly each month in a Greek Bank account in your name on the first day of the month, call it a pension in gratitude from Her Majesty's Government. You'll be provided with all the details of those before you leave here for Athens in a few days. With those sorts of sums you actually won't need to work for the rest of your life really. Well, except for us occasionally, of course."

"For you? What will that-"

"Entail, what will that entail? Don't worry," he told her again. "Nothing very dangerous at all really, all very low level. Offering your analysis on some communications we may have intercepted, and possibly occasionally engaging in conversation, as well as other activities, with people we are interested in. Not too dissimilar from what we understood you've been doing for the Ruskies, I guess. What we've been watching you do for a few years for them. You'll get a full briefing and debriefing each time of course, for each operation you're involved in."

He turned to head towards the door once again, but turned around once more to add, "Oh, and I don't expect I really have to tell you this, but no social media at all from now on, especially not under your new identity. We've obviously been monitoring you and checked and you don't appear to have been a user of it under your previous identity. Expect the Ruskies are as tight about that as we are, so that shouldn't be much of a hardship for you, and anyway it's for your own safety.

It all seemed very vague, but she was a little concerned over his use of the phrase, "other activities", as well as his comment, "What we've been watching you do for a few years." Although, Athens, and an expensive apartment, wouldn't be too unpleasant at all, neither would what he'd told her about the money.

The next day the woman hair stylist arrived at the Safe House to cut and dye her hair, and order some clothes online which the new Sophia picked out. Two days later they arrived, along with a full set of luggage, all delivered by vetted secure MI6 staff operatives, including the woman hair stylist.

She spent the next two weeks going over and over her new life history, her 'Legend', learning it word for word, but trying not to sound too mechanical when repeating it. At the end of the two weeks another man and a woman she'd never met before turned up at the Safe House to test her on it over two days. She was fine, very relaxed, and they seemed happy with how she answered their questions on her new life history. She had always had a good memory, particularly in her academic studies, and at one point she felt as if she actually believed what she was saying about the new her.

At the end they told her there were no problems and that the woman who'd met her at St. Pancras International would pick her up at ten the next morning to take her and her luggage to Heathrow airport for their flight to Athens. She was to be her handler, her contact at MI6 in London eventually, but would go on the flight to Athens with her. When they arrived there they would be met by one of their operatives in Athens to take the two of them to the apartment in Glyfada. Her handler would provide Sophia with a new mobile and all the necessary secret encrypted contact details for it, as well as for her new MI6 provided laptop, plus the details of both her new bank accounts, while she stayed with her for two days. After that she'd leave to return to the U.K. As well as her handler in London at MI6 she would also have a handler, a contact, in Athens, also a woman, who would be there at the apartment to meet both the women when they arrived. In relation to the bank accounts though, she was told that the monthly payments, what they referred to as her 'pension' from Her Majesty, would be made to the Swiss Bank account for security reasons and to avoid any possibility they could be traced easily if made to the Greek account. The Swiss account would be more secure and much more difficult, practically impossible, for anyone such as other foreign Security Services or police to check on or investigate. She could simply transfer whatever funds she needed from there as and when she did.

Everything went smoothly and she settled into her new life as Sophia Orlova well, adapted to it easily. She spent most of the time in Athens, but occasionally took trips over weekends and sometimes longer to some of the Greek Islands, including Crete, Kos and Lesvos, near the Turkish coast. She loved the spring and summer sunshine of her new life and swimming in the clear blue sea. Even the winters were nowhere near as severe as in Moscow.

Over the next five years what she did for MI6 was pretty low level stuff, nothing very dangerous or exciting, not that she minded that. From time to time MI6 in London, or her Athens handler for them, contacted her to ask her advice and analysis of something they'd picked up about the Russian Security Services or projected Russian Foreign Policy activities. However, there were no longer any academic conferences to attend and see what information she could pick up from foreign academics as she'd done in the past for the Russians. That would have been far too dangerous in terms of her being recognised by any Russian academics attending, or others sympathetic to the Russians and in contact with the Russian Security Services.

So, by 2019, and over the previous five years, she now had a good life in Athens in a good flat and with a nice balance in a Swiss Bank, as well as a very considerable regular monthly income which MI6 set up for her.

Over those five years she'd not even been required at any time to do anything which could be described as her in any way becoming 'active' for them, MI6; not being 'an active operative in the field', as it was termed. However, that changed in what was to become a dramatic fashion at the start of the second week of October 2019.

Her Athens handler called at lunchtime and told her she would be picked up by her at seven-thirty the next morning as she was booked on the ten o'clock flight to London Heathrow. It was just to be an overnight stay in London as she was booked on the four o'clock flight back to Athens the next day.

She probably knew better than to ask, but nevertheless started to reply with, "But what-"

She never got to finish.

"I'll fill you in on the way to the airport. You'll be picked up at Heathrow and taken to head office, and after that to your hotel. Then you'll be picked up the next day in time for your flight back. See you at seven-thirty in the morning."

With that she rang off, leaving Sophia somewhat bewildered. Why was she suddenly being summoned back to London? She knew what 'head office' meant, the River House and MI6, but she hadn't been back there or even to London in the five years since she arrived in Athens. For almost an hour she wracked her brains trying to figure out if she'd done something wrong, made some mistake. But there was nothing. If it was nothing though, or even something basic, something simple she wasn't even aware of, why couldn't it be sorted out in Athens with her handler? Her superiors at MI6 must surely be aware that for her to go back to London, and risk being seen there, recognised even by chance, would be dangerous for her. In the end she decided the best thing to do was to simply pack an overnight bag, try and forget about it all, and try and get a good night's sleep until her handler picked her up in the morning. Hopefully, she would tell her more on the way to the airport.

She didn't though. All she told her was that she was told to get her on a plane to London quickly as there was a particular project that she was especially suited for, and it required briefing her in person at the River House.

"Project, what project?" Sophia asked.

"No idea, that's all I was told, get you on a plan to London straightaway, and there's really no point in asking me anything more because I don't know anything more," was the only answer she got throughout the whole journey to Athens airport.

At Heathrow she was met by her London handler, the same woman who five years previously had taken her to Athens. The handler made a quick call and as the two women emerged from

Terminal 5 a black limousine pulled up ahead of them and took them straight to MI6 headquarters at the River House, or to give it the proper name, the Secret Intelligence Service Building on the banks of the River Thames by Vauxhall Bridge.

The handler told her she could leave her overnight bag in the limousine as it would take her to her hotel later. Having checked in at reception, and been given their lanyard security passes, she was taken up to the fifth floor in a lift by her London handler and then down a long corridor intermittently flanked on either side by various unmarked doors. Eventually they reached a very imposing, highly polished, oak door that was clearly more imposing looking than any of the others. Her handler knocked once and a female voice inside simply said, "Enter." They went into a fairly large office and the woman, clearly some sort of secretary, although probably her job title was much grander, told them, "Ah, yes, come this way. Sir Michael is expecting you."

She got up from behind her desk, walked over to an equally imposing, highly polished, oak door and tapped on it once. This time a very upper-class sounding male voice said, "Enter," and she opened the door, then held it open to let the Sophia and her handler into a much larger room, before leaving and closing the door to go back to her office. The room the two women were now in could hardly be called an office. It was much too big for that, and with a much larger and more impressive desk than the secretary's. As well as the desk there were four wingback dark green velvet upholstered armchairs situated around a dark wood coffee table. On the coffee table were a silver tray, an expensive looking teapot, two equally expensive looking cups and saucers, and a bone china plate of biscuits.

There had been no name plate on either the Secretary's door or the one to the room they were now in. All she knew from the Secretary's comment was that the tall, upright, straight backed man in front of her now with swept back grey hair and wearing a dark pin-striped suit and waistcoat which was clearly bespoke tailored was Sir Michael.

There was no attempt by him to introduce himself further as he walked over towards them. He merely said, "Please, take a seat."

Sophia assumed that her handler knew who he was, as well as his position in MI6, but she wasn't about to ask either her or the man at that point. She thought it better to just sit and listen to whatever she was at last about to be told about this 'project' her Athens handler had referred to in the car on their way to Athens airport.

As she sat down in one of the chairs he added, "So good to meet you at last, heard good things about you, jolly good things actually. You've been doing some good work for us over the past five years, and of course, brought us some very useful info and intel when you decided to come across to join our side."

He was talking in the typical upper-class clipped style and accent. She knew very well that this was just the preliminary small talk of a certain type of English gentleman; patronising to say the least. But she just nodded and remained silent.

"Would you like some tea? English breakfast, not good black Russian tea I'm afraid. Wouldn't do to have that in this place of course."

He grinned a little in her direction as he finished, but didn't wait for her to answer and started to pour her a cup, then asked, "Milk?"

She was beginning to feel a little uneasy over all the pleasantries. She knew very well from her Russian Security Service training that they were usually just a lead up to something much more difficult and serious.

She wondered what was coming as she replied, "Black is fine, thank you," and reached over to take the cup and saucer from him. Oddly, she thought, he made no attempt to offer her handler any tea. Obviously she was someone much lower down the pecking order than him.

She wanted the pleasantries and small talk to end so he'd get on and tell her what this was really all about. Instead though, he reached for the plate on the coffee table and said, "Biscuit, my dear? They are jolly good, dark chocolate digestives, my favourites."

She declined, took a sip of her tea and decided to take a leap to try and move things along.

"I understand you have a new project you want me to undertake for you, the Service I mean?"

He took a biscuit himself, took a small bite, and then sat back in silence in the deep soft upholstery of the armchair to digest it.

Eventually he said, "Yes, quite a small thing really, but we think you are the ideal person to sort it out for us, given where you are and your history. The real one, I mean, not the one we concocted for you."

She sat in silence, trying to relax and knowing better than to interrupt and ask questions at that point, while he took another sip of his tea.

He sat back in the armchair again and this time crossed his legs.

"Yes, well the thing is this really. I suppose I should fill you in a bit on the history of the situation. It's a situation we find ourselves in, the Service, and it could all be a bit embarrassing for us politically if it were to come out, be made public."

Her mind was racing. She had no idea what he was referring to, and particularly how it involved her, the "ideal person to sort it out," given where she was and her, "history", as he put it. Was it something to do with her previous links to the Russian Security Services? She definitely wouldn't be happy at all with that. In her new life and identity she'd done her best to give the impression, at least, that she'd put all that behind her. She decided the best thing was to stay silent and let him go on.

"It really all started in a small village, a tourist place called Lindos on Rhodes back in 2016," he started to say. "Don't suppose you've ever been there, but as you are in Athens now, not too far away, only half-an-hour or so flight to Rhodes, well ...."

While he paused to take another bite of his biscuit she now realised that was what he meant by, "the ideal person to sort it out for us, given where you are," she now realised.

"Anyway, we'd been looking for this bloody Irish woman for some time; an IRA agent, an assassin," he continued. "She'd infiltrated MI6 as a double agent, and subsequently we discovered she was responsible for passing on information that resulted in some of our operatives being killed. In addition, she did some killing herself for the IRA, particularly one of our best people just before she disappeared off the radar, the Irish woman. She disposed of the woman who actually recruited her to MI6 years before, supposedly her best friend at university. We're pretty certain that she pushed her under an underground train at Oxford Circus Station here in London. Basically, while she was still acting as a double agent she virtually destroyed that woman's life, even went so far as to have an affair with her husband and made sure she found out about it, not that he was a saint anyway though. So, the Irish woman destroyed our operative's, that woman's, personal life. Then when we discovered she'd been operating as a double agent for the IRA for years, having been recruited and recommended by the same woman, her best friend, that destroyed her, our operative's, professional life too. The woman, one of our best operatives, had a nervous breakdown and left the Service as a result of all that. However, that obviously wasn't enough for the Irish woman and the IRA, and that's when she pushed her under the tube train. Oh, she was clever alright. There was nothing clear on CCTV on the station platform, but we did spot what we are certain was her on Oxford Circus station concourse minutes before it happened. She did it alright."

Sophia was now looking worried. Apprehensively she interrupted, asking, "Are you going to ask me to find her, the Irish woman, and deal with her? I haven't really any experience in ... I haven't really done any of that sort-"

He grinned slightly again as he shook his head and told her, "No, no, certainly not, my dear. We know that, and anyway, it's not her we're after now. She's long gone from Rhodes, to god knows where."

She let out a small sigh of relief.

"But we did actually locate her, find her, back in the summer of 2016 in that village Lindos, on Rhodes, or at least we had a tip-off about her possibly being there at that time from one of our contacts, our informants on the island. He wasn't actually in Lindos though. He was in Rhodes Town, but he picked up from one of his contacts in the Lindos area that there was an Irish woman in Lindos at the time who appeared to fit the description of the one we were looking for. She was supposedly investigating her family's past and relatives, possibly Greek on one side of her family. So-"

Sophia was again a little confused as she interrupted. "But if she's not there now what-"

He looked across at her out of the top of his eyes as he reached for the plate of biscuits again. It was a look that indicated that he wasn't used to being interrupted.

Instead of continuing though he simply asked her, "Are you sure you won't have one of these biscuits? They really are rather good. From Fortnum and Masons, I always insist on these."

She declined again, but thought it best not to try to finish her question.

He took a bite out of another biscuit and then after he swallowed it reached for the last sip of his tea.

Eventually he continued with what he was saying, as though he'd not been interrupted.

"So, we sent one of our best operatives you see, to Rhodes and Lindos to deal with her. You know what I mean obviously, but-"

Sophia couldn't help herself though, couldn't stop herself from interrupting yet again.

"So that's what you meant when you said she was 'long gone from Rhodes'? She's dead? Your operative dealt with her?"

"Hardly, unfortunately no, on the contrary, and, as I said, we've no idea where she is at the moment, even if she's still alive or dead. It was our operative who was killed in Lindos, late one evening in a back alley. We don't know if he even located her there, or even if the Irish woman we were tipped off about by one of our informants on the island was her. That woman vanished soon after the body was found. I think we can pretty well certainly assume it was her, the IRA woman we'd been looking for. The local police didn't appear to have much of a clue what happened, and they obviously weren't aware he was one of our people. We certainly weren't going to disclose that. We got one of our high-up contacts in the Foreign Office here to get in touch with the British Embassy officials in Athens and the Hellenic Chief of Police in Athens, basically on the basis that the guy who died was a British citizen and on the pretext of trying to ascertain just what the Rhodes police investigation had discovered about the way he died, plus getting his body back to London as quickly as possible. Our Foreign Office contact was told the Rhodes Police thought it was most likely an accident. There were some steps with uneven surfaces and their scenario was that he slipped and cracked his head on a wall and then the ground. Apparently there was a considerable amount of his blood on the wall and the ground around the body. The police simply thought he was a tourist, although they were seemingly a little suspicious that there was no identification on him, no phone and no indication where he was staying. From that they also queried how the British Embassy knew then that he was a British citizen, but eventually, after some diplomatic pressure, the Hellenic Chief of Police ordered the local Rhodes police to shut the case down as an obvious accident and his body was returned to London. All in all, a somewhat unfortunate and embarrassing situation politically for us, the Service, you understand."

Sophia still didn't really have any idea quite how all that could possibly have any connection to her and what she was going to be asked to do now, the 'project'. She tried once more.

"But, so … what … how is that-"

She never got to finish. He hadn't.

"As I said, all very embarrassing you understand?"

She didn't quite understand completely, but just nodded.

"Consequently, we had to hush it all up. We had no proof of course, but were pretty sure that the killer was the Irish woman we'd been looking for, the IRA agent or by then, ex-agent possibly. At least there was no indication it was one of your former lot, FSB or GRU or whatever section of the Russian Security Services."

Now, again she was trying to figure out, if that was the case, what all this had to do with her? If it didn't involve the Russian Security Services what was this 'project' her handler had told her she was wanted for? Once more she couldn't wait.

"But I still don't see what this has got to do with me? How do I come into, fit into all this?"

He got up out of his wingback chair with another chocolate digestive biscuit in his right hand and walked over to the floor to ceiling window to peer out over the Thames.

Her patience was running thin. Was this just all an act by him, to test her over something he'd eventually get to? She waited a little longer for an explanation.

After he'd put the last part of the biscuit in his mouth and swallowed it he turned back to look across at her.

"Yes, yes, that's good question, my dear, a very good question."

He hesitated and headed back to sit in the armchair

She waited in silence.

To her growing frustration and irritation he reached for the tea pot to pour himself another cup of tea and asked if she wanted another. She declined.

Then he simply repeated, as if to emphasise it to her, "Well, all very embarrassing for us, the Service, if something like that got out, in the media for instance, one of our operatives being bumped off in that way. You do understand."

She nodded slightly again in silence. She thought it best to agree so that he would continue, even if she still was not certain she understood fully.

"Of course, as I said before, with the cooperation of the Hellenic Chief of Police in Athens we managed to hush it all up. We certainly didn't want it getting out, getting in the media, the press and the rest, not the Greek media, and definitely not the British. All far too embarrassing and politically very sensitive for the Service, us in MI6, with the Irish situation at the time."

She wasn't at all sure what he meant by, "the Irish situation at the time"? She couldn't recall anything. Something related to Brexit and Northern Ireland perhaps? But she didn't really have a clue. So, again she just nodded slightly in silence, although she was still none the wiser where she came into all this.

He took another sip of his tea, then seemed to let out a slight sigh before going on.

"Anyway, that's still the problem now really, our dilemma, it possibly getting out, becoming public knowledge. Although, to be more accurate, it's a problem that has re-surfaced, re-emerged you might say."

"Why?" she asked finally. "But why now? Why has it resurfaced now, how, in what way?"

"As I said before, we had a contact on Rhodes back in the summer of 2016, a reliable informant usually, still do actually, the same Greek guy. Jolly good usually, in Rhodes Town though, not in Lindos where our man was bumped off in 2016. Of course, it was made to look like an accident, but we didn't buy that, too much of a coincidence our man being there and this mysterious Irish woman. Anyway, yes, yes, so why now? Well, our same Greek informant in Rhodes Town reported that he'd been told, heard from someone he knew in Lindos, that there was a witness to the murder of our man in 2016. He said it was just a rumour of course, although from a pretty reliable source he had in the village, Lindos."

She couldn't wait any longer. She was now becoming increasingly exasperated at the time he was taking getting to the point of precisely what they wanted her to do. She tried to hurry him along by interrupting and jumping to an assumption of what the point of all this was. What her connection to it was, why she'd been brought to London for it.

"So, you want me to go there, Lindos, and check out if the rumour about a witness has any truth, any foundation?"

He got up and walked back over to the window, then turned and told her, "Not exactly, partly, indirectly that's it."

She frowned. She was even more confused now.

Still standing with his back to the window he stared across the room for a few seconds at her sitting in the armchair and then said, "Look, by chance we have a man of ours there in Lindos now. Well, he's sort of one of ours. He's not exactly a full-time operative, never was really, but he's done some work for us in the past occasionally while he was in the same line as you were actually, while he was at a university in England. He's finished with that now though, the university stuff, his employment there, and he's in Lindos. Been there all summer, writing a bloody novel supposedly. We like to keep a check, keep tabs on all the people who have done work for us in the past, even those who were only part-time operatives. So, as soon as we got the report from our informant in Rhodes Town about the witness rumour in Lindos, and being aware that this guy who used to do some things for us occasionally was there for the whole summer, we got in contact with him and told him to do some digging about the rumour, see if there was any substance to it. Of course, he wasn't exactly keen, said he'd put all that stuff he used to do for us behind him when he left the university. We, shall we say, persuaded him on what we wanted though. We do have certain pressures we can apply if necessary."

He allowed a small smile to creep across his lips as he hesitated for a moment before telling her in a very serious voice, "You know, my dear, they say you never actually really leave the Service, even when you think you do, because the Service never really leaves you. I expect that you know that though. I expect it's the same with your former employers, the Ruskies."

She nodded slightly again, and shifted a little uncomfortably in her seat. Then trying to reassure her he added with another slight smile, "Not in your case of course, with the Ruskies I mean."

He hesitated yet again before going on, "Hmm ... yes, of course not. Anyway, the thing is this guy in Lindos now has given us nothing, nothing at all on this witness rumour."

"But perhaps it's just that, a rumour, and that's why he hasn't been able to turn up anything," she suggested. "You did say Lindos is a village, and there are always plenty of rumours and gossip in villages isn't there? Everyone knows that."

"Possibly, yes possibly, that's a possibility I suppose."

He returned to the armchair and sat down again before adding an explanation of where she came in to it all at last.

"But that's where you come in, my dear. We thought as you're nearby in that lovely apartment in Athens we set you up in you could just pop over there to Rhodes and Lindos for ten days or so perhaps. It's only a thirty minute flight or so. Just sort of check up on him on the quiet so to speak, plus see if you can pick up any of the gossip in the village about the supposed accident three summers ago and any possible witness. As he's been there all summer since May it is the case that he's more likely to have picked up any gossip or rumours in the village on that, if there really are any, than someone there just for a holiday like yourself for ten days. You may do, of course, hear something on it in the village, but I'm sure you can easily get close to him and find out if he's actually been doing what we wanted him to, see if you can get anything out of him on it."

"In ten days? But I don't know him. Why would he tell me anything, even if he has found out anything on this rumour?"

"Well, that's the beauty of it, my dear. You do know him. Well, you've met him briefly at least. That is why it's all so convenient, you being in Athens, him being in Lindos, and you've met before."

Once more he got up and walked over to the window as she asked, "Where, how?"

This time he didn't turn around. He simply continued staring out across the Thames as he told her firmly, "At that conference in Moscow when he told you the contact number for our operative there. I suppose in many ways you have him, David Alexander is his name, to thank in some part for you getting out of Russia and the nice life you have now in Athens."

"But that was for what, a minute or slightly more, and he didn't even introduce himself."

He turned away from the window to face her across the room.

"Come now, you know how it works. He wouldn't introduce himself then would he, far too dangerous? Anyway, that's why this is so perfect. So, you have to go to Lindos for a holiday for ten days straightaway. That should be long enough to do what we want. We'll arrange it all for you. Your handler in Athens will. Flights, a nice hotel, probably just outside the village, transfer to the hotel and back to the airport, plus we'll even give you a nice sum of spending money. All you have to do is find him and find out what he knows, what he's found out, if anything. It's only a small place, a small tourist village, so you should be able to find him fairly easily. Don't go asking around about him though. Don't ask lots of the local people if they know him, staff in the bars and restaurants in the village, or the owners. He's been there all summer so it's likely a few of the locals will know him. If you go asking around the place about him there's a good chance it'll get back to him, and that will definitely spook him. If you do find him make sure you make it look like a coincidence. He may well remember you, or he may not. It was five years ago at that Moscow conference, and you've changed your appearance a little. Although, I suppose we did some of that. Make it look initially as though you don't recognise him. Give him time and see if he recognises you, and obviously don't let him think you are working for us now. We don't want him thinking that and that we've sent you to check up on him. By all means tell him you're living in Athens now and have a new life and identity, but not that you do anything for us at all. Make him think that you've left all the working for the Russian Security Services, as well as us, behind you. Get him to trust you. I'm sure you can do that can't you?"

She nodded again slightly as she told him, "That's what I've been well trained to do."

He took a photograph out of a light blue A4 folder on the coffee table and slid it across the table towards her saying as he did so, "In case you don't remember what he looks like, this is David Alexander."

"Ok, but no I can't say I do remember much of what he looks like. After all, it was five years ago, and as I said before, I only saw him and spoke to him for about a minute at that Moscow Conference."

"You are the obvious choice for this, and quite convenient really, you being in Athens."

She didn't know what to say. She knew that in reality she had no choice, and anyway, when it came down to it ten days in the sun on Rhodes didn't seem so onerous or dangerous.

He didn't wait for any reply in agreement from her. He walked over to sit behind his desk, buzzed his secretary on the intercom and told her when she answered, "Good, we're all done here."

PART FOUR:

THE VICTIM, THE INVISIBLE MAN AND THE OTHER WOMAN

17

Antika

Two days after her overnight trip to London and the River House Sophia checked into the Acquagrand Hotel just outside Lindos after her early morning flight to Rhodes from Athens. She'd never even been to the island before, let alone the small picturesque tourist village of Lindos. So, where to start looking for David Alexander in the village was a mystery to her at that point. She told herself that luckily Lindos wasn't very large, although from what she'd read online from various social media sites there appeared to be quite a few bars and restaurants.

She was going to be there for ten nights, but the season was tailing off, and although she'd been told in her meeting in London that David Alexander had been there all summer she had no idea when he was likely to leave, or even if he was still there in Lindos. She hadn't been told if he was, or if so, when he was likely to leave. It appeared MI6 in London had no idea about that.

She decided to try and get a feel of the village that first night. Perhaps ask one of the hotel receptionists if they could recommend any bars or restaurants and go and check them out, although she figured that if he was there the whole summer he wouldn't necessarily be using the restaurants regularly, at least not every night.

As she'd been instructed in her meeting at MI6 in London, she shouldn't ask about him in the village, ask some local which bars he was likely to drink in, as she was supposed to be checking up on him discreetly; seeing if he was doing, or making any attempt to do, what MI6 required. If she started asking around and it got back to him it might spook him, and Lindos was a village, gossip travels. The other side of that though was maybe she would pick up some of the gossip, something on the 'accident' three summers before and the supposed witness. Then she possibly wouldn't have to find or meet this guy David Alexander at all.

A week went by and she had absolutely no joy in her search for him, nor even on overhearing anything, any conversations, about the accident three years previously. It was after all though just that, three years ago. She never heard the name David Alexander mentioned at all anywhere, not in the bars and restaurants in the evenings nor on the Lindos beaches. She went to the long sandy Main Beach on three afternoons and to the smaller Pallas Beach on four other days. She was starting to think it a bit odd that someone who had supposedly spent the whole summer living in the village was proving so elusive to find, or even hear his name mentioned.

Once or twice her frustration pushed her towards being tempted to ask about him in a couple of the bars she had a drink in. However, in the end she reminded herself that wouldn't be a good move. On a couple of evenings in that first week her Athens handler called to check on any progress, but all she could tell her was that there was nothing to report, adding that she was starting to seriously doubt if he was still there in Lindos or even on the island. The handler told her they had no record of him leaving the island, at least not on any flight from Rhodes airport. She wasn't aware just how they had access to that information, but she wasn't about to ask. In fact, by the end of that first week she'd virtually switched off from her MI6 'project' of trying to find David Alexander in the village. She'd come to the conclusion that it was best to just relax and enjoy the sun, the beaches and the swimming. In fact, she was getting a rather attractive tan.

Three days before she was due to go back to Athens she decided that for a change she'd go to the beach at St. Paul's Bay or the edge of the village. She'd heard good things about it from the hotel receptionist, but hadn't tried it so far. It was another relatively smaller one when compared to the Main Beach in Lindos Bay. It was a popular venue for weddings with its very Greek setting and a small traditional white Greek Orthodox chapel at one end of the picturesque bay. As with all the Lindos beaches the water was a clear inviting cool blue. The beach was still busy despite it being the middle of October, while the temperature was around a very pleasant twenty-six degrees. Luckily she found an empty sunbed and a parasol in the second row back from the sea. She immediately made for a swim in the cooling water of the bay. As she emerged from it and headed for her sunbed she did a quick scan along the beach just in case there was any chance of spotting him. However, there was no sign of anyone who looked remotely like him. The overwhelming majority of the sunbeds and parasols were occupied by couples of two women, two men, or a man and a woman. As far as she could make out there were no men alone at all on the beach. She made herself comfortable on the sunbed, put on some sun cream after she dried off a little, and simply relaxed to enjoy the rest of one of the last few afternoons of what had now appeared to have developed completely into a holiday.

Fifteen minutes or so later a woman's voice from the other side of Sophia's sunglasses disturbed her restful half-dozing relaxation by asking, "Would you like anything to drink?"

She lifted her sun glasses onto the top of her head and squinted her eyes before raising her right hand up to shield the sun from her face. The attractive waitress looked to be in her mid-twenties, had long dark curly hair tied back in a ponytail, and was holding a tray in one hand down by her side. The logo Tambakio was displayed on one side of the white t-shirt she wore above her equally white shorts, signifying she was a waitress from the restaurant and bar at the far end of the beach.

"Oh, yes, that would be good, thanks, fresh orange juice with some ice, " she replied.

A few minutes later the waitress reappeared with the drink. As Sophia reached into her beach bag to find her purse the waitress told her politely, "It's five euros, plus ten euros for the sunbed and parasol."

The waitress turned to walk away having been handed the fifteen euros, but Sophia decided to try just once more to find the elusive David Alexander, discarding her resolve not to directly ask anyone in Lindos about him.

"Excuse me, do you work here every day and live in the village?" she asked.

A slight, confused frown spread across waitress' face as she turned back before replying, "Yes, every day since the start of May, but I get a couple of days off each month. We have to work while we can in the season."

"So, you're from Lindos then?"

"No, Albania, but I've lived here every summer for the past five summers, and work here as well as most nights in a bar in the village."

"Sounds like hard work."

She grinned slightly before replying, "Yes, yes, it is, but there's no work in the winter months from October to the end of April, so you have to work and money when you can."

"You must get to know quite a few people who are here for the whole summer then, people working here, as well as any even just staying here, not necessarily working I mean?"

"Quite a few, yes, but mainly the bar and restaurant workers."

Sophia decided to take a chance, take another leap in the dark.

"Just Albanians and Greeks or …?"

She hesitated for a moment before adding, "What about any English people? Do you know any of them who work or just live here?"

"A few English people who work here, although there used to be quite a lot more here working all summer before, but with Brexit it's much more difficult. They have to get work permits and visas, and I think there's some sort of limit to the number of days they can stay, not just here but in the E.U.. All that takes time, there's a lot of bureaucracy."

Sophia wasn't thinking about young English summer workers in the bars and restaurants at all. That's not what she meant, why she asked, or was interested in. She decided to take the plunge and be more direct.

"What about a guy, an English guy in his late thirties, I met him a few years ago and he said he came here regularly, recommended it to me actually, David, David Alexander his name was?"

The waitress frowned slightly again. She was clearly increasingly unsure why she was being asked this, and was a little wary as it was beginning to sound like a bit of an interrogation.

In addition, she didn't know his full name, his surname, but an English guy called David lived in the apartment across the courtyard from the apartment her and her boyfriend rented. Despite him living there all that summer she didn't actually know him very well. Their paths rarely crossed as she worked through most of the day on St. Paul's Bay beach and in the evening in a bar in the village. Even when she did see him in the courtyard it was only momentarily to say hello as she was heading to work in the bar in the evening, or was returning from work on the beach to rest for an hour and shower, change and go off to work in the bar. She decided it was probably best not to reveal even that to this woman she hardly knew though. She really didn't want to get involved in whatever the reason was that the woman, who she'd only just met fleetingly and served, was asking about someone who possibly could be her neighbour. So, she decided she wouldn't ask her why, and she wouldn't even mention it to her neighbour, David, either, not least because he might not have actually been the English guy the woman was asking about.

But having finally taken the chance of actually asking someone from Lindos about him directly Sophia wasn't going to leave it there.

"So, do you, know this guy David Alexander?"

"No, I don't, I don't know anyone here of that name."

Feeling a small pang of guilt though, she added, "There is an English guy around that age I'd say, late thirties, who I think has been here most of the summer, although there are a few English guys around that age and older who've been in the village all summer, mostly working."

"Do you know where he stays, in the village?"

"No, no idea," the waitress lied and decided it was clearly time to walk away. "Now if you'll excuse me I have to get on with my work serving."

"Sure, yes, sorry, just one more question. That English guy you mentioned do you happen to know if he drinks in one of the bars in the village regularly?"

The waitress stopped, half-turned and replied, "Most of the English guys who live here drink in quite a few of the bars regularly I think, like Bar404, or the Courtyard Bar, Giorgos, or even Antika some nights, but not one in particular. Now, I'm sorry, I do have to go."

She walked off along the beach towards the restaurant and bar at the end while Sophia laid back down on her sunbed and a very slight smile of satisfaction spread across her lips.

As Sophia lay on the sunbed in the warm sunshine and gazed out at the stunning beauty of the bay she was running over in her mind whether it would be worth actually trying some of those bars again which she'd been to before, or perhaps try the one she hadn't actually been to, Antika in the centre of the village. Or maybe even just give up looking for David Alexander altogether and simply inform her Athens handler there was no sign of him whatsoever in Lindos, just enjoy the final couple of days relaxing in the fine weather and the lovely surroundings. Could she really do that though, give up looking for him and tell her Athens handler there was no sign of him in the village. Wouldn't that be dangerous if somehow they later discovered she was lying, couldn't that threaten her quite cosy good new life in Athens?

She'd seen all those bars mentioned by the waitress during her various evenings in the village following dinner. She'd been into three of them, but there was no sign of David Alexander, and she'd never even overheard his name being mentioned in nearby conversations. Consequently, she decided that after dinner that evening in one of the restaurants in the village she'd try the one bar the waitress mentioned which she hadn't actually been into, Antika.

In the taxi she from her hotel into Lindos Main Square she decided she would go once again to the Village House restaurant for her dinner. She'd already been there twice during her stay and really enjoyed the food. The service was good also, very friendly towards all the customers it seemed. To be honest that was actually the case in all the restaurants she'd been to in the village, but she had got on particularly well with one of the waitresses in the Village House, Marianthi. Just like Sophia she lived in Athens, at least through the winter, and then worked in Lindos in the summer. Athens gave Sophia something to talk to her about. At one point on the second evening she went there she did think of asking her if she knew a David Alexander in the village, but she quickly thought better of it in case she did, and well, and it got back to him from Marianthi that a woman was asking about him. Anyway, she got on well with Marianthi, who even suggested they meet up for a drink back in Athens sometime in the winter. So, she wanted to go back to the restaurant to see her one more time before she left.

As she took the short stroll through the narrow white walled alley from the Main Square to the restaurant she started to realise just how calm and relaxed she felt, much more so than she had for some time. Lindos was obviously good for her. Something she thought many of the tourists in the still quite busy alleys must have shared. The October mid-evening air was still pleasantly warm, so much so that she'd chosen to wear a simple sleeveless knee length cream dress with a wide red belt at the waist, all of which nicely highlighted her by now fine tan. If nothing else she'd had a very good holiday she told herself, even if she hadn't managed to find David Alexander.

As she entered the restaurant through the Lindian stone archway and into the small courtyard she was greeted by the owner, Ari in his regular friendly way. He was a quite tall, slim, dark haired man in his mid-forties, dressed in a white shirt with the sleeves rolled up, a pair of black jeans and black trainers. He was also Albanian, but had been in Lindos for many years. On the first occasion that she'd dined in the restaurant there was a range of different nationalities dining there and she overheard him conversing with some of them in their native languages, including a little Russian. From what she heard she concluded that he could obviously speak some parts of at least five other languages besides Greek and his native Albanian. She wasn't about to speak in Russian to him though, nor let on that she was from there originally.

"Good to see you again," he told her. "Marianthi was only saying yesterday evening that she wondered if we'd see you again before you leave. She'll be pleased. She's serving on the roof terrace. Go on up and she'll find you a table."

She made her way up the wrought iron flight of stairs to the rooftop terrace. There were around ten tables on the terraces either side of the staircase, plus another four on a further terrace up a few steps. Almost all of them were occupied, but as soon as Marianthi spotted her she came over to greet her and lead her to a vacant one, telling her as she did that she was pleased to see her again before she leaves.

She had a delicious Prawn Saganaki with feta, recommended by Marianthi, as well as a glass of cold white wine. While saying goodbye to him as she left she congratulated Ari on the delicious food. Then, as she said goodbye to her, Marianthi reminded her that they would definitely meet up in Athens during the winter. As a result they quickly exchanged mobile numbers.

It was approaching ten o'clock as she made her way through the by now quite busy Lindos alleys full of tourist evening drinkers. As she'd decided earlier, she was heading for the one bar she hadn't checked out before which the waitress on St. Paul's beach told her she thought David Alexander might drink in, Antika Bar in the centre of the village. It would be one last try she told herself.

The interior of Antika was quite modern, although the exterior frontage onto the alley was also comprised of traditional Lindos stone. Within a few yards of the entrance there were four stone steps leading up to the main bar area with a few high tables and stools. To the right almost all along one side was the modern looking bar, and beyond that at the far end there were more steps leading up to an outside terrace area with table and chairs. Just before the bar, also to the right, was another set of stone steps leading up to another terrace, one side of which looked down on the alley below. That whole upper terrace area, along with a large section of the bar area below was open with no roof and a perfect view of the clear Lindos night star-ridden sky.

The bar was quite busy on the upper terraces as well as in the bar area. She made her way towards the bar through the high tables and some of the people standing around them or sitting on the stools. At the far end of the bar there were three young Greek-looking guys, but towards the middle of it there was one guy alone. From the back she couldn't make out if it could be David Alexander so she headed to stand at the bar close by to him. With a very quick brief glance she realised it was him.

She remembered the instruction from her meeting at MI6 in London that she should make it look like a coincidence. Consequently, she picked up the cocktail menu card on the bar and proceeded to appear to study it. She thought there was a chance that he wouldn't recognise or remember her anyway due to the changed colour and style of her hair, part of the change of her identity by MI6.

For a minute or so it seemed she was right about him not recognising her, so she decided to try and push contact between them along a little. She asked one of the barmen quite loudly could he recommend a good cocktail. It was all she could think of rather than speaking directly to David. She hoped it would provoke him into responding for the barman. It worked.

He turned his head towards her and before the barman could answer interjected with, "They are all good when he makes them. He's my next door neighbour here, Ledi, so I better recommend any of them he makes."

She was feeling pleased with herself. Not only had she found the elusive David Alexander, but she'd discovered that she still had one of her old talents, one of her old skills, of how to engage a man in seemingly innocent conversation.

She turned her head towards him, deliberately fixed a stare on his face for a few seconds, and then told him a simple, "Thank you," accompanied with a slight smile. Another one of her old talents, her lingering eye contact, easily suggested to him there was more to it than a simple, "Thank you."

His reply of, "You're welcome," was accompanied by a returned slight encouraging smile.

Despite the changes to her hair, she was hoping he'd recognise her first. That was the plan, to make it appear a coincidence. However, he never said anything more and they both stood at the bar in silence with only the sound of the music in the bar between them while Ledi made her cocktail.

She couldn't decide the best thing to do. Should she say something about recognising him or not? In the end she didn't need to. He was obviously thinking about the same thing. After a couple of minutes he decided to go ahead and ask.

He turned his head towards her. He knew, if it was her, their previous meeting was in a rather diplomatically delicate situation. His voice betrayed his hesitancy as he asked, "Erm … Excuse me, but didn't we meet at a conference years ago? I … err … I think I … err … helped you with something, Well sort of anyway. It's Alexandra isn't it?"

Inside she was smiling. She hadn't lost it, all her old talent. But she wanted to make it look like a coincidence and didn't want to spook him. So, she made sure there was a blank, expressionless, cold look across her face. She didn't respond immediately, didn't even turn her head towards him, but continued to stare at the back wall behind the bar. For a very brief moment she wanted to let him think that he'd made a big mistake and she wasn't the same woman at all. She was enjoying the game. She always did, but for a while recently she'd thought that she might have forgotten that.

She bit the inside of her lip for a few seconds more until she leaned into him slightly and said very quietly, "Please, it's Sophia Orlova now, for obvious reasons, as I'm sure you understand. Alexandra Ivanova is no more."

"Of course," he told her, realising that was obviously her new identity given to her by MI6. Almost whispering he added, "You obviously got out."

"Yes, thanks in part to you and the initial contact," she replied, also in a very low voice, purposefully adding an encouraging smile as she finished. She decided that having found him at last she would jump right in and try and maintain contact to see if he'd found out anything on what MI6 wanted about a witness to the supposed accident in 2016.

"I should thank you properly. Maybe dinner one night while I'm here?"

"Oh, err … no … err … no that's really not necessary."

"I see. At least a drink then," she insisted.

"Well I've only just got this beer. Maybe I'll have another in a while, thanks."

"It's the least I can do after the way you helped me. It's David isn't it?"

She obviously knew it was, although she'd made a mistake. She hadn't quite recovered all her old talents. He never actually introduced himself at the Moscow conference. So, she wouldn't have known his name from there.

Luckily he was too sucked into wanting to engage in conversation with her, this lovely woman standing near him at the bar, to notice or think about that.

"You remembered that from just one conversation we had. I think it was five years ago. That's impressive," he replied.

It wasn't really impressive at all. She'd been given his photo just over a week before at MI6. Although she wasn't supposed to tell him that, of course, nor that in reality she'd actually been sent to check up on him and what he was supposed to be doing in Lindos for MI6..

"I never forget a name, or a face, and that one conversation did turn out to be quite important in my life after all."

She knew the first part of her sentence was a lie, although not the second part. Another smile from her followed as she finished telling him that. She was determined that having finally found him she would use all her talents and assets. She wasn't going to let him go easily.

She sucked on the straw from her cocktail as he told her, "We didn't get the chance to have a proper conversation at the conference, for obvious reasons. I knew a little bit about your work speciality from your academic publications. With what I was being asked to do I guess I thought it best not to linger too long or try to have a longer conversation."

"No, that wouldn't have been a good idea, for either of us. We, us Russians, were being watched and monitored all the time at the conference. The State Security Services were terrified that what eventually happened with me would happen. Of course, they were right, it did. I think they thought there might be even more who did what I did."

"Hmm ... that must have been tricky, but-"

She didn't let him finish what she assumed would be more questions about her defection. She didn't want their whole conversation to just focus on that. She was trying to figure out a way of how to get it round to what she'd been sent to find out, what he'd found out, if anything, about the supposed accident in 2016 that killed the MI6 operative.

"I'd rather not talk about that anymore, and certainly not here," she told him firmly. "It's all in the past, my past life, another life altogether."

"Yes, I understand, of course it is."

There was a silence while he reached to take another swig of his beer. Then he changed the subject, although not to what she was there to find out. There was no reason he would, of course, and she was continuing to struggle in her mind to find a way into that subject, a way to prompt him in that direction.

Instead, he moved the conversation on to asking about where she was from in Russia originally. She had no idea why, but she told him, "St. Petersburg."

That was a lie, and an almost instinctive answer. Another of her old talents and ways had obviously also returned. In fact, she was from Lipetsk, a city around three hundred miles south-east of Moscow.

She asked if he'd been to St. Petersburg and anywhere else in Russia and was somewhat surprised by his reply.

"A few times, I was lucky enough to go a few times for my university work back in England, to conferences and for academic research. St. Petersburg three times, Moscow a couple of times including the one when I met you very briefly, Smolensk, which I really liked, as well as a couple of places in the Northern Caucuses, Nalchik and Vladikavkaz."

She raised her eyebrows as she told him, "Northern Caucuses, Nalchik and Vladikavkaz? They aren't places I'd expect an English academic to have visited. Why did-"

"Now it's my turn to say, don't ask, Alexandra."

"Sophia, please," she corrected him, with an irritated edge to her voice as she quickly looked around to ensure no one had overheard him use her former name.

"Sorry, yes, of course," he apologised.

She thought she probably knew the answer anyway to the question she was about to ask when he interrupted. Those weren't the sort of places a normal tourist, or even an academic, would visit, but she knew he had connections with MI6, so assumed that was the reason why.

He added that for his academic research he'd also visited Tbilisi and Minsk, in Georgia and Belarus, when they were part of the Soviet Union before it collapsed.

She assumed that they were also supposedly for his academic research, but in reality were for other reasons related to his MI6 links, at least in part. She wasn't about to ask him about those however, even though in relation to MI6 she appeared to be getting no nearer to moving the conversation on to what she needed to, what she wanted him to talk about. What he asked next did help her a little in that respect, however.

"I presume you're here on holiday, but where do you live now? Or shouldn't I ask, as I guess it's part of your new identity? Perhaps you'd prefer not to tell me where Sophia Orlova lives now? Would that be safer?"

She was taken a little by surprise by his change of direction, but at least there was some connection to Lindos in the conversation now, a little closer to what she wanted to talk about and hoped their conversation might get to.

"Yes, I'm here on holiday, just for ten days. But there's no problem telling you where I live now."

She appeared more at ease as she darted a slight smile across her bright red lips in his direction. Inside she was beginning to feel more optimistic about eventually finding out what she needed to.

"In Athens, I have a flat there and work as a translator."

The translator part of that was another lie, but she didn't want him asking anything more about what she did in Athens for work, or if she didn't work what she lived on. As she finished telling him that she employed some of her old skills and talents once again. She reached to squeeze his forearm gently with her hand and added temptingly, "You should come to visit sometime."

It was obviously an enticing comment, designed as a back-up just in case she didn't get out of him what she wanted to know at this time, or rather what MI6 wanted to know. It was also designed to test just how comfortable he was talking to her and whether he was actually playing the same game as her. After all, she knew from what she'd been told at MI6 in London that he worked for them as well. She was testing him to try and gauge from his reaction to her suggestion whether he was at all suspicious of her and if her turning up in Lindos and Antika was really a coincidence.

He didn't respond to her invitation, just stayed silent and took a drink of his beer. She took that as an indication he was at least a little uneasy and suspicious.

They were engaging in some sort of shadow boxing, dancing around subjects they each were trying to avoid talking about, or at least avoid disclosing much information about to each other.

She was good at it, but then so was he. She knew he worked for MI6 at times, and was supposed to be doing just that in some way in Lindos, as she'd been told at the River House in London. She thought that gave her the upper hand as she gave him no indication she was still working for them.

However, his dealings with MI6 had taught him to be initially suspicious of almost everything and everyone, and her next question pushed him straight into his realm of paranoia and suspicion. She thought that asking it was her very clever way of gently leading him back to talk about any links he had to MI6, and hopefully eventually what he was supposed to be doing for them in Lindos.

She picked up her cocktail once again to finish it. After she placed the empty glass on the bar and nodded to Ledi for another she turned to face him to ask bluntly, "So why did they choose you?"

"Choose me for what?"

"To pass on those contact details to me at the conference. Why you?"

She lowered her voice almost to a whisper and added, "Why did MI6 choose you?"

Surprise was clearly evident all across his face as he hesitated answering. That gave her the opportunity to throw another probing question at him, trying to hopefully get to the point of what she really wanted to know.

"Had you worked for them before? Did you work for them before?"

"I ... err ... no ... I, that is-"

She didn't let him finish.

"After all, you did say you'd been to all those places in Russia. Nalchik and Vladikavkaz are hardly regular places on the tourist trail are they?"

She deliberately made the leap from him passing the MI6 contact information on to her at the Moscow conference to a link with his Russian visits to the unusual places for tourists of the cities of Nalchik and Vladikavkaz. She was clearly inferring there was some sort of connection between the two, and that he had a much greater and closer connection with MI6 than he was prepared to disclose, which of course she already knew. She wanted to see how he would react and if in doing so he'd tell her more, hopefully eventually finally getting out of him what she was there to find out.

He'd also worked for MI6 though. He knew how these things, these types of conversations, could develop. Consequently, he was now becoming increasingly suspicious about her and the direction she was taking their conversation in, almost driving it in. It felt like it had now developed into a bit of an interrogation, rather than just a couple of coincidental acquaintances chatting over a drink.

He may well have just been being completely paranoid, but one thing he was certain of was that she was bloody good at what she was doing. He was beginning to be convinced it was deliberate. She was bloody clever at it.

He took a final swig of his beer, ignored the obviously probing part of her comment about his visits to Russian cities that were not, "on the tourist trail," and then told her while trying to sound casual about it, "My academic background and expertise on Russia. I guess that's why they chose me, approached me, as well as partly I suppose because I'd been there quite a few times."

Determined to sound as light-hearted about it as possible, he added with an ironic smile, "Plus, I had actually been invited to the conference, which was a sort of requirement and an advantage in choosing to approach me. There was obviously no point in trying to get someone to pass the contact details on to you who wasn't actually going to be there and hadn't been invited was there?"

As he finished telling her that she asked where the toilet was and he pointed her in the direction of an archway on the other side of the bar. While she made her way towards it through the groups of drinking customers he was thinking that this was a woman who knows how to play people. She'd obviously been well trained in that. The question going through his brain now was by whom? Was it by MI6 after she'd defected and was now working for them, or by the Russian Security Services before that, or maybe both? Whichever it was, he decided it was time to leave before she could start probing further and throwing any more awkward questions at him.

When she returned he told her it was good to meet her again. That he was glad everything worked out so well for her and he could help, but that he'd had a few late nights recently and was feeling tired, so was off to bed now.

She seemed surprised, but squeezed his arm and told him, "That's a pity. Perhaps we will meet again before I leave?"

She kissed him on one cheek while deliberately placing her left hand tenderly on his other one, and then whispered softly in his ear, "I hope so. I would like that very much."

As she drew her head back he could almost feel the stare of her penetrating steel grey eyes drilling down deep into his soul.

He gulped hard and then partly nodded as he barely spluttered out, "Yes, maybe. Well … err … goodnight," and then left.

He felt extremely virtuous as he made his way back to his flat across the small square with the tree and the low white wall in the centre of the village. He'd resisted temptation well. Perhaps he'd actually finally given up seeking the 'lightness' of encounters with women that were merely sexual. He thought that he had no doubt what she wanted. He was wrong. What he thought she wanted, them to sleep together that night, was only a means to get what she really wanted to know.

While she finished her second cocktail she tried to engage the barman, Ledi, in what she wanted to appear to be simply the usual meaningless conversation about Lindos, the bar, and regular customers. He was busy making drinks so it was a broken up intermittent conversation, which suited her as it eventually allowed her to ask quite directly, "What about the guy I was just talking to, David? He's a regular is he?"

"Fairly regular, he's been here all summer, so he comes in quite a lot."

"Always alone though, like tonight?" she asked.

Ledi smiled to himself slightly as he looked down at the order sheets the waitresses had brought in order to see what drinks he needed to prepare next. He assumed that question was her fishing as she was interested in David personally and wanted to find out if he drank regularly in the bar with any woman in the village. That wasn't her reason for asking, of course.

"Yes, usually," he told her as he reached behind for a couple of cocktail glasses from a shelf.

"He drinks in a few bars in the village regularly then?"

She was fishing again, but still not for the reason the barman thought.

"Quite a few. Most of the people who live here for the whole summer go to a few different bars. Although, so I've heard, there seems to be only a couple that they, as well as some of the restaurant workers, locals, go to for a late drink after the music stops in the bars at one, the Courtyard and Lindos By Night. Sometimes as he leaves here and says 'goodnight' he adds that he's off for one drink in the Courtyard. I think he knows some of the British restaurant workers in the village who drink there late after they finish work."

"The Courtyard?"

"The Courtyard Bar, just to the left from here and left again about thirty metres up the alley that's alongside Pal's Bar. There's a large sign on the side of the bar that can be seen once you get to Pal's."

It wasn't a bar she'd tried before, no doubt why she hadn't come across David Alexander before during her stay in the village. If he drank there regularly late at night throughout that summer the staff would obviously have known him. If she could believe what he'd told her when he left, that he was off to his bed, he wouldn't be there now though. Nevertheless, she decided she would go there now and see what else she might be able to pick up from the staff about David's late night drinking partners there, particularly the British restaurant workers Ledi had mentioned.

It was only just approaching one o'clock and the music was still playing in the Courtyard Bar as she entered. It was pretty busy in the bar, around twenty people, as well as more sat outside in the courtyard itself and up on the roof terrace from what she could see from the screens at one end of the bar. Most of the customers inside the bar were couples, however, and looked more like tourists than restaurant workers. She made her way towards the far end of the bar and took a seat on an empty stool.

As soon as she sat on the stool the owner, Jack Constantino, came along to that end of the bar and said, "Good evening." As he didn't recognise her as someone who'd been in the bar before he added, "I'm the owner, Jack. What can I get you to drink?"

She'd already decided on another cocktail and as she picked up and quickly scanned the cocktail menu card Constantino commented, "Haven't seen you in here before. Just arrived?"

She glanced up from choosing her cocktail.

"No, been here a few days, but someone I met a while ago recommended Lindos for a holiday and also mentioned your bar as a good place for cocktails, so I thought I'd better get around to trying it eventually."

Pointing to a cocktail on the card she said, "I'll have one of these, please."

While the owner went off to the opposite end of the bar to give her cocktail order to the tall, dark haired cocktail barman, Dimitris, she quickly looked around, scanning the customers in the bar again, confirming they all appeared to be tourist couples and not restaurant workers in the village.

"Who was it? Sounds like one of our regulars. We get quite a lot of people who come to Lindos year after year and regularly come to the bar while they are here," Constantino asked as he returned to her end of the bar.

"Err … sorry?" She misunderstood for a moment and thought he was asking who she was looking around the bar for.

"You said someone you met, a friend, recommended Lindos and the bar."

"Oh, yes, but I don't think I said he was a friend, just someone I met, an acquaintance I suppose is the best way of describing him."

Jack Constantino nodded as she went on.

"I think he may be here in Lindos now actually. A friend of his told me he's been here for the whole summer. His name is David."

"David Alexander? Yes, he's been here all summer, if that's who you mean. And he is still here now, was in earlier tonight. He comes in most nights, usually drinks with some of the Brit restaurant workers when they come in after they finish work."

"Anyone of them in particular?" she asked quickly.

That caused Constantino to frown slightly, not really seeing why she asked that, but anyway he told her, "Alice, Alice Palmer mostly. She's been here working over the last four summers. They seemed to get on well quite soon after he came in May this year. They drink a lot together late on quite a few nights after she finishes work in the restaurant, even going to some of the clubs apparently."

At that point Dimitris arrived with her cocktail, which she told him was impressive. He said something to Jack in Greek and they both went to the other end of the bar to presumably sort out something, an ingredient, Dimitris needed more of for his cocktails.

Twenty minutes later she was just finishing her drink and thinking of leaving for her own bed when Jack Constantino came back along to her end of the bar, asked if she'd like another drink and with a nod of the head in her direction added, "That's Alice at the other end of the bar with some of the people she works with. She's got to know a lot of the locals over her four seasons here."

She was with two women and a man, all of whom appeared younger than her. Sophia thought they looked Greek. As Constantino had indicated they were probably locals. They were all seated on stools, no doubt resting their weary legs after a busy night in the restaurant. She'd obviously come straight from work as she still had the restaurant's black t-shirt on bearing its logo, along with a black fairly short skirt and flat sensible lightweight slip-on shoes. Her long dark hair was tied in a pony-tail.

Sophia told him, "No, thanks, no more cocktails for me tonight. I'm off to my hotel and bed."

She paid him for the cocktail and while she waited for her change glanced briefly again along the bar at the group. She was thinking over in her mind what the bar owner had told her twice now; that this woman, Alice Palmer, had been working in Lindos, and presumably also living there, over the past four seasons. She picked up that information and processed it in her brain straightaway. That meant she would have been here in Lindos in the summer of 2016. If only through her work in the restaurant among the locals, she must surely have heard any rumour in the village about the supposed accident being not that at all, if there was such a rumour.

Sophia was also now thinking that if Alice Palmer was as friendly with David Alexander as Jack Constantino implied he would certainly know she was here in that summer of 2016. So, if he was actually doing anything on what MI6 had required him to do in Lindos this summer he would surely have asked her about it. Sophia's mind was racing ahead now. What if this woman, Alice Palmer, was actually the witness MI6 were trying to find in Lindos and eliminate? The one who could publicly and politically cause them great embarrassment who David Alexander had been asked to find during his summer in Lindos. Constantino had said David and her got on very well together, and regularly went late night drinking together, including to some of the clubs. What if, as Constantino implied to an extent, there was more between them, David and this woman, than just late night drinking together? From her own experiences and what she liked to refer to as her talents, Sophia knew herself that pillow talk can be quite loose and dangerous when people are relaxed and off-guard; when they think they can trust the person they are lying next to. So, what if she'd told him in one of those moments one night here after they'd had sex that she knew the accident in 2016 wasn't that at all, it was murder and she'd seen it, been the witness the rumour was about. If David Alexander had become as involved in some sort of relationship with her, sexual or otherwise, as Jack Constantino implied, then that would explain why he hadn't reported anything to MI6 about the murder, even if she'd told him she was the elusive witness in the rumour.

All of that was supposition, of course. Perhaps, she was jumping ahead of herself. She could hardly ask Alice Palmer, or even David Alexander, if that was indeed the case. She could try and get into some sort of conversation with Alice, although she had no real idea how she would be able to guide that around to talk about the supposed accident in 2016. She'd had no real success in that respect earlier in her conversation with David Alexander in Antika. In any case, she wasn't about to approach Alice Palmer that evening while she was with a group with others there in the bar. She could hardly ask her bluntly, "Were you the person who witnessed the murder here in the summer 2016?"

Equally she definitely wasn't going to try to start up a conversation with her about David Alexander, even later somewhere else. If Alice Palmer was that friendly with him that would almost certainly get back to him from her and that would undoubtedly spook him, perhaps even to conclude that someone, probably MI6, was checking up on him. And that would doubly be the case if she'd aroused any of his suspicions through some of the questions she was asking him earlier in Antika and he put the two things together. As a result there would be no chance of her getting anything out of him on what he may or may not have discovered in the village about the murder of the MI6 operative, particularly if it did relate to Alice Palmer.

Either way she came to the conclusion that she'd done enough investigating and hypothesising for the evening. Anything more would have to wait. Tomorrow would be her last chance to go to one of the beaches in the village. After making it into Lindos in a taxi from her hotel in the morning she would do a quick wander through the village on her way to Pallas Beach just in case by chance she came across David Alexander outside one of the cafes.

She said, "Goodnight," to Jack Constantino and made her way through the narrow alleys back to the Main Square and a taxi back to her Acquagrand Hotel.

Her luck was in the next morning. Instead of going the shorter way directly to Pallas Beach from the Main Square she decided one more time to try and find David in the village, appear to coincidentally bump into him once again. She wandered all along the main alleyway through the village passing the Red Rose Bar and then Yannis Bar in the small square with the tree in the centre with the low white wall surrounding it. She took the left alleyway from there and eventually arrived at Café Melia. There was no sign of him outside any of those having a mid-morning breakfast or coffee, nor as far as she could see, inside.

As she took the alley on the right side of that square by Café Melia to head back towards the centre of the village and then down the slope to Pallas Beach she had virtually given up finding or seeing him again before leaving the next day for Athens. However, when she reached the end of that alleyway there he was, seated outside Giorgos Café bar with another guy who looked English, and eating breakfast.

Giorgos was busy with the mid-morning trade of a range of nationalities, some Brits, but also a smattering of Germans and French day trippers from Rhodes Town. Even though it was the second weekend of October the village was still buzzing with day tourists enjoying the warm autumn sunshine while they browsed the many small shops or headed towards one of the beaches. Much to David's surprise the Brit, German and French nationalities passing by or enjoying their food and drink in Giorgos were added to by a Russian he now knew as Sophia.

He couldn't avoid seeing her as she emerged from the alleyway directly opposite, and she had obviously spotted him.

Trying yet again to make it appear a coincidence as she approached the two men's table she asked, "Hi, are the breakfasts good here?"

"Very, the English ones are at least," David told her. "On your way to the beach?"

"Yes, I like to swim in the bay. The water's so clear, and still very warm."

He nodded and then pointed to the guy with him, Jason, to introduce them.

"This is Sophia. I met her a few years ago. She's from Athens."

She looked relieved when he used the new name.

Jason nodded, saying, "Hi," as he turned back towards David, bit the inside of his mouth and nodded again slightly to him in approval.

"I heard there is a good Italian restaurant in the village. Is it?" she asked.

"Is it what?"

"Good, is it good?"

"Oh, yes, sorry, yes it is, very good, Gatto Bianco, across the square from the remains of the ancient Amphitheatre," David confirmed, adding, "Do you like Italian food?"

Unlike the evening before, this time the conversation between them was going precisely where she wanted it to, the direction she thought she was gently nudging it in. He was falling for it. It was an obvious invitation that he couldn't resist.

"I love it," she responded, followed by precisely what she intended. "Will you join me tonight, around eight-thirty? I said I owed you a dinner, remember."

Standing behind him, Sophia couldn't see it but now Jason was grinning broadly across the table at David and his eyes were widening with every second.

"Oh … err … tonight? Well, I was going to have dinner with Jason tonight, so-"

"That's ok, we can have dinner another night, no problem," Jason interrupted.

She didn't wait for David's confirmation, instead told him, "Good, I'll see you at the restaurant at eight-thirty then. Nice to meet you, Jason, Bye, see you later, David."

With that she turned to head off quickly down the alley in the direction of Pallas Beach feeling pretty pleased with herself and now being able to be a lot more relaxed for her final day in the warm sun and the clear blue sea on Pallas Beach.

When she turned up at the restaurant that evening he was already there. She looked stunning in a very smart, not inexpensive, low cut, short bright red dress and a thin silver necklace. The bright colour of the dress showed off her nice tan to perfection. If anything, he now felt under dressed simply in white shorts and a dark green polo shirt.

They were shown to a nice table on the roof terrace overlooking the Amphitheatre Square, and of course with the fine view of the illuminated Acropolis looming over the village.

They ordered some Italian white wine and a pasta seafood dish each with a salad. David wasn't exactly comfortable being with her, but he reckoned it was only dinner, and was determined it was only going to be that. Dinner with another woman, even one as lovely as Sophia, wasn't in his plans at all. His mind was too preoccupied still with thoughts about Alice Palmer. Even when Sophia reached across the table a couple of times to take and squeeze his hand while they enjoyed their good pasta, one time asking pointedly where his flat was in the village, he was very restrained, only telling her it was in the centre, disclosing no more detail. In fact, it was only just around the corner from the restaurant, literally no more than thirty metres away. However, he certainly wasn't going to tell her that. He reckoned he knew full well what was in her mind, and was determined to avoid it, avoid sleeping with her.

After they'd finished their meal and the wine the waitress brought them a Lemoncello Italian liqueur each. In her mind she was tussling one again with how, if it was at all possible, to try and get the subject around to the supposed accident in Lindos in 2016. He was right about her intentions in asking where his flat was in the village. She had been working on the assumption that if she could get into his bed with him she might just be able to get him somehow on to that subject in any post-sex pillow talk. She reckoned she'd always been pretty good at that, and was hoping she hadn't lost that one of her talents, which she'd used a few times for the Russian Security Services. However, as getting into his bed clearly hadn't worked she tried a different tactic.

"I've really enjoyed my holiday here. It's been very relaxing after Athens. It's very different to Athens, of course," she started to say.

She tried to lighten what she was trying to provoke some discussion about from him by letting out a very small laugh before adding, "Not least, of course, there aren't many slippery, rough paths and alleyways in the centre of Athens, unlike Lindos, except up at the Parthenon and the Acropolis in Athens I suppose, but not in most of the centre of the city. After I saw you this morning I nearly slipped over on my way to the beach. It can be quite dangerous in some of the alleys and on the paths in here, don't you think? I suspect there must be a few unfortunate accidents."

She thought that might at least prompt him to mention the supposed accident in 2016, but he didn't respond at all. Those comments of hers did appear a little odd to him, and provoked some very slight suspicion again in his mind, but he dismissed that quite quickly as simply paranoia.

With no response from him she shifted the conversation onto her next move.

"It'll be a little difficult to get back into the crazy rush of a capital city after I get back there. It's been great here. I can definitely see why you would want to spend the whole summer here. Perfect for your writing, and I expect you've got to know quite a few of the local people, including some of the restaurant and bar workers?"

This time he did respond, but only with a brief, "Yes, some."

She decided to engage a little further in her fishing expedition, and definitely a little more directly.

"The Courtyard Bar owner, Jack I think his name is, told me last night that you've been spending some time, quite a bit he said, with an English woman who works here in the summer. He said she's been here four summers working?"

"Yes, Jack, that's right, and Alice, who's been here four summers now apparently."

His paranoia returned a little, although he was trying to balance that against assuming perhaps he was simply over reacting as all she was doing was repeating what was merely part of the usual churn of village gossip she'd heard from Jack Constantino.

He skipped over her particular mention of Alice by adding, "There's a few of us, me and some of the Brits and locals who work in the restaurants and bars, who meet up sometimes late on for a few drinks after they finish work. By the time they finish, mostly around one, they find it difficult to go back to where they're staying and try to sleep, so a few drinks helps that. Quite often they meet in the Courtyard, or in the lower bar up at Lindos By Night. I've got to know quite a few of them through the summer."

He was somewhat concerned and suspicious over her mention of dangerous Lindos paths and accidents, and then Alice, but on the whole still put it down to his paranoia. It was her first time in Lindos, her first experience of some of the uneven and slippery paths, and she said she almost slipped over herself that day on her way to the beach, plus it was Jack Constantino who she said mentioned Alice. Maybe after all it was simply his paranoia.

She had one last move to try. She wasn't giving up, although this was a longer move in the game she was playing. She knew it wouldn't pay off that night.

"As I said, Lindos has been great, very relaxing, and very different from Athens. But I expect you know that. I'm sure you've been?"

She didn't know if he had, of course. It was a gamble. It turned out to be a good one, at least to some extent.

"Funny really, all the times I've been here to Lindos I've never been to Athens. Through the airport on connecting flights to here once, but not into the city at all."

As soon as the words came out of his mouth she knew that was the opportunity she was looking for, hoping for.

She took her chance, stared straight across with her piercing steel grey eyes into his, and instantly responded as enthusiastically as she could sound with, "You should come soon. Come on your way home, when you go back to England from here."

"Oh, I … err … I-"

He was stuck for just what to say, how to decline politely, but she didn't let him and was insistent.

"Come, please just come for a few days on your way home. I will be your guide. I'd love to be, and I'd love to see you again. I'm a very good guide," she added jokingly, followed by a bright smile and an ironic, "And I'm very cheap."

At that time, lovely as Sophia was, and as much as he would have liked to see Athens, the Acropolis and the Parthenon, all he could do was just smile and nod his head slightly. He knew that would definitely not be a good idea in terms of any possible further relationship with Alice. It was bad enough him having to leave Lindos and go back to England soon for the winter, but he was pushing his luck if he thought she would easily believe he was stopping off in Athens on his way home simply because he wanted to see it as a tourist. Not that he had any intention of telling Alice, or even at that point stopping off in Athens, but for Christ's sake his tourist Athens visit would be to see the very woman she got so uptight about when he told her about MI6 getting him to contact the woman at the Moscow conference. This was one of those times to say nothing, or at least, as little as possible and be non-committal.

After his very slight nod of the head he merely told her, "I'll see. I'll have to check a few things."

He was deliberately vague, but Sophia appeared to accept that, much to his relief. Not that she backed off at all that evening. He reckoned he knew perfectly well what all her reaching across the table to take and squeeze his hand while staring pointedly into his eyes was about, as well as her asking where his flat was in the village and inviting him to Athens. He didn't think of himself as a vain man, but it seemed pretty obvious that she wanted them to sleep together that night, or if not, then in Athens if he did stop off there on his way back to London. However, he exercised strong self-control, self-restraint, and resisted the temptation. The old David Alexander with his 'lightness' in sexual encounters with women would no doubt have done so. But now he thought he'd put that part of his old life and all that entailed behind him, especially having now finally at last slept with Alice Palmer. Even though he felt she'd cooled somewhat towards him after that it was still her, Alice, he was most keen on and he wasn't going to risk damaging anything between them by sleeping with the woman he was politely having dinner with, Sophia. He didn't want to risk there was any chance if he did it would get out around the village, and no doubt back to Alice. That would certainly destroy any hope he had of a meaningful relationship of any 'weight' and fidelity with her.

Consequently, he didn't respond to Sophia's obvious advances, but instead acted like a proper English gentleman and asked for the bill. She insisted on paying it though, as a way of thanking him she told him, for what he did for her at the Moscow conference. He walked her back through the village to the taxi rank in the Main Square and put her in a taxi back to her hotel, after telling her "Goodbye" with a kiss on the cheek.

When she got into her room at the Acquagrand she called her Athens handler on her burner phone straightaway, telling her that despite dropping a few hints over dinner with him she had found out nothing concrete from him about the witness, or even if there had been one.

"He's either being very clever and keeping anything he's found out to himself, or he simply hasn't found out anything," she told her. "Whether that's because he's not really looking, not trying to, or there just isn't anything, I don't know, I can't tell from him."

There was no response, so she added, "Personally, I think it's most likely the latter. He hasn't discovered anything."

"Is that it then? That's all you've got from almost ten days there? Top brass at the River House won't be pleased, won't be pleased at all."

The handler was angry, not least because she was going to be the one to have to report that to London.

"Surely there must be something you've found out that I can give them? Anything? Anything to lighten their response. It'll be me getting the bollocking, not you. You can just go back to your cosy life here in your nice flat."

That prompted Sophia to try and give her some hope.

"Look, I know you're angry obviously. The only possible thing you can tell London that might help is that I invited him to stop over in Athens when he leaves Lindos on his way back to London for the winter, in a week or so I think. He didn't say he would, but he did say he'd think about it. He said he has to check a few things first."

"Ok, I'll throw London that bone to gnaw on. At least that might keep them off my back, or our backs, for a week or so until we see if he does come to Athens."

The handler calmed down a little as she told Sophia flippantly, "You had better practice your pillow talk then my dear if you want to get out of him what he knows."

Sophia wasn't happy with that comment at all, but thought it best not to respond. Instead, she threw in another piece of information she'd picked up from Jack Constantino. Not that she really thought it was relevant, and David hadn't really responded to it when she mentioned it over dinner. But it was information of sorts, and at least showed she hadn't simply been lying around in the sun doing nothing.

"Oh, and apparently David Alexander has been spending a lot of time in the late evenings throughout the summer drinking, and who knows what else, with a British woman who works in a Lindos restaurant. The woman's name is Alice Palmer. It may just be a complete coincidence, but she's been working in Lindos for four summers. This one and the previous three, which means she would have been in the village in the summer of 2016. I've found out nothing to think it was anything other than that though, a coincidence. According to the owner of a bar in the village I was talking to last night David Alexander and this woman, Palmer, seem to get on well together. Throughout the summer they've been going off drinking together in the clubs in the village. The bar owner told me that quite regularly they'd meet in his bar after she finished work in the restaurant at around about one o'clock, have one drink together there, and then tell him they were off to one of the clubs. If Palmer does know anything about the murder though, she either hasn't told

Alexander, or if she has, he's kept it to himself and obviously not told London."

"Do you think Palmer could be the witness then? She was in the village at that time."

"I don't know. I haven't discovered anything, or heard anything suggesting she was just because she happened to be working here. I expect there are probably quite a few people here now, working here this summer, who were here in the summer of 2016. I just thought it might be something the River House would be interested to know. Who knows, it could simply be that David Alexander has been a little easily distracted by his, shall we call it friendship with her, while he was supposedly trying to find out for the River House if there had been a witness to what happened in that summer of 2016. And I can't say I've uncovered anything to suspect that this Palmer woman was the witness. So, I've absolutely no reason to think she was."

"Ok, I'll let the River House know about the Palmer woman. They may want to do a check on her generally, just in case. See if there's anything dodgy on record for her in the U.K. Presumably though, if she's been working in Lindos for four seasons she will have all the necessary required documents for that, work permits and the rest, and the Greeks will not have turned up anything dodgy. Because of that, the River House might decide it isn't worth the time and bother checking up on her, especially when I tell them you said you've not managed to discover anything suggesting she even remotely could be the elusive witness. As you also pointed out, there must be quite a few people working in Lindos now who were also there in 2016. So, like you, they will probably put it down to a coincidence Palmer being there then and now."

"Yep, I think so."

"Ok, I'll report to the River House that although you're back to Athens tomorrow you haven't given up on Alexander as there's still a chance he may stop off in Athens. Plus, if so, there's a possibility you may get to use your pillow talk technique and get something out of him they want."

Sophia ignored that last comment once again and simply replied with, "If that's all. It's quite late and I have an early flight in the morning, and have to pack yet."

"Sure, be in touch for any update once you get back on his possible stopover. Goodnight."

18

Athens and 'lightness of being' again

The evening after Sophia left to return to Athens was when Dianne Arnold dropped her bombshell to David about Alice Palmer sleeping with Simon Chapel earlier that summer. His reaction was initially one of anger with Alice. That soon turned to anger with himself over his own stupidity for even considering any sort of 'weight' in a possible relationship with her, rather than sticking to his idea of 'erotic friendship' and 'lightness' in sexual encounters with women.

Almost illogically, he'd become somewhat infatuated with Alice throughout that summer of 2019. But had she simply only wanted the 'lightness' of an 'erotic friendship' with him after all?

"Friends, good friends, very good friends," was what she'd told him they were quite a few times throughout most of that summer, adding that was all she wanted. But they'd slept together twice in those dying weeks of the summer of 2019. Not once, but twice. So, it definitely didn't seem like a one-time thing to him, and in different ways and through different things she'd said to him he got the impression she didn't think it was either. Although it seemed her attitude towards him had cooled somewhat after the second time they slept together.

Consequently, now as well as confused he was angry, although mostly with himself. As a result his view on a stopover in Athens to see Sophia on his way home changed dramatically, and the 'lightness' of sexual encounters was firmly back on his agenda.

He spent the day on Pallas Beach after Dianne told him about Alice and Simon Chapel going over and over it in his mind. Eventually, he decided he'd call Sophia that evening and take up her invitation to be his tour guide around Athens.

She acted a little surprised over him calling, but it was just that, an act. She was sure he would after their dinner in Lindos.

He told her he was going to be in Athens for three days on his way back to London at the end of the following week, from Friday the twenty-fifth.

That was greeted with silence at the other end of the line. She never said anything. She was making him squirm, and was determined not to sound too keen. She didn't need to. This part of her plan was working.

"So, if you're around, and your offer to be my guide still stands, I'd love to meet up for you to show me the Acropolis and the Parthenon, as well as the rest of the interesting things," he added to break the silence.

He obviously couldn't see the smile that had crept across her lips over his, "rest of the interesting things," comment. But she reckoned she knew very well what he meant, and yes her plan, and another of her talents, was definitely working.

"Sure, yes, of course, that'd be great. Good, I'll look forward to it," she told him, deliberately sounding much more enthusiastic in order to reassure him.

He told her he'd get an early flight so they could possibly meet around lunchtime and she could give him her Acropolis tour on Friday afternoon. She agreed, and told him that if he sent her a text telling her which hotel he was staying in she'd meet him there at around eleven-thirty, if that fitted with his flight time.

As she sounded more enthusiastic now he decided to push his luck a little.

"I'm sure you know a few good restaurants, so perhaps I could repay you for being my guide by taking you to dinner on Friday evening?"

"Yes, that'd be great, see you at the end of next week."

With that she rang off. No sooner had the line gone dead than he was already beginning to wonder if in anger he'd actually done the right thing. But anyway, it was done now. He was that guy once again, the one who believed in the 'lightness' of sexual encounters with women.

As soon as their conversation ended she called her Athens contact, her handler. Being careful over the phone she informed her she couldn't see her or her friends in London the following weekend of the twenty-fifth as she had a visitor from Lindos coming. Her handler knew exactly what she meant and simply replied, "Don't worry; I'll inform our friends in London. I'm sure they'll look forward to hearing how your weekend went with your visitor."

His early seven o'clock flight from Rhodes to Athens was on time and at eleven-thirty on that Friday morning of the twenty-fifth he was sitting on one of the long couches in his hotel reception area with a view of the entrance.

Even though it was almost the end of October Athens felt hot, hotter and more stifling than the still warm Lindos with its closer and more open proximity to the sea. According to the weather app on his phone the temperature outside was twenty-four degrees. Pleasant, but in the city it felt hotter. Because he expected to be climbing up to the Acropolis and the Parthenon looming over the city that afternoon with her he decided shorts would be fine, along with a cool cotton light blue short-sleeved shirt and his trainers.

Eleven-thirty came and went. It was almost a quarter to twelve and he was now beginning to wonder if she'd changed her mind and wasn't coming. However, she was deliberately late. She wanted him a little unsettled.

His concern disappeared as he spotted her stepping out of the revolving entrance doors. She looked good again, very good, even better than he recalled her looking that night in Antika a few weeks earlier. She was wearing a sleeveless plain light grey dress with a loose wide black leather belt just below her slim waist. The dress was very short, highlighting perfectly her fine tanned legs all the way down to the flat light grey leather sandals. As she entered the lobby and spotted David she removed her large sun glasses and placed them into her small canvass shoulder bag, while simultaneously smiling across at him.

"Welcome to Athens for your first time," she told him, then bent down to kiss him on the cheek. "But maybe not your last?" she added enticingly.

"That depends if I like it, I guess," was all he could think to reply.

"Well, many people here call it the ugly city, but I love it. Maybe you will. As I told you that night over dinner though, it's not like Lindos of course. Let's go and see."

His hotel was in the centre, quite near the Plaka. So, they took the short walk to the bottom of the hill and up to the Acropolis while she asked if his flight and hotel were ok, and made an occasional comment about the historic sites they passed as well as the Acropolis and Parthenon they were approaching. She was right. She was a quite good guide, which he complimented her on. There were quite a few tourists around, but nowhere near the crowds he'd anticipated, obviously down to the time of year.

After they wandered around the various parts of the site at the top, taking in the Acropolis and the Parthenon mainly, they made their way back down to find somewhere for lunch and a cold drink.

They found a place with shaded outside tables and she ordered for them both, demonstrating her fine Greek, which he again complimented her on.

"Well, I've had almost five years to learn here," she told him, adding how much she liked living in the 'ugly city'.

When the food arrived it was a Greek mezze for them to share. But then the waiter returned with some bottles of water and, much to David's surprise, an ice bucket in which sat a fair sized bottle of Ouzo.

"Wow! This, now?" he said as he glanced at his watch and added, "It's just gone two in the afternoon. If we drink all that I don't think I'll be able to stand, let alone make it back to my hotel and out for dinner tonight."

She laughed. "We don't have to drink it all, David. That's not the idea, just a couple of glasses each with the ice and the water. You are in Athens. It's what we drink here. It's good. It'll make you even more relaxed."

She reached across the table to squeeze his hand telling him, "Just relax, enjoy the surroundings, as well as the company of course. Don't worry, I won't let you get too drunk for dinner tonight." She ended with another quick smile across the table.

He struggled through two glasses laden with plenty of ice and water, accompanied by a few good helpings of some of the food to try and soak up the Ouzo..

Sophia insisted on paying for their lunch. It wasn't something David usually agreed to. However, she reasoned that she'd been the one who ordered the Ouzo and insisted. He eventually agreed, telling her he insisted on paying for dinner that evening then, plus pointing out she'd paid for their dinner in Gatto Bianco in Lindos last time.

"Of course, David, if that's what you want. I've booked a nice restaurant by the sea that I know."

He didn't know Athens at all, so he couldn't figure out where that could be, but if it was as nice as the place where they'd had lunch it would be fine. Perhaps it was the Ouzo, but as she'd suggested he was feeling more relaxed. Maybe that's what she'd planned.

After the lunch they wandered around the Plaka for part of the rest of the afternoon. From time to time she tucked her arm in his. He was starting to think it was a very pleasant way to spend a Friday afternoon.

They arranged to meet in his hotel lobby that evening at eight-thirty. He was there ten minutes earlier and seated on the same couch in his light beige chinos, plain white short-sleeved shirt and smart boat shoes. He wasn't sure at all what sort of clothes might be required in the restaurant she'd booked. He didn't think to ask, although the clothes he'd taken to Lindos for the summer never included any formal trousers or shoes, let alone a tie. Apart from the pair of chinos, all he had taken was shorts.

She turned up looking immaculate yet again, stunning in a simple but effective, outfit. She carried herself as though she knew that very well. She was wearing a knee length halter neck quite low cut black dress with a thin silver chain around her neck and black sandals, this time with a heel. Her small black leather bag hung nicely on her bare tanned shoulder.

This time she greeted him with a small kiss on the lips and then she asked him to get one of the receptionists to call a taxi to take them to the restaurant in Piraeus. The taxi ride took around twenty-five minutes, during which she again tucked her arm in his a couple of times as she pointed out some of the significant sites they passed on the way.

The restaurant was good and their table had a great view over Piraeus Harbour and the twinkling lights of some of the moored boats. They ordered some fresh fish each along with the nice bottle of white wine she wanted.

As they finished their wine he paid the bill and asked the waiter if he could call them a taxi. When the waiter told him of course he would, and then asked him where to, before David could answer she told the waiter Glyfada. He knew that wasn't in the centre of Athens where his hotel was, but presumed that was where her apartment was and of course just wanted the taxi to drop her off there first. However, when the taxi reached her apartment she had other ideas. As her handler had suggested, she was going to try as much as possible to use her pillow talk techniques to try and find out from him what MI6 wanted to know.

As the taxi pulled up outside her expensive looking apartment she took hold of his right hand, squeezed it again, and turning her head to face him stared intensely straight into his eyes as she told him, "You are coming in for one more drink aren't you. A nightcap, I think you call it, or maybe at least a coffee. We can't let our night end here."

It didn't actually sound like a question, but more of an assumption, bordering on a demand. All he could do was nod in agreement and then reach to pay the taxi driver.

When they got inside he was impressed, very impressed, with the apartment. He was thinking that this certainly wasn't a cheap apartment, and definitely not in a cheap part of Athens. She had obviously been treated very well by MI6. The floor in the lounge was real wood and the lounge was expensively furnished with modern bright furniture. He was even more impressed when she walked across the lounge to open the curtains and a pair of floor to ceiling large glass sliding doors to reveal a large terrace with wonderful views.

She walked out onto the terrace pointing out, "You can just about see the illuminated Acropolis and the Parthenon in the distance in the centre of the city." Then she turned around to face him and asked, "Now that nightcap. Would you like some wine?"

"That'll be fine," he replied, as he followed her into an equally modern, bright, expensive looking extensive kitchen.

After she poured them both a glass of cold white wine they returned to sit on the large leather couch in the lounge. However, the wine was barely touched by either of them. Within ten minutes, after a few minutes of meaningless chit chat, David's tour of the apartment was complete as they adjourned at her suggestion to her bedroom. Seconds more and they were both naked on her king size bed exploring each other's body for the next half-an-hour or more.

He knew he shouldn't compare, but after having had sex with Sophia he definitely didn't feel the same as he had after he'd slept with Alice that first time. Was it guilt over his return to 'lightness' in his relations with women, or because he felt he'd cheated on Alice?

Sophia on the other hand appeared to be more than satisfied from what they'd just done as she lay with her head on the pillow next to him.

There was a silence between them for a time that was drifting into becoming an awkward one. David was actually wondering how long he should lay there before suggesting he would leave when she asked him another surprising question.

"Do you actually know why they, MI6, wanted me to defect? What they wanted me for?"

As she asked him she continued to lay flat on her back and stare dispassionately up at the bedroom ceiling.

He turned his head slightly to look at her.

"No, nothing, they told me nothing, I was just to be the messenger and give you the contact number. To be honest, I didn't want to know."

"Nothing at all?" she asked once again, remaining motionless alongside him and still focused on the ceiling.

"No, nothing at all, other than it was you I was to contact. They simply gave me your photo and precisely what to tell you, just the contact number and absolutely thing more. They actually told me not engage in any other further conversation with you then or throughout the rest of the conference, even over anything academic. They insisted on that firmly. From what I knew about you academically, I just assumed that it was something to do with information which they knew you had access to from the Russian Security Services, information on Russian foreign policy intentions in the Far East, particularly China and North Korea, which would be of use to them."

"So, you knew who I was then?"

"Only from some academic articles of yours I'd read, a couple that were of interest to me because of my courses when I was at my university in England. I didn't know much more about you, other than that you were a Professor in the International Relations department at your university. That was in those academic journal articles of yours I read. When MI6 wanted me to pass on the contact number to you I assumed you must be someone important to be a Professor at one of the largest universities in Russia. That was the limit of what I knew about you personally. I really didn't want to know anything more, as I said I just guessed that you must have had some connection with the Russian Secret Services for MI6 to be interested in you."

She turned on her right side to face him. Still resting her head on the pillow she asked, "So, you thought I was a spy?"

She allowed the barest of smiles to creep across her lips as she finished asking him that, signifying to him that she was teasing him to some degree.

He decided to play along, although he had a much more serious look on his face as he asked, "Were you?"

She ignored his question, but went back to his previous assumption as to why MI6 were interested in her and getting her to defect. She lifted her head up off the pillow and rested it on her right hand for support with her elbow and upper arm now on the pillow.

"To some extent, you're right, it was to do with information that I had access to from the Russian Secret Services on Russian government foreign policy intentions in the Far East, particularly China and North Korea. That was certainly part of the reason MI6 were interested in me and wanted me to defect."

She was staring into his eyes, watching closely for his reaction to what she was about to tell him to see if it would shock him, although it wasn't the pillow talk she intended at all. It wasn't really going to get him on to what she was supposed to be finding out from him.

Her voice now was cold and calculating, almost detached as she told him, "But it was also because I could give them, MI6, information on people, the names of people in the U.K. and the Far East, mainly Russians, but some others, all Russian spies who they could try to turn to spy for them, or, of course, kill."

She thought that was at least about intelligence agents being killed, but was about as close as she'd managed to get so far with her pillow talk on the subject of what happened in Lindos in 2016.

She was right about one thing. It did shock him. He had no idea that what he did for MI6 at that Moscow conference was part of that, would lead to that. His head was starting to spin with it all. What he did led to, or could have led to, people being killed, was a lot more than what he had told Alice Palmer in Rhodes Town on that August afternoon. He certainly wouldn't be telling her any of what he'd just heard, including of course how and where he'd heard it; in Sophia's bed. Indeed, there was a lot more in his past about him and MI6 that he could have told Alice on that August afternoon in Rhodes Town, but avoided doing so. Now he could add what Sophia had just told him to that; his part in leading to people being killed.

Sophia could see he was shocked at what she'd done that he'd contributed to. But she carried on, with an even more dispassionate tone in her voice.

"As soon as they got me out of Russia and into one of their 'Safe Houses' just outside London I gave them a list of names. In return, of course, they gave me a new life, a new identity, all necessary documents, even a new birth certificate in my new name, U.K. passport, and a whole new family history. They referred to it as a legend, making me a completely new and different person, whose family managed get out of Russia just after the collapse of the Soviet Union, when the new me, Sophia, was very young, just twelve. Alexandra Ivanova instantly became Sophia Orlova, and that's me today."

As she knew he also worked at times for MI6 on operations, like when he gave her that contact number at the Moscow conference, she assumed he probably knew about some of that, about a legend, although not necessarily all that in relation to her case. He did, of course. But she thought and hoped it might just possibly be a way to get him, and their pillow talk, onto something that could link to, or develop towards, what she was trying to find out he knew about any witness to what happened in Lindos in 2016.

She was still lying on her side staring at him with her head propped up on her right hand as she told him, "Anyway, if you do some things for the Security Services, like you did with that contact thing for me, you must surely know people get killed sometimes, David, agents or operatives or whatever they label them. And you must know that not everyone's identity who you come across in that is real."

"Ermm ... yes ... yes I suppose so," was all he could think to say, or was prepared to say in answer to that.

He wasn't sure at all that he really wanted to know all she'd just told him. She was revealing a lot about her new identity and how MI6 had arranged it, much more than he needed to know or was comfortable with.

However, she knew that very well and was deliberately determined to do so. It made him vulnerable in all sorts of ways.

"In my new life here I even made some new friends, Greeks. It was one of them who suggested that I should go to Rhodes. I did some research on the internet, liked the look of Lindos very much, so decided to go, and of course, met you. So, here we are."

That wasn't exactly true, unless her "new friends" could be classed as the people in MI6. As she finished she lay back down with her head on the pillow.

"How do you feel about all that," he asked?

"Well, I saw that there were a few Russian tourists in Lindos, so that made me a little nervous at times in case by chance someone might recognise me, just like you did I suppose."

She looked up at him and saw he had a confused frown on his face.

"Oh, sorry, you mean you and me here? I thought you meant Lindos. We don't really know each-"

"No, not me and you here," he interrupted. "I meant how you feel now about what you did, what you gave to MI6 that resulted in people possibly, probably being killed."

She pulled herself up to sit with her back against the bed headboard. Now, at last, their conversation was heading in the direction she aimed for, and wanted.

"I did what I had to do, David, for self-preservation, to get out of Russia. With anything to do with Security Services, British or Russian, people get killed. Did you not think that might be the case when you did what you did for MI6 by giving me that contact number?"

It was another cold statement, devoid of any hint of contrition whatsoever, but she hadn't finished, hadn't quite made the connection she was looking for.

"Surely you must have had some idea why MI6 wanted me to defect, and that there would be consequences for some people from that, maybe even people getting killed. Ok, so you've been in lovely picturesque Lindos with its tourists all this summer, and I don't suppose there are Security Service agents or operatives there at all, so it's difficult to compare, but you must know it's different to that in Moscow or London, or even here in Athens. They are everywhere in those cities, believe me."

He didn't react at all. He wasn't sure how to, and he certainly wasn't going to say anything he knew about the MI6 guy getting killed in 2016. Anyway, she still wasn't finished probing or fishing. She had one more piece to play.

"Even in Lindos though, you don't really know if people are who they say they are. Not just their identity, but what they say they do for a living. It's a holiday place, people can be anyone they like. Take that woman Jack in the Courtyard Bar told me you'd become very friendly with, Alice, what do you really know about her other than she says she's been working there for four seasons, and why is that? Why did she leave England to come and work in Lindos in particular? Perhaps she had to? Perhaps she's got something to hide in her past, like we all have?"

She'd loaded the question, loaded the gun nicely, and now she'd fired it at him. Her mention of Alice prompted him to respond.

"Alice? Well, everyone I've spoken to in the village, including Jack, says she's been there for four summers so that must be true. But no, I don't know why she left England."

That wasn't true though. He did, but they were both playing the 'economical with the truth' game now, although neither of them appeared to be aware the other was.

"Probably she just wanted to live and work somewhere warm and happened on Lindos. I don't really know, but I'm sure she's got nothing to hide she's running away from."

Another lie, but Sophia had him precisely where she wanted him now in this game of chess. She decided it was time to go for check-mate.

"But how do you know that, David. Have you asked her? Have you even had a conversation about it, why she left England, what she's running away from? Perhaps in pillow talk like this when you slept with her? Have you?"

She propped herself up resting her head on her right hand to face him as she asked that last thing.

"What? Err … no … no," another lie, "and I don't know what she's running away from in England, if anything at all, which I'm sure there isn't."

Now he felt very uncomfortable. Initially, he briefly thought Sophia's question of had he slept with Alice was just jealousy. Very quickly though the consequences of the whole situation he now found himself in overtook that and was right at the front of his mind. What on earth had he bloody done? Not just that evening in Athens with such a hard-hearted, seemingly emotionless woman, but also for MI6 back at that conference when he passed their message on to her. And what had he done coming to Athens at all and deceiving Alice, just because he was so angry with her over what he'd heard from Dianne that Alice had done with bloody Simon Chapel earlier that summer.

He'd been bloody stupid in once again pursuing the 'lightness' of a meaningless sexual encounter simply because of his anger with Alice over what he'd been told she'd done with Simon Chapel. It certainly appeared that was all Sophia wanted, the 'lightness' of a sexual encounter, and in his anger over what Dianne had told him he thought that was all he wanted.

That wasn't all Sophia wanted, however. Their sexual encounter, and any subsequent pillow talk, was simply the means through which to get what she really wanted, and what MI6 wanted her to find out.

He was sure now that he didn't want to spend the whole night there in her bed. To his surprise and relief nor did she want him to. Just after three, as he lay wondering how he could make his excuses to leave, she told him she would call him a taxi to his hotel. After he kissed her goodnight in her apartment doorway and climbed into the back of the taxi, a great feeling of relief swept over him, followed immediately by remorse at his total stupidity.

As they'd arranged before he left her apartment they met again the next day. She could feel he'd changed towards her, in that he was nowhere near as open as he'd been the previous night in her bed. Consequently, before he left for London she got nothing out of him about the possible witness to what happened in Lindos that summer of 2016, if he even knew anything more. She never mentioned Alice Palmer again during his Athens visit, nor did he.

She dismissed Alice as the possible witness and reported to her Athens handler once again that she got nothing out of David Alexander during his stay in Athens. Her handler passed it on to the River House in London, for Sir Michael. When the handler said, again flippantly, "Your pillow talk skills not working as well as they used to then?" Sophia again ignored it. Instead, she repeated that she thought any talk of a witness was merely just all gossip and rumour, and that there was absolutely no substance to it that she could discover from Lindos or from David Alexander in particular.

Two days after he got back to England David got a call from his MI6 handler instructing him to come into the River House for a debrief on what he'd learned during his summer in Lindos about what happened there in 2016. He tried to put it off, telling his handler there was nothing more to report than he'd already told them, which actually was nothing at all. However, his handler was insistent he should come in at ten in the morning two days later for a proper face-to-face debrief. He said nevertheless the top brass had insisted on that.

David had no choice. So, as instructed, with some trepidation, he went. He knew his questioner's probing in the debrief could be difficult, but he carefully ensured he never reported anything more than he'd already told his handler previously throughout the summer. He purposefully didn't report what Alice had told him, and obviously not that he knew she was the witness. He was still struggling with his personal dilemma over that and any relationship he might have, or wanted to have, with her. He also never reported what happened between him and Sophia, which raised their suspicions somewhat as she'd already reported that to her Athens handler, who relayed it to the River House. Although Sophia had said she'd got nothing out of him. He, of course, still had no idea that when she was in Lindos she was also working for MI6, or that additionally she'd raised Alice Palmer's name with them as being very friendly with him.

What he did report at his River House debrief though was that he was going back to Lindos next summer, in 2020, probably from March. As soon as he did that he realised it was a mistake. They wouldn't let the possible witness issue drop and that perpetuated it. He was instructed to keep listening in the village for any more rumours about any witness when he went back. The point was made firmly to him again that they couldn't let it drop completely as the witness could still emerge at any time in the future and embarrass them. They were convinced there was one and that it wasn't just rumour and gossip, despite what both David and Sophia reported. Consequently, their investigation was still officially open, but put on hold, with the exception of what David was instructed to continue to do when he got back to Lindos the following summer.

PART FIVE:

2020

19

March

Alice Palmer stayed in Lindos for the winter while David Alexander went back to UK via his short diversion in Athens. They exchanged texts regularly and there was the occasional Skype and Facetime between them from somewhere open with a Wi-Fi connection in the village. Basically, that amounted to the Red Rose bar in the centre or the Lindos Ice Bar up the hill in Krana.

   Through the winter he tried to put his guilt over Athens behind him, concentrating on meetings with his publisher and editor, and making suggested changes by the editor to the first draft of his novel. He had no further contact with Sophia after he left Athens. His guilt re-surfaced though over Alice's reply after texting her to wish her a Happy Christmas in Lindos. She texted back, "Happy Christmas to you too. When are you coming back? I miss you. X."

   He arrived back in Lindos at the start of the first week of March, on Monday the 2nd. There weren't that many people around in the village at that time, certainly hardly any tourists. A few of the bar and restaurant owners, along with some of the shopkeepers, were starting to get their properties ready for the start of the upcoming summer season following their winter hibernation.

It wasn't until the Friday evening of that first week that Alice and David met up. They exchanged a few texts after he got back and he suggested they meet up. But she put him off, and kept doing so until that Friday evening. He thought that was a bit odd, but eventually put it down to her blowing hot and cold, sending mixed signals, much as she'd done throughout the previous summer. To some extent that continued when they met on that Friday evening. He had received her encouraging text at Christmas, of course, telling him she missed him, and his first impression on that Friday evening was that she was pleased to see him. As the evening wore on, however, he sensed an underlying tension between them emanating from her.

They went for a drink in one of the only two bars that were open at that time, the Lindos Ice Bar. Quite a few of the locals from in and around the village were there. For many of them it had been their regular drinking spot throughout the winter months; a place to meet and play cards or just chat. Alice and David knew quite a few of them from their visits and summers in the village. Over a fair few drinks they caught up from some on how the winter had been. The bar seemed to stay open for as long as anyone was prepared to carry on buying drinks and consuming them.

As it got late the tension coming from her began to increase. Something was wrong. He had no idea what. Unusually for her she hadn't mentioned what it was, and he decided that for now he wasn't going to ask, but instead pick his moment. Their first meeting didn't seem the best time for it.

At the end of the evening they walked down the hill into the village together. As they reached the Main Square she suggested, "Let's sit on the bench over there looking out over the bay for a bit. I'm not actually very sleepy, and I haven't had that much to drink. It's not as though I've been doing much during the day and evenings here at this time of year, not like in the summer when I'm working. Even if I go to bed now I won't sleep."

He was about to learn what was bugging her, what the tension was about.

Lindos was a village, and like in all villages gossip travels, or at least some gossip does. The particular gossip about David and his Athens stopover at the end of October only partly originated in the village, and only eventually. He was caught out as a result of Sophia meeting and becoming friendly with the waitress at the Village House Restaurant, Marianthi, during her Lindos stay the previous October. She worked there throughout the summer, but lived in Athens during the winters. They kept in touch and when they met for a drink in Athens just before Christmas Sophia told her that an English guy she met in Lindos called David, a writer, had come to visit her for three days at the end of October. She made it pretty obvious to Marianthi that they'd slept together.

Unfortunately for David, therefore, the details of his regrettable Athens visit didn't remain only between him and Sophia, or even just in Athens. Dianne Arnold also worked at the Village House restaurant with Marianthi, and they kept in touch throughout the winter as Marianthi wanted to come back and work at the restaurant for another summer. On one call between them she repeated to Dianne what Sophia had told her about David's visit to her in Athens, including that they'd slept together. Like Alice, Dianne stayed in Lindos through the winter and quite regularly met up with her for a drink up at the Lindos Ice bar. On one of their nights up there in January she couldn't wait to tell Alice what she'd heard from Marianthi.

Alice wasn't happy about that at all. It was actually jealousy that was making her angry now. When David left Lindos at the end of last summer she had obviously been drifting into the realm of the 'weight' of fidelity and responsibility in the relationship between them. Was that what she wanted? Was that what her Christmas message, and the phrase "I miss you. X" meant? She wanted to convince herself it didn't and it wasn't jealousy making her angry. However, as they sat on that bench in Lindos Main Square on that Friday evening her anger towards him over what Dianne had told her she'd heard from Marianthi suggested the opposite.

When Dianne Arnold had told her about David and Athens, and Sophia, her emotions swung between devastation and disappointment on the one hand, and feeling justified and relieved on the other. Deep down she knew she always expected it, to be let down by a man. What she found difficult to comprehend however, was why she felt so hurt this time. Why did it seem so serious and matter so much to her? She didn't think it could again. That was something she didn't want to acknowledge at all, wasn't prepared to. All those emotions had been swept away though, crowded out now by anger as she'd met and was about to confront him. She almost spat out at him what she'd been told with aggression, bordering on venom, oozing from her lips.

What else could he do but own up to his stupidity? He sighed and then took a deep breath.

"She lived in Athens, and yes, she was on holiday here. I went to Athens on my way back home last October to see her after she left here. It was stupid, a stupid thing to do, Alice."

Even then, however, he didn't go so far as to tell her that Sophia was also the woman from the Moscow conference five years ago he'd told her about that August afternoon in Rhodes Town. He conveniently convinced himself that was information about Sophia's new identity that he simply could never share with anyone.

He didn't need to tell Alice that though. She guessed that they might be, but he lied and denied they were the same person.

"Wait a minute, how stupid am I," she started saying, raising her voice again. "Marianthi told Dianne your shagging friend in Athens was Russian. She lived in Athens, but was Russian."

He stayed silent. He knew the conclusion Alice was about to draw, what she was about to say.

"The woman you told me about at the Moscow conference, the one you passed the MI6 contact number to, she was Russian too," Alice continued. She looked him straight in the eyes as she said loudly, "It was the same bloody woman, wasn't it, your Athens shag and the woman at the conference?"

He stayed calm, frowned a little and looked incredulous as he said forcibly straightaway, "What? No, of course bloody not. How did you get to that conclusion? There's a lot of bloody Russian women in the world, Alice. And that was nearly six years ago, the conference in Moscow and that woman I passed the MI6 contact number to."

She looked at him sceptically as she said, "And I asked you that afternoon in Rhodes Town last August if you slept with the woman at the conference in Moscow, and you said you didn't."

"Because I didn't, Alice."

That was true, he didn't then, but he lied now.

He still convinced himself he couldn't confirm it, that she was the same woman; partly because of the need to keep Sophia's new identity secret and safeguard her, and who knows where it might end up through the Lindos gossip conveyor belt. What if Alice told Dianne, who then would no doubt tell Marianthi and it could easily end up back in Athens, where Sophia was living, and even possibly reach the Russians there. Also, of course, that definitely wouldn't help his position with Alice, and any possible relationship between them,

Then somewhat pathetically and half-heartedly he did try to justify to Alice what he'd done with Sophia by mentioning what he'd heard about her and Simon Chapel. But that just made her even more angry as she pointed out that what she stupidly did by sleeping with him on one night was much earlier in the previous summer, before she slept with David, whereas he slept with Sophia after Alice and him slept together.

The previous summer they'd shared a lot of long nights of drinking, clubbing and talking, often finished off wearily in the bright sunlight of the new dawn with a slice of pizza from Nikos by the tree in the little square in the centre of the village. This though had been a completely different experience. Instead of the calm, relaxed, but tired conversations between them of the previous summer's sunrises, this time they'd argued over each of their indiscretions, sometimes loudly, on a bench in the Main Square.

Eventually the silent tension between them was palpable. It was so thick in the night air it would have needed a very sharp knife to cut through it. The interminable silences were becoming excruciatingly long as they both continued to stare out into the distance of the bay.

Her anger hadn't dissipated though. It was as much about what she'd allowed herself to do, her emotions do, as anger with him. That was just bubbling away silently inside her and exploded again as she suddenly screamed at him loudly, "You were angry over what Dianne told you about me and Simon bloody Chapel, a bloody one night stand, a fucking meaningless one night stand. But instead of talking to me about it you scurried off to Athens to fuck that woman. So, what was it, some sort of revenge fuck? Good was it? Hope it was worth it? Was it? Was it?"

Small traces of a single tear trickled down each of her cheeks, the result of a mixture of anger and disappointment. David sat there not having any idea what to say, how to answer? He had no answer. It was now becoming increasingly obvious to him that she cared about what he'd done, about him, a lot more than he thought back then, back in October when he'd stupidly decided to go to Athens. She wouldn't let on back then, wouldn't go so far as to tell him that, how much she cared about him. Although he did recall one unexpected moment outside Café Melia a few days before he left when she asked him to stay in Lindos with her for the winter. However, when he replied he couldn't she didn't seem that bothered. He clearly misread that as well. That was Alice Palmer though. Once she'd taken a chance in exposing her feelings, even the smallest one, she would retreat into her defensive shell again if she didn't get the response she'd hoped for, and after that she would get angry with herself for laying herself open to rejection.

He stammered as he struggled to answer her question, not really having one that was in any way credible, his voice virtually echoing with a plea to her for some sort of leniency, some sort of understanding.

"No ... no ... it wasn't ... it wasn't good. It really wasn't. But okay, yes, I guess it was some sort of meaningless revenge fuck. I thought-"

She didn't allow him to finish. "That's just it though, David, isn't it. You never thought at all did you? Your dick did your thinking for you!"

Her anger wasn't dissipating one iota.

He sighed heavily. All he could do was respond quietly with, "I guess so."

He returned to staring out across the bay in silence for a few seconds before trying to finish telling her in a low, regretful voice what he previously attempted to say.

"Look, Alice, I just thought that you and me … well, that there was no future in anything between you and me. You didn't seem interested in anything serious. That's how it seemed to me. Every time it looked as though that was what was developing you ran away, not just physically, but emotionally. To me it seemed like you were scared of something, scared to commit. Perhaps that was because of what happened to you in the past, with your ex-husband, and I can understand that. I don't know, but that's what it seemed like to me, that it was pointless, hopeless. I tried, god knows I tried, all summer, and I tried to tell you a few times how I felt, but you seemed frightened of any sort of meaningful commitment, even avoided talking about it. I know it's not an excuse, but I'm just telling you how I felt, what I thought was or wasn't happening between us, that's all."

She calmed down a little and her voice was breaking up with emotion as she told him, "Those couple of times, the sex, it was good. I know it was. You know it was. It was special. Don't get me wrong, it was. But it was always me who initiated it, and in fact I felt I was getting mixed messages from you because you seemed so reluctant. It was, wasn't it, the sex? Good, I mean?"

She didn't wait for his reply, but sighed heavily, a resigned sigh, before telling him, "I guess I knew in reality it was a mistake to go any further with what we had between us, to go any further than being just very good friends. I was afraid of precisely this, that somehow everything would eventually be spoilt, messed up. I should have stuck to my 'friends, very good friends' thing and known that taking a chance and wanting more would end in a disaster."

It seemed she was saying it was a mistake to go beyond the 'lightness' in their relationship, a mistake to go beyond any 'erotic friendship'. Maybe that was really what he thought too.

They sat on the bench together for another five minutes in complete silence, just staring out into the bay in front of them. Clearly they were both emotionally exhausted. Then she simply told him she was going off to her bed, gave him a slight kiss on the cheek and told him, "Goodnight."

He sat there for another four or five minutes trying to go over in his head what had happened over the past hour. Finally, he decided he was too tired and drained to process it all. Not least because additionally also lurking in one corner of his mind was his dilemma over what he should or could do about Alice and MI6, or more accurately, what he knew he couldn't do and definitely didn't want to do because of his personal feelings about her, tell them she was the witness they were looking for.

After that night on the bench in the square she avoided him, wouldn't even talk to him on the phone or return his texts. Every time he called it went to voicemail. He left a couple of messages saying he really needed to talk to her, but she obviously ignored them. The restaurant she worked in hadn't opened for the season yet so he couldn't go and see her there, and somehow, even though the village was small, he never bumped into her. He went round to her apartment a couple of times and banged on the door, calling out her name, but there was no answer. He had no idea if she was in there or not and was simply refusing to answer the door to him. He asked a few of the locals in the village if they'd seen her, including the woman he got to know quite well who ran one of the supermarkets near his flat which he used regularly and that he knew Alice used, but no one said they'd seen her. He started to think that perhaps she'd left Lindos?

He despaired. How could he have been so stupid as to do what he did by going to Athens? If she was still in the village then surely in a few weeks as the season started he would see her. The restaurant where she worked would open, and if nothing else he could go and find her there.

However, both Alice and David's world, and everyone's world, got much, much worse, and suddenly changed dramatically. His despair and frustration over Alice paled into insignificance in comparison. On the twenty-third of March the Greek government announced a full national lockdown in response to the Coronavirus pandemic that had spread to Greece, including to the island of Rhodes.

20

Lockdown

Initially from the 23rd of March only short trips to one of the small supermarkets allowed to open in the village were permitted and always while wearing a mask and with social distancing. The village was a collection of deserted white walled alleyways and boarded up shops, restaurants and bars. Despite the comforting warmth of the spring sunshine it felt bleak and desolate, reminiscent of an English seaside town in the depth of winter. It was a time of year that should have been full of optimistic expectancy and anticipation of the coming summer tourist season. Normally there would have been plenty of busy activity as the shopkeepers, as well as the bar and restaurant owners, prepared their properties for the forthcoming season due to start in early to mid-April, depending on the calendar of the Greek Orthodox Easter. The outer and inner walls of some of the shops, bars and restaurants would have been being given a new coat of paint and any exposed woodwork spruced up. With lockdown they all remained closed. The village was very quiet. After the Greek government lockdown announcement there was to be no start of the 2020 tourist season at the usual time in Lindos or anywhere in Greece.

    Isolated in his Lindos flat with no internet connection, and consequently without even access to U.K. radio or press for news, it took David a couple of days to fully obtain details of the extent of the lockdown regulations in Greece. Any internet connection in Lindos was very unreliable and only intermittent even at the best of times, even with mobile phone roaming. The woman serving in the little supermarket he used regularly near his flat told him initially about the lockdown. The Greek government actually announced it on Sunday 22nd of March, to come into effect from the next day. By chance he happened to go into the supermarket early that evening to get some milk and the woman told him about it, although she didn't have all the details. Consequently, although he'd decided he would contact them as little as possible throughout the coming summer he had to relent and call his MI6 handler in London to find the details of the Greek lockdown regulations. That was just one of the unforeseen difficulties of finding himself in a countrywide lockdown situation in a foreign country and with virtually no access to the internet.

Only a handful of Brit ex-pats were around, those like Alice who had stayed in Lindos through the winter and lived in the village. Like David she found herself stuck in Lindos at the start of the Greek lockdown.

It was quickly clear that no one had any idea just when the 2020 summer season might begin in Lindos and across Greece, as well as most of southern Europe, if it ever would. The virus was in control of the holiday calendar, and politicians and governments, including the Greek one, were battling to stay ahead of its effect. The island of Rhodes was actually not too badly affected in terms of the number of cases of the virus, but cases in the countries from where most of the tourists to the island came were soon increasing rapidly, especially Britain. Also, on the Greek mainland the number of cases quickly began to grow, particularly in Athens.

The few bar and restaurant owners in Lindos who David occasionally encountered on his way to the supermarket in the first couple of weeks of the lockdown going to or coming from their premises to check all was okay with them all briefly told him the same thing while carefully social distancing, that they had no idea when the season might get underway. They were all downbeat and full of pessimism, with no expectations whatsoever that it might actually ever do so. All seemed resigned to the sad anticipation that the 2020 season would be a write off. Aside from those brief encounters and conversations the only sound in the village he experienced was ones of echoing emptiness.

Usually at this time during the four years Alice Palmer had been living and working in Lindos she would be starting work at the restaurant. Not serving customers yet, but helping the owner and his wife get things ready and set up for the coming season, and for when the first tourists would start to arrive in early to mid-April. This year the restaurant wouldn't be opening in April and nobody really quite knew when it would. Consequently, there was no work for her, and that meant she wasn't getting paid. Through the winter months from November until March she usually lived on her savings from the summer season. She was careful, and budgeted that way through the summer. Even though her wages were hardly excessive, she lived on some of that during those busy months and saved her tips as extra for the winter when there was no work. Because she was good at her job, always chatty and friendly in the restaurant, the customers, the tourists, liked her, and gave her some good tips, which helped her through the winter.

In the first week or two of the lockdown it felt at times as though the village itself was sad, as though its feelings were hurt from missing the usual hordes of tourists. As exercising outside was allowed as long as it was near where you lived, to relieve the boredom and get some fresh air Alice walked down to the Main Beach on a few days, then slowly along it a couple of times, sometimes more. It was odd, strange, with no one there except her. In summer it would usually be filled with multiple sun beds, parasols and lots of tourists, as well as multitudes of tourists having lunch or a late breakfast in the restaurants and cafes at the back of the beach. Now there was no one, and the restaurants and cafes were all sporting their winter shutters. With no idea about an end in sight to the pandemic, strolling along the empty beach clutching her flat espadrilles in hand and occasionally dipping her feet into the chilling sea she wondered if there would be anyone at all that summer on the Lindos beaches. If so, how would Lindos, its tourist businesses, and its people survive, including her?

One day while she walked on the Main Beach in those first couple of weeks even the usually calm clear sea in Lindos Bay appeared agitated, as if in sympathy with the village and its people over the unknown and unpredictable turmoil looming over it and them in the coming months. The waves appeared angry, rhythmically crashing onto the deserted beach as she watched the dark foreboding storm clouds of that particular day gathering overhead. It was a forlorn vision in such a usually beautiful and happy place. Perhaps, it was one reflecting the impending turmoil about to engulf not only Lindos and its residents, including the bars, restaurants and shop owners, but the whole of Greece and far beyond? Initially, that's how the scene before her registered with her.

Alternatively, she wondered if the angry waves and the uncertainty of the gathering dark storm clouds overhead were merely a symbolic representation of the turmoil and doubt within her over her relationship with David Alexander, even though her anger over what he'd done in Athens had actually by now subsided somewhat. It had been a few weeks since their argument on the bench in the square and she had deliberately avoided any contact with him. She dwelt on that for almost an hour as she meandered back and forth along the deserted beach. It was somehow beautiful in its stark, dramatic emptiness, framed by the rough sea in the bay and the dark clouds overhead. There were plenty of worse places to be in the world right now, and plenty other things to be angry about rather than what David had done the previous October.

Perhaps the visits to the Main Beach with its quiet emptiness, along with the loneliness of the lockdown, mellowed her in terms of her anger with him, and after a couple of weeks she decided she needed a friend. She needed someone to talk to, even if only on the phone, someone to get some support from through the lockdown and its accompanying boredom. That turned out to be David. In reality, he was virtually the only option. Who else could she turn to? In fact, there were one or two others, including Dianne Arnold. She knew Dianne would be supportive, but she also guessed she would press her about David, going over and over what she knew about his Athens visit. She decided she couldn't face that right now, even though only on the phone.

He was surprised when she called. Having left plenty of voice messages and sent numerous texts in the weeks after their argument, as well as before and after the start of the lockdown, all with no response, he'd almost given up.

Her voice was tentative at first, simply asking how he was, how he was surviving the lockdown. He asked her the same after he told her he was okay and was trying to use the time for some editing he had to do to the second draft of his novel. She told him she obviously had no work as the restaurant hadn't even begun to prepare for the season when the lockdown was imposed. Then she told him about her walks to the Main Beach and how strange it all felt down there.

He noticed quite quickly that she seemed determined to avoid any conversation about their argument on the bench in the Main Square. He was relieved, and certainly wasn't going to raise it.

Basically, they both realised that in the circumstances they only had each other. Not physically because of the lockdown, but in terms of communication verbally by phone. Even Skype or FaceTime between them wasn't possible as neither of them had an internet connection or access to Wi-Fi in their accommodation, and of course none of the bars and cafes that had it were open. The lockdown was draining, physically tiring, tedious in an empty small tourist village like Lindos. Of course, it had to be so, but the usual winter emptiness of the place in terms of people and tourists had been stretched by another few months at least. The spring sunshine brought only some slight relief. From the 4th of May, after six weeks of lockdown, Greece began to gradually lift some restrictions on movement and to restart business activity.

After that date David and Alice did manage to meet a few times, always outside. Neither of them was really completely sure of the rules of lockdown, so they initially agreed that any meeting or contact should be minimal, as that was what they at least believed was allowed. Usually they went for a walk down to one or other of the deserted beaches, Pallas, the Main beach or St. Paul's Bay. Initially it seemed there was still some lingering tension between them just below the surface over their indiscretions the previous summer and autumn. Just like the Main Beach on Alice's walks during the full lockdown all of the beaches looked odd without their large numbers of sunbeds and umbrellas and the multitudes of tourists. They sat on the sand and talked for an hour or more, usually about what they'd heard about the news from the U.K. or what they'd heard from locals occasionally in the village about the situation on Rhodes or in Greece generally. They continued to studiously avoid any talk of their argument and previous indiscretions. Always when they were walking or sitting on the beach they kept socially distanced, one-and-a-half or two metres apart roughly. Although, at times he desperately wanted to touch her, grab hold of her hand, hug her and kiss her.

One day on St. Paul's while they were sitting talking she reached over to take his hand. He knew that because of the Covid regulations and social distancing strictly he shouldn't, but he took it and squeezed it as they exchanged a smile. It seemed they both simply couldn't resist doing so any longer.

"I'm glad you're here," she told him. "I know we shouldn't do anything more, but I just wanted to touch you, hold your hand if nothing else is possible. I'm happy you came back. I really don't know what I would have done if you hadn't, if I had been here alone through all this craziness, the lockdown and the pandemic."

He watched her closely, never taking his eyes off her as she told him that with her eyes tearing up slightly but firmly fixed on his face. He could hear the concoction of emotions of agony, frustration, yet also happiness in her voice, and see it plainly on her face and in her eyes. He felt the same.

He nodded slightly and allowed a small smile of satisfaction to grow across his lips as he replied, "Me too, I'm glad I came back, and that I'm here with you."

She squeezed his hand as he told her that, and then let out a small chuckle.

"What's funny," he asked?

"Oh, silly really, but according to all the novels and movies an English woman is supposed to come to a Greek island to meet a Greek man, not an English one. Clearly I never read the script."

He smiled as he replied simply, "Clearly," while thinking how good that sounded to him, an optimistic sign perhaps? Maybe all the anger of the previous summer and autumn was behind them, paled into insignificance by the effects of the pandemic and the events in the wider world. Maybe the 'weight' in their relationship was gradually slowly returning.

They sat in silence for half-an-hour, grasping hands and gazing out into the empty bay with two small fishing boats anchored in the shallow water bobbing up and down very slightly with the movement of the sea. Moored at the jetty below the small picturesque Greek Orthodox chapel was a slightly larger tourist boat, originally moored for the winter, but obviously remaining there because of the lockdown.

Despite all the craziness and sadness that was happening in the pandemic stricken wider world, for those few hours of that peaceful St. Paul's Bay afternoon in the early May pale sunlight all was silent and calm around them. The only low sound was the crystal clear sea lapping gently on the shore at the edge of the beach. Stretched out before them was the view of the high rocks on either side of the entrance to the bay from the open sea with a few birds swooping between those and the water of the bay below. For a few moments, those few hours together, they were completely detached from the madness of the pandemic, cocooned from it within their own company, as well as by the beauty and solitude of the deserted St. Paul's Bay. The panorama of the beautiful bay and the tranquillity all around them felt light years away from the Covid pandemic madness and tragedy engulfing the world.

It wasn't only David and Alice, and any relationship they may have had, that suffered during the weeks and months of the various stages of the lockdown. They were starved of company of course, deprived of being drinking buddies and possibly more, but so were many people in the village. Most of all though it made David realise how much he felt starved of her, her company, her smile, even in some way her defensive aggression. Despite the long days of continuous sunshine for most of the lockdown, he felt they were in a constant cloak of frustrating darkness as far as their relationship was concerned. It was a darkness that seemed never ending; a bleak unremitting darkness in a beautiful picturesque place, Lindos. The lockdown meant they were further away than ever from resolving their relationship and what it meant to each of them, 'lightness' or 'weight'? The pandemic and the lockdown denied them the time and opportunity to explore that.

21

After lockdown

Restrictions on entry to Greece for international travellers were finally lifted in mid-June and entry restrictions on British tourists were set to expire on the 15th of July. Consequently, there was a more optimistic atmosphere in the village as the shop, bar and restaurant owners began to prepare their premises in anticipation of tourists returning in a few weeks.

As the village began to come alive some shops opened up first and then gradually a few bars, cafes and restaurants as some of the tourists started to appear by the middle of June, although not yet from the U.K. When some of the cafes opened, as well as their walks to the beaches David and Alice met for coffee at Giorgos and Café Melia.

One afternoon in the middle of June when they were at St. Paul's Bay Alice said she was supposed to be starting work back at the restaurant the next week. However, he was puzzled when she added that she wasn't sure about it now, whether she wanted to. She seemed vague and uncertain about it. Something was clearly bothering her.

Before he could ask her why she wasn't sure she went on to talk about their walks to St. Paul's together during the earlier part of lockdown, how deserted it was and peaceful. Then, to his surprise she changed the subject completely. She started to ask about the Russian woman at the Moscow conference he'd passed the MI6 contact number on to.

That made him nervous, thinking she might start bringing up his Athens mistake again, and ask about that and the Russian woman there. Was that was what was clearly still bothering her on that afternoon.

It wasn't and she didn't bring up him and Athens. She only asked if he ever found out the truth about why MI6 wanted the Moscow conference Russian woman to defect.

"That afternoon in Rhodes Town you said you thought there was more to her activities than just some academic expertise that they, MI6, wanted. Did you ever find out what that was?"

He simply shrugged his shoulders and told her, "No, best that I didn't know."

What she asked next suggested she appeared obsessed with it, especially his comments about MI6. It prompted him change his perception of perhaps what was bothering her. Maybe she still had concerns about the Irish woman she saw commit the murder in 2016 and wanted reassuring?

"Yeah, I guess so." She waited a few seconds, then added, "When I told you that afternoon in Rhodes Town about seeing the Irish woman kill that guy and that I heard something between them about MI6 you told me I shouldn't worry about the woman finding out I'd witnessed it and coming back to kill me because MI6 would have killed her by now."

"Did I actually say that? I can't remember exactly what I said now."

"Yes, I'm sure. How come you know so much about MI6, David, so much as to be able to make a comment like that?"

She looked at him with suspicion written all over her face.

"Why would you think I do? Even if I did say that, and I really can't remember I did, it was just an assumption. I don't really know. How could I? I was just trying to put you at ease I guess, help your peace of mind that's all."

That wasn't true, of course, but despite his attempt to dismiss it and make light of it, seeds of doubt were still swirling around in her mind. She wasn't totally convinced by his explanation by any means.

During the next couple of times that they met for coffee he could sense it was obvious her unease at his explanation over his MI6 comment hadn't gone away. She became more insular and detached, even while they chatted over some of the more mundane daily occurrences in the village as it started to emerge from the lockdown.

He decided he would tell her a little more, needed to, but not in such a public place as one of the cafes or even one of the beaches, that were now starting to get more tourists on them. He suggested that they go for a walk up to the monument on the hill above the northern end of Lindos Main Beach one morning, before the sun got too hot. There wouldn't be many people around up there, if any. The monument was a stone shrine dedicated to Ioanni Zigdi, a Greek politician who was born in Lindos in 1913. He told Alice that he'd never been up there, but always wanted to as he'd heard it had great views over the Main Beach and the village, and it was only a short walk up the hill.

"Why not, I've never been either. It'll make a change from St. Paul's and the Main Beach," she agreed.

Although it wasn't yet noon when they got up there it was still quite hot under the mid-June sun. They sat for a while drinking from their small bottles of water while looking at the stunning panorama of the village and Main Beach below. His assumption was correct. There was no one else around, just the two of them. For a while they chatted about the beautiful view and being lucky to be in Lindos. He waited and then picked his moment.

"You know you asked about me and MI6, how I knew so much about them. Well, to be honest, there is more, a little more I can tell you, a little more I think I should tell you, want to tell you."

She turned away from looking at the view to face him. Her face was blank, expressionless. She said nothing. Silently she was thinking she knew that there must be more. Perhaps he was about to redeem himself, and her trust in him.

"After what I did, passing the contact details onto the Russian woman at the conference, MI6 tried to formally recruit me to their Russian Department, Russian Desk they called it. They said it was because of my academic Russian background and all that stuff, my expertise on Russia. But I turned them down, told them no. It definitely wasn't something I wanted to get into. I never signed anything, nothing like the Official Secrets Act or anything. The guy from MI6 who approached me to pass the contact details on to the woman at the conference only asked me verbally. He said it was off the record and asked if I would be interested in working for them officially at Thames House, MI6 headquarters in London. They call it the River House because, well, because it's by the river."

He shrugged a little and smiled slightly before continuing.

"When I told him no he said that was okay and that the conversation had never happened as far as he and MI6 were concerned. I'm actually not clear, or sure, if I should be telling you this, Alice, Official Secrets Act and all that, even though I never signed anything. It never got that far, just the one brief conversation. That's why I never told you all of it before."

She wasn't sure whether to be relieved over what he'd finally told her, or disappointed and angry that he hadn't told her before. Somewhere deep in the back of her mind she couldn't help wondering if there was even more he wasn't telling her, which there was, of course, but he knew he definitely couldn't, shouldn't, tell her that.

Her face betrayed her confusion.

"I see, and is there more, David?"

"More?"

"Yes, what I asked you about before at St. Paul's. Do you actually know more about what happened to the Russian woman who defected?"

He did. He knew quite a lot about what happened to Sophia, of course, but he wasn't about to tell her all of it. He hesitated slightly as he began to tell her. He was figuring out just how much he could tell her, how much he should tell her. Above all he wanted to make sure she never connected the woman at the conference as being the same woman as Sophia.

"Yes ... err ... well, yes and no really. I don't know what happened to her after she defected. They, at MI6, wouldn't have let on to anyone about that as I guess they would have given her a new identity and a new life. Not that I was in any position to, but it would have been pointless asking, plus I wasn't really bothered. Why should I have been? She was nothing to me. I was just asked, told, to deliver a message to her with the contact details so she could defect."

Was he being a bit too defensive on that last point, protesting a little too much he wondered? Alice simply stared at him, listening in silence. He ploughed on, hoping what he was going to tell her next would distract her from dwelling too much, if at all, on the new identity stuff.

"I did have that conversation with the guy from MI6 after she defected though. It was the same conversation in which he asked me to go and work in their Russian department. I don't know if he should have told me, but I asked him why they wanted the Russian woman to defect. Was it because of her academic stuff or more? I didn't expect him to tell me. I was surprised when he did."

"And what was it for?"

He bit his top lip and his face contorted slightly into a frown.

"They wanted a list of names from her. They knew she did some work, as the guy put it, for the Russian Secret Services and had access to some information and names MI6 were interested in, wanted. Apparently some of them were in the Russian Secret Service who she knew would defect. Some of them were in Russia, but some were spies in the U.K. My MI6 contact guy told me that the ones in Russia would be worked on, encouraged and helped to defect. But he also said that some of the ones in the U.K. already, the spies who they knew would never defect, would likely be eliminated."

He looked her straight in the eyes as he added, "Killed."

He could see straightaway she was shocked. Her mouth was half open and it was all over her face. She thought he might have been holding something back from her, but she had no idea it would be something like that.

He tried to respond instantly to her obvious shock by telling her how he felt about it; his obvious remorse.

Still staring straight into her eyes he added, "It haunts me, believe me it does, being responsible, even indirectly, for people being assassinated. I don't feel good about it, Alice. How could I? You're the only person I've ever told about it. It's a secret that I've had to carry within myself ever since, a dark secret that I know I probably shouldn't even be telling you. MI6 wouldn't be happy about that at all, me telling anyone. But you asked, and I wanted to be honest with you. By telling you that I want you to know that you can trust me."

She reached to take his hand, told him, "Thank you for telling me," and then kissed him tenderly on the lips.

Even now though, he knew that he wasn't telling her the whole truth, and not simply the fact that the Russian woman at the conference and Sophia in Athens was the same person. He had an even darker secret deep inside him than that in addition to what he had just told her about MI6. He knew he couldn't tell her that. He daren't. It related to her.

22

July: "Sometimes life just happens"

By mid-July even British tourists started to arrive, so the village was much busier. Not the usual volume of tourists for the middle of July, but most of the bars and restaurants had opened and were doing a reasonable trade. At the end of June Alice's restaurant opened, but with fewer tourists than normal in Lindos she was finishing nearer to midnight than one o'clock. She was back to meeting up with David regularly after work. The clubs had not opened after the lockdown ended, so their late nights were restricted to late drinks in Jack Constantiono's Courtyard Bar or, less often, Lindos By Night Bar. That meant there were far fewer late nights that turned into early mornings for them.

The only very late night stretching into early morning option was on Friday and Saturday nights at the open air club, Arches Plus, on the road down towards the Main Beach. That stayed open until six-thirty or even seven in the morning. Because it was the only club open in the village, as well as on that part of the island, it was always very busy. As both David and Alice knew Valasi, the owner well from their Lindos stays, and from frequenting his other club in the centre of the village, Arches, they had no problem getting in no matter how busy it was.

They met up a few times during the day for coffee or for a late breakfast at the usual places, Giorgos and Café Melia. Generally she seemed more at ease with him again, which he put down to his partially true revelations up at the memorial above the Main Beach. Things were going well between them once more. The trials and tribulations over his Athens diversion appeared to be well behind them. Although he was still wrestling with a particular dilemma over her and what he was supposed to be doing in Lindos for MI6, one he couldn't share with her.

On the second weekend of July, on Friday the 10th, his feeling that things were once more going well between them was considerably enhanced, or so he thought initially. They met at the Courtyard Bar after she'd been back to her flat to change after work. Around two-thirty she suggested they move on down to Arches Plus and he agreed. On the walk down there she reached over to take his hand, smiling broadly.

Soon they were inside and getting their first drinks at one of the bars. It was crowded, very crowded, seemingly even more so than usual. Perhaps it was because of the increase in the Brit tourists as the summer season was finally beginning to open up.

They'd only had one drink when she surprised him by saying, "Let's go," and added loudly over the music, "It's too crowded. I don't feel comfortable here when it's this crowded, especially with all the Covid shit."

"Okay," he agreed. As he did so he took her hand and led her through the crowded club.

"Phew! That's better. How can it be so bloody hot in there when it's open air," she said as they emerged outside.

The view of the bay across the road was magical, sparsely lit up by the small lights twinkling on the few boats moored in the bay.

"It is a warm night, and it is July, Alice, plus it's more crowded in there than I've ever seen it. Probably because there aren't that many clubs open on the island, I guess."

She was still clutching his hand as he suggested, "Pizza?"

She never answered. Instead, she told him, "It's always a beautiful view isn't it," and started to walk across the road towards the low iron railing opposite, still clinging on to his hand and taking him with her."

"Yes, stunning," he agreed as they reached the railing. "Don't usually see it like this though do we, lit up in places in the middle of the night by the lights from the boats moored in the bay."

She let out a small chuckle before agreeing, "No we don't, it's usually the sun coming up and daylight by the time you're ready to leave."

She was teasing him. A good sign, he thought. So, he reached to put his arm around her shoulder and hold her close to him.

He thought he'd misread the situation again, however, when she pulled away slightly, shrugging off his arm after a minute in silence while they stared out across the bay.

"I'm not ready for this yet, David. I don't want this right now," she told him quite firmly.

In a few seconds the romantic moment evaporated. Or so he thought.

Another long half-minute passed as they both stood gazing out in silence at the picturesque sight of the bay before them.

He was bewildered, frozen, although not from the air around them at all, and wondering quite what to do next. Suggest pizza again, or just say goodnight and go off to bed. A few seconds later he was even more bewildered. But that was the conundrum that was Alice Palmer. He should have known that by now.

She turned her face towards him. As she looked at him in the surrounding darkness her bright eyes were darting and studying every part of his face. It was as if she was an artist checking out his features and searching for inspiration. She obviously found it.

She reached up to put her left hand behind the back of his neck, pulled his head down into hers and kissed him with a warm, soft, gentle, lingering kiss.

"But I … ," he started to say as she pulled back from the kiss and they parted.

She stopped him by placing two of her fingers onto his lips while gazing into his eyes enticingly.

After a few seconds she removed her fingers and he tried to speak once again.

"You just said …"

She stopped him again by kissing him once more.

This time as she drew back from the kiss she told him, "Sometimes life just happens, David, and you just have to let it. Don't over analyse it. Just go with the moment."

He was speechless. All he could do was nod in agreement. This was one confusing woman indeed. Beautiful as far as he was concerned, inside and out, but bloody confusing.

So, life did "just happen" again for the two of them that night. For the first time since the previous summer they slept together, had sex. Or made love, with all the 'weight' that involved? Perhaps that was the way it could be described. He thought so, although he knew there were other complications and barriers to that now because of the instructions he'd been given by MI6 again before he came back. Consequently, it couldn't be that straightforward. Whether she shared his view that what they'd done was make love that night, and not simply had sex as part of another episode in their 'erotic friendship', was another matter.

23

"Sometimes crap just happens"

It was close to ten when Alice left David's flat the next morning. Then she called him at one suggesting a late breakfast at Giorgos and a few hours on Pallas Beach.

"Sounds like a good idea," he told her.

Going to the beach together wasn't something she'd often suggested throughout the previous summer. In fact, he could only recall it happening a couple of times.

All seemed well between them all afternoon, with a few swims in the cooling clear sea and some nice sun. As she left him at five-thirty to go off to get ready for work she told him, "See you later. I'll text you to find out where you are when I finish work, but I think I can guess which bar you'll be in."

"Maybe I'll surprise you," he told her.

"No, you won't, you'll be in Jack's, as usual," she said with a smile and a small kiss on his cheek as she left to make her way up the hill from Pallas.

She was right. He was in Jack Constantiono's Courtyard Bar. Despite what she'd told him she didn't even bother to text, just went back to her flat to shower and change into some bright green shorts and a loose white t-shirt before going to the bar.

As she arrived the owner was telling David a rumour he'd heard was that the Greek government might introduce a midnight curfew on all bars and restaurants in the country sometime in the next few weeks if the Covid situation didn't improve, or in fact, continued to deteriorate.

"Bloody great, we've only just started to pick up on the tourist trade in the restaurant," Alice chipped in.

"Well, I guess it'll mean you'll finish earlier," David suggested.

"Not really, will be pretty much the same by the time we've cleared up, and where the bloody hell will we be able to get a drink after that? All the bars will be closed by then."

Alice didn't look happy at all at that news as she reached to take the first drink of her vodka and coke. What Jack told the two of them next made her even more unhappy.

"Oddest thing, Alice, you probably wouldn't remember her, probably never met her, but there was an Irish woman here four summers ago trying to trace her Greek father. She had no idea who he was, but her mother worked here for a couple of summers in the seventies and that's when she got pregnant with her."

Alice quickly placed her drink down on the bar as a look of concern spread across her face. David was too busy focusing on Jack and his story to notice her changed expression, and Jack was too engrossed telling it to notice the change.

"No, can't recall meeting any woman here doing that," she interjected with a quiet tone in her voice trying to downplay it.

"Anyway, it's a long story," Jack continued. "Basically, I introduced her to my mother and grandmother who were able to help her about some things in and around the village at that time her mother worked here."

David had begun to link the dots together, particularly as he glanced at the concerned look on Alice's face.

"So, what's odd about that, Jack?" he asked.

"Well, I haven't heard anything at all from her since that summer, not a word since she left. I thought that maybe she'd let me know how she got on with the rest of what she was trying to find out about her family, particularly the Greek side in the village, especially after my mother and grandmother helped her so much. They asked me a couple of times if I'd heard from her. And she never actually said goodbye when she left, just left without even saying goodbye to anyone in the village from what I gathered. Then yesterday, out of the blue, I got a text message from her, asking how I was, how the village was, and saying she must come back someday soon."

David knew exactly what Alice was thinking as he quickly glanced sideways at her face. Simultaneously she did the same and as their eyes met concern was clear on both their faces.

Jack never noticed. As David said, "Yes, I suppose that is odd," he obviously merely assumed it was his story that had created the changed expression on both their faces.

They finished their drinks and left together. As soon as they got outside the bar Alice stopped walking, turned to face him, and said quietly, "It's her, isn't it. I know it's her."

She was distraught as she added, "I knew it, I knew she'd bloody come back looking for me."

He never really actually believed what he said next, but he thought it was the only way to calm her down.

"You really don't know that. How do you know it's the same woman you saw?"

"She was bloody Irish, David."

Her voice was raised now. She wasn't calming down at all. A couple of people outside Pal's Bar at the bottom of the alley finishing their last drinks, as well as a couple sat at the small table munching their crepes from the crepe shop opposite, heard her and turned to look up the alley at them.

"Just calm down," he told her as he placed both his hands on her shoulders. "Even if they are, were, both Irish it doesn't mean the woman Jack is talking about and the woman you saw kill the guy in the back alley are the same woman. There are plenty of Irish tourists in Lindos all the time."

"But it was the same summer, 2016, David. That's a hell of a coincidence don't you think?"

"Yes, the same summer, but how many Irish female tourists do you think were here through that summer, Alice, bloody hundreds, maybe even a lot more? And you don't even know if the woman, the killer, saw you anyway. Even if she did, why would she wait four years to come back to find you? Why now?"

She hesitated for a few seconds and took a deep breath.

As she did he added, "It can't be the same woman. It really can't. That wouldn't make sense would it, to wait this long?"

She nodded slightly. "Maybe, maybe you're right, but you know from what I told you, from what happened that afternoon in Rhodes Town when I overheard an Irish accent, that I get nervous about it, paranoid."

There was a worrying frown all over her face. He put his arms around her shoulder and pulled her into him for what he hoped would be a reassuring hug. They stood there at the top of the alley like that for a long half-minute.

She moved away slightly as he told her, "Look, if it makes you feel better, safer, why don't you come back to my place for tonight? We don't have to do anything, just sleep, and I'm sure you'll feel better in the morning."

"I … I … err … ," she hesitated, obviously thinking things through and still dwelling on what Jack had just told them.

A few seconds later she told him firmly, "No, no, not tonight, David. I think I need to be alone to think all this through."

"Are you sure?"

She nodded slightly once again, then replied, "Yes … err … yes, I am. I don't think I'm in the mood to be with anyone right now. I need to think this, and a few other things, through and decide what to do next."

"What do you mean-"

He started to ask, but he never got to finish his question. She was back into her disappearing act mode of last summer.

"I'll tell you tomorrow, text you or call you in the morning and we can meet for breakfast. I'll tell you then, after I've figured it all out in my head."

She quickly kissed him on the cheek, told him, "Goodnight," and rushed off down the alley.

He woke up at nine the next morning and her text suggesting breakfast at Giorgos came through just after ten. He was hoping that when he got there she would be more relaxed about what they'd heard from Jack Constantino after a good night's sleep. However, when he arrived she was already there with her coffee looking like the worried frown had stayed with her all night. He ordered a cappuccino from Tsamis, as well as a couple of croissants.

"No breakfast for you?" he asked her.

"Only coffee, can't face anything else at the moment."

"Did you sleep ok? Manage to put all that stuff Jack was on about out of your head?"

She looked sceptical as she glanced silently across the table at him for a few seconds out of the top of her eyes.

"Hardly, how could you expect me to after that?"

"I suppose so, but look it's probably nothing, just-"

He was trying to reassure her yet again, but never got to finish.

"I'm leaving, leaving Lindos, leaving Rhodes, leaving the island," she blurted out.

He slumped back in his chair, stunned. That was the last thing he'd expected to hear from her.

She reached for her coffee as he asked with an air of desperation in his voice, "What? When? Why? But I thought after Friday night that we had a connection again."

She shrugged as she placed her coffee cup down on the table, but initially said nothing in response for a long ten seconds while he stared at her in bewilderment.

"Is this all because of what Jack told us last night? It's really nothing, I'm sure, just-"

Again she didn't let him finish.

"It's worse, David, much worse than just that."

"How could it be? I'm certain what Jack said is nothing."

She sighed and then took a deep breath before telling him, "Remember I said the other night that sometimes life just happens, well change that to sometimes crap just happens, and usually just when you think everything is going so well."

He shook his head in bemusement, but before he could say anything she added, "Look, David, I didn't tell you, what with everything going so well between us, but a week ago I got a call from a friend, well sort of a friend, a woman I worked with back in the restaurant in Sheffield, and-"

"The one where you stabbed the guy in the leg?" he interrupted.

"Yes, David, that one," she told him firmly, clearly a little agitated that he wouldn't let her finish.

"We've hardly kept in touch, and it's been a while now since I left, but anyway, she's still working at the same restaurant and she said someone had been in there asking about me, a customer. Asking about me by my full name, not just Alice, and wanting to know from her, as well as a couple of others who still work there, if they knew where I was now. She said it was a man, middle-aged she thought, and she told him she didn't know where I was, which is true because I've never told her or anyone back at the restaurant. I thought it was maybe someone from the Probation Service because of what happened with me stabbing the guy in the leg and being put on probation, but that was over four years ago and surely they would have come looking for me before now. But now, after what Jack told us last night about the Irish woman, I'm wondering if the two things are connected."

She took another deep breath before adding, "So, that's why I'm leaving, because of both those things. Whether they are connected or not I don't know, but if I leave and go somewhere else without telling anyone here where, I figure then no one can find me or let on to anyone who comes looking for me here, like the Irish woman, where I am."

For a few minutes when she finished he was speechless. Not least because although he had no idea if she was right about the Irish woman Jack had told them about last night being the killer Alice saw that night back in 2016, he was pretty sure that the guy who was a customer in the restaurant back in Sheffield asking about her was almost certainly not from the Probation Service, but from MI6, checking up on the background of this woman, Alice Palmer, who they somehow had discovered had spent a considerable amount of time with him the previous summer. Someone from MI6 was on a fishing expedition trying to find if she was likely to be the elusive witness they were looking for.

While he was trying to deal with that conclusion running through his brain all he managed to ask her was, "Leaving, but where to, not the U.K.?"

"No, I obviously can't go there because of skipping the probation, another island, maybe one of the smaller ones."

He leaned forward to rest his arms on the table and tried to push her for more detail, "Which one?"

But she wouldn't budge, not least because she didn't know. It seemed like a spur of the moment thing.. Even though perhaps she'd been dwelling on it all night she hadn't thought it through that much.

"I haven't decided yet."

Then the unpredictable, surprising Alice Palmer resurfaced.

"Come with me, David."

Her eyes clearly told him that she meant it as she stared anxiously across the small table waiting for his response. He didn't respond to that directly though.

"But why now? Just because of what Jack told us last night? You said you knew about the guy asking about you in the Sheffield restaurant a week ago."

He knew the answer to that was yes, but she didn't admit to it.

She didn't really answer his question. Instead, she tried to sound as matter of fact as possible as she told him, "Time to move on, I've actually grown tired of supposedly living the dream here now. I've been here living and working for almost four seasons. Want to try somewhere new."

"Really?"

He raised his eyebrows. He knew that wasn't true, or at least not the real reason. She knew it too.

She took another drink to finish her coffee and then lifted the empty cup in Tsamis' direction standing in the doorway to signal that she'd like another. "And one of those please, Tsamis," she added as she pointed to David's croissants.

Now it was David who was frowning as he once again slumped back in his chair at her lack of a real answer. Eventually, seeing his despair from his face and body action she admitted what he guessed.

"Okay, David, yes, perhaps it is a bit because of what Jack told us last night. I know it might just be a coincidence, like you said, and not the same woman, but I'm tired of worrying, always looking over my shoulder in case that bloody woman shows up. I know that she might not have, probably didn't see me that night. But all the time I'm here I keep thinking she knows where to find me if she did see me, which is why I want to go somewhere new, somewhere different. At least I'll feel safer and be less worried there. Plus, who knows, maybe the guy in the restaurant asking about me is somehow connected to her, part of the same organisation or whatever. I told you that night in the alley I heard MI6 being mentioned in the fight. Perhaps, the Irish woman, the killer, was part of the IRA, and maybe the guy asking about me in the restaurant isn't from the same organisation as her, but from MI6, although I don't have any idea where he, they, would have got my name from. It's just all too complicated and muddled, David. I need to go somewhere no one connected to what happened here in 2016 can find me, whether it's the IRA or MI6 or whoever."

He had a pretty good idea she was right about the guy asking about her in the restaurant being from MI6, as well as how he, they, would have got her name, from Sophia, but he wasn't about to tell her that. She asked about Alice that night in her bed in Athens, saying Jack Constantino had told her David had spent a lot of time with Alice through that summer of 2019.

Instead, he asked again, "So, where?"

"I'm not exactly sure. I told you, perhaps one of the smaller islands, more remote. Just come with me and we'll decide together. Let's just go the day after tomorrow, not tell anyone at all here, and decide when we get to the Rhodes Town ferry port."

She was leaning forward across the table and anxiously almost pleading with him. He'd never seen or heard her do that before. Her voice was bordering on a whisper now.

He stayed silent, not responding at all as Tsamis arrived with her second coffee and the croissant. He was still facing a real dilemma. One that he couldn't tell her about, daren't, or even start to explain. Besides which this was all too much of a shock, all too quick, too much to take in. She hadn't prepared the ground at all. Was this merely typical Alice Palmer? Always running away?

She took a bite of her croissant and then a swig of the coffee before telling him, "But if you won't come with me I'm not going to tell you where I'm going, not that I know that right now to be honest, David, or even let you know where I end up. I don't want anyone to know. I'll feel safer that way. I need to find somewhere I feel completely safe, a safe place for me."

He sat there in a daze, shattered. Despite the bright hot Lindos July sunshine his mind was a hazy fog. Just a couple of nights ago they'd slept together again and he thought everything was good between them, a new beginning. But now there was this. Deep down he knew this was always a possibility. That it might come eventually and he would then have to face up to the possibility that there was no way he could be with her or go with her. However, he never anticipated it would arise so soon. For reasons known only to him he daren't go with her, for the safety of them both.

"I do understand, Alice. I do. I'm disappointed, and that's an understatement. But I know what you mean. I guess we all need somewhere we can go to, retreat to, where we know we're safe. I haven't told you this before, but I know I have mine, somewhere I can go off to when I need to and have at times in the past; disappear for a few weeks or more and feel completely safe. A place called Scilla, in the deep south of Calabria, right on the toe of Italy, that's my own little safe place. An Italian friend of mine, well his father really, has a hotel there, U'Bais, and I know I can turn up there almost any time. They even give me a room they refer to as my 'usual room', and I know they won't tell anyone I'm there. I call it my safe place, and so does my friend whose father owns the hotel, as well as even some of the staff."

Her eyes were pleading with him to go with her. She didn't need to ask him that again. He could see it.

"But I can't, I can't come with you. I have to go back to London for my novel," he told her.

He knew that was only partly true, and certainly wasn't the main reason. Despite his immense disappointment, one very small part of him could only be relieved that she was leaving. He knew that there was something he would have to do eventually if she remained in Lindos. Something he was being forced to do, instructed and expected to do. He'd put it off again at first when he returned in early March, just as he had through the last part of the previous summer. Then lockdown enabled him to put it off longer. The people at MI6 reluctantly accepted that. They had to. They had no choice because of the lockdown. Anyway, that's what he told them. He'd wracked his brains over how to get out of it, out of doing what they wanted. Now, thankfully, by leaving Alice had provided him with an option, a way out, what seemed to be a solution to his dilemma, even if it wasn't ultimately what he really wanted and it meant he couldn't be with her. As much as he really wanted to he couldn't go with her, or even tell her the real reason that he daren't.

The cold, defensive and indifferent part of her character resurfaced as she replied, "I see, okay, of course. I'm gonna leave the day after tomorrow then. That'll give me time to sort a few things here, with the restaurant and my landlord and that, although I'll tell them I've got to go back to England because of a family emergency."

"Oh, that soon, I-"

He never got to finish.

"Right, I need to pay Tsamis for this inside and then it looks like I've got plenty to do, to sort before work tonight. I'll text you and we can meet later tonight or sometime tomorrow."

She took a quick slurp of her coffee, went inside to pay, and she was gone.

He checked the usual places for her late that night, but there was no sign of her. No one in the Courtyard Bar or Lindos By Night had seen her. The next morning in his flat he got a text from her at eleven suggesting they meet at five that afternoon before she started her final night working in the restaurant at six-thirty. He replied, suggesting Café Melia, and she agreed.

It was an awkward meeting. Initially she displayed no emotion at all. He knew deep down that she had to leave. It was for the best. However, it didn't prevent him from being sad, disappointed. For the first few minutes as they ordered coffees the conversation was stilted, forced. Clearly neither of them knew quite what to say. It appeared obvious that they both wanted to avoid re-opening the whole conversation about wanting him to leave with her, or indeed, why she wanted to leave at all, felt she had to.

After their drinks arrived she asked unexpectedly, "So, is the great novel finished then?"

He was taken by surprise by her question.

"Err ... oh, yes, almost ... err ... Yes, just a few very brief final touches and then it will be. Then I'll have to go back to London to finalise a few last things with my publisher, like cover design and the rest. Hopefully it'll be published by September."

"That's good then." She flashed a quick smile across at him and a small nod.

Meaningless small talk wasn't what he wanted, or expected. He wanted to talk about them, whatever it was that was between them. He knew how he felt now, but he still wasn't entirely certain if she thought what they had now, what she really wanted, was the 'weight' of a relationship and the fidelity and responsibility that involved, or simply the 'lightness' of an 'erotic friendship'. He did think, though, tried to convince himself that asking him to leave Lindos with her meant now she wanted the first one. He did too.

He tried to bring the conversation around tactfully to that, or so he thought.

"Perhaps we could meet up later in the summer, on whichever Greek island you end up on? That would be good. I'd really like that. I'll be heading back this way, Greece I mean, late September for a month anyway, I think."

She ignored his suggestion. Instead, she asked, "So, what's it about, this novel? I think you said last summer it was about relationships."

He hesitated for a few moments, took a sip of his coffee, and then looked straight across the table into her eyes as he answered, "It's ... err ... us ... it's about us."

That took her by surprise, although she was trying not to let it show.

"Oh, I see, and is there a happy ending?"

As she asked that he thought he detected a slight tone of regret in her voice.

"Don't know. You tell me, Alice."

She didn't answer, just reached to take another sip of her coffee as she looked across at him out of the top of her eyes.

"You know the ancient Greek, Homer, wrote that life is a never ending odyssey," he started to tell her as she placed her coffee back on the table. "He wrote that it's a search for adventure, for new experiences, and for meaning. Are we, whatever it is that is between us, never ending, a never ending odyssey, or just a fleeting new experience do you think? You tell me, Alice, what you think the meaning is of whatever is between us?"

As he finished speaking he stared hopefully across into her eyes once more. It wasn't as simple as all that for Alice however, and he knew deep inside that in reality it couldn't be as simple as that for him either. There was a large barrier that prevented something between them being anything other than a fleeting new experience; MI6 and what he was supposed to be doing for them which was directly about her, although he'd never reported that. It was a real dilemma for him. He was searching over and over for a way to overcome it, and had been for months, through the final months of last summer and the first part of this one. But he was still at a complete loss how to, and he certainly couldn't tell her what it was. That wouldn't solve anything anyway. He was simply desperately trying to finally find out how she felt about him now, and about any relationship between them. He had to finally know. Perhaps it would help him find a solution.

"I don't know, David," she told him.

She looked away to stare into the far distance across the square towards the old Amphitheatre, shook her head slightly from side to side, and then took a deep breath before she continued.

"I really don't, don't know. I can't get some of the things that happened last year between us out of my head, what you did in October. Sometimes I try to convince myself I can, like when I asked you yesterday to come with me, leave here with me. Sometimes I try to believe that over time I will, but I can't just dismiss and forget it all quite that easily after what happened to me in the past with my ex-husband. Unfortunately the bad things are as much a part of what is between us now as the good times. I, we, can't just remove them from our memory can we? That's just not possible."

"But-"

He tried to interrupt. He thought they were questions and she was asking him to help resolve her dilemma, the things that troubled her. She wasn't. She hadn't finished explaining what was troubling her about what might be between them.

She briefly looked back towards him then turned away again to stare straight ahead. She appeared determined not to make any eye contact with him as she continued.

"Trust is big thing for me, David. You know that. I've told you that plenty of times. Lies destroy trust. They actually prevent people from really knowing us, knowing who we are and being able to understand us. If you can't understand someone, the truth about who they really are, how can you help them, support them, really love them?"

As she turned her head to look back into his face traces of two small tears were running down her cheeks.

"And I know you lied to me, David. I didn't want to believe that you did when Dianne told me about it all, you and Sophia in Athens. Believe me, I didn't. But part of me knew it was true because that's what I always expect now, expect to be let down. And you did let me down. Oh, I know you can say that you never actually directly lied about Athens, but you did only say you were flying home. There was no mention of Athens, let alone her, of course. So, for me that's a lie by omission. Whatever, even so it was a lie, and destroyed what trust I had in you. When you came back in March I thought I could get over it, put it behind me. I tried, believe me I tried, struggled with it all through lockdown. Yes, I was glad, happy even, that you were here for me then. I told you that, and you told me the same. But most of all what you did, and your lie over Athens, not only destroyed the trust between us it also made me question whether I actually knew and understood you at all at a difficult time like now when who knows what is going to happen here for the rest of the season with this bloody virus still swirling around the world, as well as with these bloody people possibly looking for me."

As she finished she reached up with her index finger to try to wipe away the small traces of tears from her cheek.

He didn't know quite what to say, how to respond. He'd never heard her talk to him as openly as that, about her feelings and the two of them. He knew that trust was a big thing for her. She'd told him that quite a few times. He had to admit to himself that he hadn't been exactly honest about a number of things. However, there was one more thing, a big thing, probably the largest, that he simply could never be honest with her about. It was at the very heart of the comment she'd just made about trust, loving someone, and knowing the truth about who someone really is. Instead, he attempted to hint at it without actually telling her.

"Secrets and lies are a dangerous thing, Alice. We all think we want to know them, find out all about them. But if you've kept one to yourself for so long you soon come to understand that by doing so that may help you learn something about somebody else, but ultimately you also discover something about yourself. And that's not usually good. That's the side effect of secrets and lies, I guess."

She misunderstood and clearly thought he was talking about her, when, in fact he was talking about himself.

"What are you on about?" She looked completely bemused, but he'd gone as far as he could.

"You'll see, maybe in time it will all become clear, Alice. But if you don't let go of your past it'll strangle your future."

As he finished he took her hand and leaned across to kiss her gently on the cheek.

He never saw her in any of the bars in the village that night, not even the Courtyard Bar, and Jack Constantino told him, when he asked, that she hadn't been in.

The next day she was gone. He had no idea where. Since she told him she was leaving he hadn't asked again, so she never told him exactly where. She never even saw him that day to say goodbye.

Now, for him it was in the past, the recent past, but nevertheless in the past. He thought it had to be. Was it a lost opportunity, a lingering, never forgotten, endless regret, or nevertheless despite that an enjoyable, happy time? One and a half enjoyable Lindos summers, on the whole. Only time and looking back would perhaps tell David Alexander which. One thing he knew for now though, had learned painfully, if you have any chance of happiness grab it with both hands, no matter what obstacles are in your way. Overcome them somehow and don't let happiness escape through missed opportunity.

His only consolation over her leaving was that he thought he had a way to make sure she'd be safe from MI6 looking for their witness. He'd do that as quickly as he could.

24

Making her safe

The morning after Alice left he walked up to the memorial overlooking the Main Beach again. This time to make a call where there was likely to be no one around. In his flat there was always the chance he could be overheard by someone from the other one across the courtyard. He couldn't take that chance.

He retrieved the burner phone taped to the underside of the draw of one of his flat's bedside tables and made his way up the hill to the memorial. It was still early morning and there was no one else around up there.

He pressed the speed dial memory number one and a voice answered immediately, "Is this phone safe?"

"You tell me. It's the one you gave me before I came back. So, unless you've-"

The voice on other end of the line interrupted with, "Okay, okay, is it done?"

"Yes, it's done. All clear here now. No sign of any suspicion. Your informant was right. There was a witness to what happened to your man here in the summer of 2016. Don't ask how I discovered that, or even to give you the name, because I'm not going to."

"We don't need or want to know how," the voice told him. "Just that it's done, as instructed."

"As I said, it's done. The witness has been dealt with, been removed, left us you could say," David responded firmly.

He was being deliberately evasive about offering any more detail, hoping that the voice at the other end of the line would think that was due to security. Nevertheless, the voice still wanted clarification and more.

"Dealt with, as in no longer around, disposed of, if I get what you mean, and there's no mess to clear up from the disposal?"

David hesitated momentarily and the voice at the other end of the line simply said, "You still bloody there?"

"Yes, yes, that's right, no longer around, and no mess for you to deal with. I've already done what needed to be done," he eventually responded.

He was becoming agitated. He took a deep breath and tried to calm himself before continuing.

"And I've never picked up any indication, or heard anything here, to suggest that anyone thinks that what happened was anything other than an accident, including the local Greek police. No sign that anyone has any idea there was a witness."

"Good, the Irish woman assassin was dealt with back in 2016, shortly after the event. Now you've taken care of the witness all the loose ends are tied up," the voice told him. There was a moment's silence and then the voice added coldly, "That's the way we like things, all neat and tidy."

"The Irish woman is dead?"

Surprise was obvious in David's voice. He'd tried to convince Alice that MI6 would have taken care of her that way after she was spooked by what Jack Constantino told them a few nights ago about the text he got from the Irish woman. Alice was convinced she must have been the killer she saw in the Lindos top alley that summer in 2016. However, the voice at the other end of the phone was just as equivocal in answering as David had just been about 'dealing with' the witness, Alice.

"Yes, she's been dealt with."

David wanted more. He pushed.

"Dealt with as in dead? When? Where?"

"You don't need to know any more than I've just told you, old boy. You know better than to ask that. I can't, and won't, tell you."

He was left wondering. Had she been killed, or was the voice simply deliberately using the same ambiguous language David just had. He knew MI6 would never admit it if the woman had evaded them, never been found. If, as he'd told Alice, she'd been killed though, then at least she would be safe, at least from her, if not MI6. Perhaps then he would be able to find her later that summer on whatever Greek island she'd run off to, tell her that for sure, and be with her. Although, he knew persuading her of that wouldn't be easy, not least because he could never tell her that he knew the Irish woman had been killed because he'd got that from MI6. He'd face that particular dilemma when he came to it, if he could find her. In reality, he was very unlikely to be able to find out for sure if MI6 had actually killed the Irish woman. They never gave that sort of information out easily, and it was definitely the sort of information that only MI6 people way above his involvement were given access to. They only gave him information on a 'need to know' basis, in order to get him to do whatever they wanted for them, like passing on the contact number to Sophia at the Moscow conference, or finding out something in Lindos for them about what happened in 2016.

Also, when during that first whole summer he was in Lindos in 2019, and MI6 contacted him and instructed him to try and find the witness and deal with them, he'd asked what reason they could possibly have for killing a witness to the murder of one of their own operatives? Even then, all he got in response from his MI6 handler was an emotionless, cold, statement.

"The fewer people who know who works for us, what they do, and why, the better, and safer for our existing operatives. And that includes people like the Greek police and others poking around trying to find out why an undercover IRA assassin would have killed one of our operatives back in that summer of 2016. An IRA assassin who had infiltrated our security services over a number of years. I'm sure you can understand that it's not exactly good publicity, old boy, for anything to come out publicly from whatever source, the Greek police, this witness, or you for that matter, to the effect that the British Security Services had been very successfully infiltrated for almost twenty years by an IRA operative and assassin. That just wouldn't do, would it? Make us look like a bunch of fools. No, the Section Head and the top brass think it's better to have everything related to that mess cleared up, cleaned up, rather than something sneaking out later, or someone opening their mouth publicly later and the whole embarrassing episode coming out. Some of the oiks and cretins in the British media would have a field day over that wouldn't they, not to mention some of our so-called friends at MI5. So, just do it, just do what we require you to do, old chap. then we can all rest easy can't we."

That was the only explanation he got as to why MI6 wanted the witness killed. He knew asking over and over again would have been pointless. Now, as far as they were concerned, by mid-summer of 2020 he'd done what they required.

Once again he was deliberately being economical with the truth though. He'd done that a few times with Alice through the past two summers. However, this time he felt he had good reason. As he stood on that hill overlooking Lindos Main Beach in the bright, warm sunshine he knew exactly what the voice at the other end of the line meant by, "disposed of", that he had killed the witness, Alice. However, there was no way he could bring himself to do that after the two summers, or at least one and a half, they'd spent in each other's company. He'd fallen well and truly in love with her over that time. Yes, he'd stupidly acted like a spoilt brat by running off to spend time in Athens with Sophia because of what he'd heard from Dianne about Alice and Simon Chapel. He regretted that more than he could ever show her or convince her. He desperately wanted to leave with her for another Greek island. She obviously wanted him to from what she'd told him in those last few days they were together. She'd even asked him to. But to do so would only mean MI6 continuing to look for her, as well as him, the two of them if they were together. He'd resigned himself to the fact that this way was best, safest for her, even if it meant he couldn't be with her now or possibly ever.

"Yes, all the loose ends are tied up, and that's the end of it all for me. I'm done with you lot now, for good. I mean it this time," he firmly told the voice at the other end of the line. All he wanted to do now was try to forget about it all, get down from the hill onto the beach and take a refreshing, soothing swim in the clear sea of Lindos Bay. Just get on with his new life in the picturesque beautiful village, for now at least.

"Of course you are, old boy, done, if you say so," the voice told him.

But then with a clearly evident heavy dose of menacing smug mockery it added, "By the way, Alexandra, or should I say Sophia, says, "Hi." I never told you before, had no need to, but we saw that you had a good time with her in Athens last October. Well, we read you did would be more accurate. She reported she certainly enjoyed it, and finding you in Lindos before that for us, of course."

David was stunned. Before he could say anything in response the line went dead.

At least he now knew that some of his suspicions about Sophia were accurate.

PART SIX:

SEPTEMBER 2020

25

A mystery missed call and a surprise call

Friday 4th of September was the final night of that summer of 2020 on which the Arches Plus club down towards Lindos Main Beach was open. In the village in the early evening on his way back to his flat after a day on Pallas Beach David had bumped into his friend of the past two Lindos whole summers, as well as of many Lindos shorter holidays before, the owner, Valasi, who insisted he had to come to his club for its final night of that summer. So, of course, when the music stopped in the bars in the village that evening at one o'clock as usual he went, intending to just have one more drink and not too late a night.

He'd spent plenty of long nights on Friday, and sometimes Saturday, evenings at Arches Plus with Alice throughout the first part of that summer, as well as through the previous summer. On many occasions they'd only left there as the fierce red ball of the sun rose and then headed for a slice of pizza in the village, often from Nikos in the small square with the tree in the centre, and then sat on the low white wall munching it.

This time though, and on any Friday or Saturday night since she left in July, he'd gone to the club alone. Of course, he met plenty of people he knew from the village there, including some of the bar and restaurant owners. Consequently, the intention of only having one drink turned into quite a few more and he never made it to his bed in his flat until just gone five on that Saturday morning.

It was gone noon when he managed to force his eyes open as he woke and the bright rays of the Lindos sun, still hot in early September, sneaked though the slats of the shuttered windows. He reached for the small bottle of water on the bedside table and took a long slurp trying to negate as much as possible the dryness lurking in his mouth. As he returned the water bottle to the bedside table he rubbed his eyes with one hand to focus and picked up his phone on charge alongside it. A few seconds after he switched it on a notification appeared on the screen that he had a missed call. It wasn't a number in his contacts though, so it simply showed as an 'unknown number'.

Replacing the phone on the bedside table he decided the best remedy for his weariness and slight hangover was a shower and then head to Giorgos for one of their very good cooked English breakfasts. It wasn't until he'd managed his first cappuccino from Tsamis in a busy Giorgos and was now waiting for his cooked breakfast to arrive that he remembered the missed call. He decided he'd try and return the call to the 'unknown number', but all he got was an obviously recorded message in Greek from the phone network. As he finished trying make the call Tsamis arrived with his breakfast. So he asked him to listen to it and translate what the message said as he tried again to return the call.

"Unobtainable, the number is unobtainable," the café owner told him. "Probably just someone, some business, cold calling to try and sell you something," he added.

David nodded and thanked him and then tucked into his badly needed breakfast and another cappuccino. But for some reason he couldn't forget about the call. He checked when it was made and was even more curious when he saw it said it was made at six a.m. that morning. He thought to himself who cold calls at six on a Saturday morning, and if it was from the U.K., as it most likely would be if it indeed it was a cold call as David's was a U.K. number, then that would have been at four in the morning, Greece being two hours ahead of U.K. time.

Even odder. He thought about pointing that out to Tsamis, but decided that perhaps the explanation was that a lot of those bloody cold calls are automatically computer generated.

So, he determined that the best use of the rest of his Lindos Saturday would be to forget about the missed call completely, go back to his flat, change into his swim shorts and a t-shirt, and head for a lazy, relaxing Saturday afternoon on Pallas Beach and a couple of cooling swims. He paid for his breakfast and cappuccinos and did just that.

Alice Palmer had been gone and out of his life for over six weeks. However, that didn't stop him wondering where to a lot of the time. He couldn't just forget her; get her out of his head, even though she was no longer in his life. He realised that unless she let him know some way or other he had no idea where she was now, and no way of finding out. When he thought about that he always came to the same conclusion that logically him not knowing was for the best in terms of her safety. As far as he knew MI6 had closed the case of the elusive witness. That was clearly the impression he got from his last phone conversation with his MI6 handler when David heavily implied he'd killed the witness. He'd heard nothing from them on that since, or anything else they might want him to do. Although, he'd made it clear to his handler in that phone conversation he was done with them. Hopefully, therefore, he could console himself with knowing Alice was safe from MI6 at least, even if not knowing where she was.

The biggest decision he thought he had to make now was whether he would return to Lindos the following summer and stay for the whole of it, as he had for the last two. He was unsure. He had some good memories of his two summers there, very good memories, but obviously some not so good, like Alice leaving because she felt she had to and he couldn't convince her otherwise. She'd asked him to go with her, of course. So, in some way perhaps that was also a good memory for him to dwell on.

He knew that in a few weeks, by the end of October at the latest, he would have to go back to London and by then he would have to tell the owners of his Lindos flat if he wanted to rent it the following summer. Some days he thought he would.

He loved it there in Lindos, and to be there for such a long period of time rather than a week or two on holiday. On other days, not very many though, he thought perhaps it was time to move on. He couldn't decide. If he knew where Alice was that would obviously help him, but he didn't.

That dilemma over the flat and the following summer kept popping into his brain over the rest of that day and his afternoon on Pallas Beach. At least it kept any thought about the early morning missed call out of his head. He decided, however, that whether he would come back the next summer or not he would relax and enjoy Lindos as much as he could for his remaining few weeks of this summer, particularly its beaches and clear blue sea.

It was another call late the next afternoon though that disturbed his plan of relaxing for the rest of the Lindos summer. He was on Pallas Beach again enjoying his Sunday afternoon, and between his almost semi-dozing he watched some of the Greek families enjoying theirs with their children. One of his periods of a half dozing nap was interrupted by him faintly being aware of his phone buzzing in the open side pocket of his rucksack. He sat up and reached for it. This time it wasn't an unknown number. It was a number well known to him; one he thought about deleting from his contacts but decided against for some reason. The notification on the screen worried him immediately. It said, 'Sophia'.

For ten seconds or so he toyed with ignoring it, but eventually his curiosity got the better of him.

"Hi," he said, trying not to let his voice reflect the apprehension he felt.

"Hi, David. How are you? I assume you're still in Lindos? I was wondering if you were and how you are. It's beautiful in Lindos at this time of year isn't it, don't you think? A bit cooler, but still great weather and not as humid as it is in August I guess, and not quite so many tourists."

Her voice was almost bubbly as she rattled off a load of those small talk comments in a matter of fact way as though she thought he wasn't aware of her efforts for MI6 in respect of him. He was, however. He knew about that from his handler's comments in their phone conversation the day after Alice left.

And David realised she would certainly know by now he was aware of what she'd been up to when she bumped into him in Antika that night in October 2019, supposedly by coincidence, as well as what she was trying to do for MI6 later in Athens when he stopped over.

But she was carrying on talking as though nothing like that had happened between them. He simply listened in silence, at first not even really noticing that she had said, "It's beautiful in Lindos at this time of year," rather than she expected or supposed it was.

He was trying to process that through his brain, and was beginning to assume that the way she'd said it only implied she was in Lindos too at the moment because English wasn't her first language, even though her English was very good. However, what she said next somewhat bluntly confirmed that the way it came across to him was correct.

"So, let's have dinner again in Lindos."

He was now totally bewildered. She really was talking as though there had been nothing difficult that had happened between them, or therefore was now. His confusion was reflected in his voice, which he also deliberately lowered so that anyone nearby on the sunbeds on the beach couldn't overhear.

"I ... err ... I ... but, you're not in Lindos are you? Aren't you in Athens?"

"No, well yes and no, I suppose. I'm still based in Athens, but I'm in Lindos again, giving myself a special treat of a few days holiday. I had such a good time there before I thought I would come back, and that it would be a perfect place to celebrate the satisfactory conclusion to a small operation I was involved in for London. You know who I mean, don't you, David? They were very generous again in rewarding me for my efforts. I suppose I have you to thank you for that in some part. I do hope they rewarded you well for your efforts too, something extra than usual for you perhaps? Or maybe I can share some, a little, of my reward with you?"

He did, indeed, know who she meant; her friends at the River House. And he had a pretty good idea what the "small operation" she referred to was. He just couldn't believe she was so brazenly telling him that though. Also, he never got any extra reward, plus what the hell did she mean by saying she could maybe share some of her reward with him? She didn't wait for his answer on that, not that he really had one.

"Yes, we can talk about that over dinner tonight, your share of my reward and a few other things I think we can help each other with. Shall we say at eight at that restaurant we went to last year, Gatto Bianco wasn't it? It was very nice, lovely setting and food, and company of course."

She was running away with trying to take control and organise his Lindos Sunday evening, and by the sound of it his life with her comment of, "a few other things I think we can help each other with." He needed time to think about what the hell she could be up to, who might have put her up to it, MI6 perhaps, and how he would deal with it. He decided he would put her off, at least for twenty-four hours and dinner.

"No, not tonight, I have things to do early evening and people to see in the village. What about tomorrow night? How long are you here for?"

"I arrived early this afternoon, only here for three nights, till Wednesday, same hotel as last year, Acquagrand. Ok, tomorrow night at eight at that same restaurant if that's the soonest night you can do."

Once again she confused him with the last part of her reply, "the soonest night." What was so urgent? He couldn't stop himself. The sooner he knew what she wanted, what she meant by, "the few other things I think we can help each other with," the better. He could then at least think things through about how to deal with whatever she wanted, what to do about her.

So, he suggested, "But what about a late drink tonight at ten? Somewhere we can talk without being overheard, somewhere outside? I will have finished seeing the people I have to see by then and then you can tell me then what this is about. We can still have dinner tomorrow night as well at Gatto Bianco."

At least that would give him a night and all the following day to think through whatever she wanted.

"Sure, ok, that sounds like a good idea, but where tonight? Where do you suggest that's somewhere outside?"

"Erm ... what about up at the Atmosphere Bar? It's got an outside terrace, and we should be able to find a table not too close to another, so people shouldn't overhear our conversation. Do you know it?"

"No, but the hotel will get me a taxi, so I'll meet you there at ten."

He was about to say, "Bye," and ring off, but before he did she added, "Oh, and David, I'm looking forward to it, looking forward to seeing you again. We can do good things together, I'm sure. Bye."

With that the line went dead and he was more confused than ever, and once again was also totally unsure if what he'd agreed to was a good thing at all.

He didn't really have, "people to see," earlier in the village as he'd told her. He was unable though to relax at all through the rest of his Pallas Beach afternoon through dwelling on, and thinking about her call, trying to go over and over it in his mind and analyse what she'd said. In the end he gave up and made his way up the hill and through the village to his flat. He showered and changed into a pair of white shorts and a red polo shirt, grabbed a slice of pizza from Nikos, and made his way up to the Atmosphere Bar at the top of one end of the village an hour early, at nine. He guessed she wouldn't be there at that time, but he thought a bottle of Mythos beer or two might help calm him before she arrived. He also thought it would be more likely at that time he could get a table that was not in too close a proximity to any other.

He was right about that. He could have done as soon as he arrived, except for the fact that as he did the jovial convivial owner, Stavros, gave him a big bear hug, told him it was good to see him and led him inside the bar for a beer.

The Atmosphere Bar was a modern looking one inside, with a large television screen on one wall opposite the bar itself. Outside the terrace ran along the whole front of the bar, with another large television screen at one end and a wonderful view of the Acropolis, especially when it was illuminated at night.

Stavros was always a good host with all his customers, many of who, as with some of the other bars, returned year after year, and in some cases a couple of times a season at least. In between talking to David from time to time he wandered outside to talk to some of the customers at the tables on the terrace in front of the bar. It was quite busy, as usual, but as he'd arrived and crossed the terrace David noticed there were a couple of empty small tables to the right that weren't quite as close together as some of the others. While Stavros went on one of his wanderings one more time to talk to some of the customers outside David took his bottle of Mythos beer and glass out to sit at one of the small tables he'd spotted when he arrived. He still had another half-an-hour until Sophia was due to arrive though and in the meantime Stavros brought him a second bottle of beer, generously, "On the house," he told him and joined David at the table for another ten minutes or so chatting.

When Sophia's taxi pulled up outside the bar at spot on ten David was sitting alone at the table as Stavros had gone off to talk to some other customers again. He hadn't seen her for almost a year, but as she got out of the taxi she still looked as good as ever to David.

Her hair was still a perfectly dyed blonde, but she had let it grow and now it was almost down to her shoulders instead of the very short cut she had immediately after her defection in order to change her appearance, and still had when he last saw her almost a year ago. She was wearing tight white shorts with a tan coloured leather belt and a white t-shirt displaying the small Boss logo in the centre, plus tan flat leather expensive looking sandals. Although she'd only arrived in Lindos that day her well-tanned long legs, highlighted by the white shorts, suggested she'd managed a good amount of sun worshipping on the terrace of her Athens apartment throughout that summer.

She spotted him as soon as she turned around after paying the driver, walked over to the table and leaned down to give him a kiss on the cheek as she said, "Hello." Stavros saw her arrive and came over straightaway to ask what she would like to drink. David introduced him as the owner and as he did so Stavros raised his eyebrows and smiled approval in David's direction. She ordered a vodka and tonic and as Stavros left them to get it she commented to David, "Well, it looks like I have the approval of the owner." She'd clearly spotted the reaction of Stavros.

"Really good to see you again, David," she told him as she briefly scanned the terrace assessing if any of the occupied tables were going to be able to hear their conversation. "Good choice of table, but we should wait until he brings my drink before we get on to what we need to discuss."

"Of course," he agreed, although wondering what she meant by, "need."

"Are you still living in the same apartment in Glyfada?"

She smiled across the table at him before telling him, "Yes, the same one, but you don't have to make small talk just to fill the silence until my drink arrives."

"No, no, I wasn't, I just-"

She didn't let him to finish. She realised she had already unsettled him. To some extent she thought through her appearance, but in addition he was obviously a little nervous at meeting her again unexpectedly. That was good, precisely the effect she wanted. She had the upper hand immediately, which was exactly what she needed for what she was about to talk to him about.

Stavros brought her drink and then left them, which was also what she wanted. She took a sip from the straw, deliberately making him wait a little longer to find out what this was about.

"Hmm, that's good, good vodka I think."

She sat back in her chair and stared across at him, her eyes piercing straight into his for a long few seconds. She was about to say that she expected he was wondering what this was all about when instead what he said led the conversation precisely in the direction she wanted.

"Reward, you said on the phone that you got very generously rewarded for your efforts in bringing a small operation to a satisfactory conclusion, and that there were a few other things you think we can help each other with."

"Yes, I did say that didn't I."

She was being deliberately coy as she leaned forward in her chair again to take another sip of her drink.

"As she sat back in her chair again she repeated, "Yes, I did."

"And?" he asked, sounding a little agitated at the game she was so obviously playing.

"And I do, I do think there are quite a few other things we can help each other with."

He wanted to raise his voice to display his growing anger at her and her games, but he knew that wouldn't be wise where they were. He'd had enough of all this sort of crap in the past, game playing with people's lives, and he was determined to put her straight on that.

Sounding as forceful and firm as he could in a low tone of voice, he said, "Look, Sophia, I am fully aware of what small operation you are referring to, but I never got any extra reward for what I did and I didn't expect one, and I certainly don't want, or expect any share of whatever you got. I don't know what game you're playing, but as you said, that operation came to a satisfactory conclusion. I'm done with all that stuff now, done with MI6 and their games, and yours, so I'm bloody certain that there really aren't things we can help each other with as you suggested."

Her steel grey eyes stared straight across into his face again for a few seconds. This time there was a lot more menace in them. She sat forward in her chair once more, slowly took another sip of her drink, and then told him, "Calm down, David. We don't want a scene here now do we."

He picked up his glass and took a drink of his beer, thinking he had put her straight and got how he felt across to her.

But he hadn't, far from it in fact.

Still sitting forward in her chair she slowly rested both elbows of her bare, nicely tanned arms on the table as she placed the palms of her hands on either side of her face and stared even more intensely across into his eyes.

"But it wasn't, David, was it? It wasn't actually a satisfactory conclusion to that operation, not for MI6. Maybe it was for your friend, but not for them. We both know that don't we. Because of what you told them MI6 think that it was, or should I say what you led them to believe. I've seen the report, don't ask how, but I've read the words you used in that call you made reporting to your handler. They still do think that of course, what you led them to believe and that it was a satisfactory conclusion, because I haven't told them what I know yet, what I've seen, proving that the operation wasn't concluded at all, wasn't resolved the way you led them to believe."

Once more she paused deliberately and leaned forward to pick up her drink for another sip while he sat opposite in silence, completely dumbstruck and shocked by what she'd just told him about seeing the report. She hadn't finished though.

She was enjoying this a lot, and enjoying his obvious growing discomfort and torment across the table from her. It had been a while since she'd done this sort of thing, had any opportunity to do it. It was the sort of psychological torture she'd been trained in by the GRU, Russia's Main Intelligence Directorate. She'd almost forgotten how good she was at it, but was pleased she hadn't lost the technique. In fact, in her training she'd been complimented by one of her trainers in the GRU on how good she was at it; a natural, he told her.

Pleased by seeing the look of shock all across his face, and that her technique was clearly working, she went in for the kill verbally. She'd softened him up nicely, but there was a lot more she wanted out of him, a lot more she wanted from him in future. Alice Palmer was just the bait to hook him. What she now knew about her, and how he'd lied to MI6 about her, was exactly the leverage over him she needed for what she wanted him to do.

As she put her drink down on the table she raised her eyes to focus straight into his face once more, deliberately paused yet again for a few seconds enjoying his discomfort at wondering what was coming next, and then told him firmly and forcefully, "So, in fact, the operation hasn't been concluded, hasn't been dealt with at all, has it? Because she hasn't been dealt with has she, David."

He struggled to find an answer, searching his brain for one that would stop her.

"Well ... I ... erm ... I dealt-"

She didn't let him finish.

"She's not dead though is she, David. She's very much alive. I saw her on the metro in Athens last Friday. I even tried to follow her, but I lost her."

He knew she was right. Alice Palmer wasn't dead. He didn't know how she knew, but now he was clutching at straws as, shaking his head, he challenged her.

"No, no, you must have been mistaken. How, how could you be sure it was her? You've never met her, have you?"

As he asked that last question there was an edge of uncertainty in his voice. But he never got his answer straightaway. He was left hanging, waiting for her answer, as at that difficult moment Stavros noticed David's glass was empty and came over to ask if they wanted more drinks. David was at least relieved by the time it gave him to think about what she'd said. He told him, "Yes, thanks Stav, another Mythos for me and another vodka and tonic."

He didn't even bother to ask her if she did want another. She hadn't actually completely finished her first one, but she nodded slightly anyway and smiled at the owner. They sat in awkward silence while they waited for him to return with the drinks. David was furiously trying to process all she'd said so far.

After their drinks arrived she once again slowly took a sip and placed her drink back down on the table, deliberately making him wait for her response to his question. She sat back in her chair, purposefully looking relaxed, confident she was now fully in control of the situation and their conversation, in total contrast to his obvious uncertainty and uncomfortable lack of control opposite.

Eventually, almost nonchalantly, she answered his question. Even then she couldn't resist continuing her game by slightly misleading him with the start of her response, giving him some hope he was right. Then she made him wait once again. She was enjoying it all, and wanted to savour the moment as much as possible.

"Oh, yes, of course, you're right, I have never actually met her, not formally so to speak, I suppose."

She reached for her drink again and as she lowered her head and sucked on the straw she looked out of the top of her eyes across at him. She was content that he still looked uncomfortable, but she thought she detected a very slight smile of satisfaction on his lips, clearly satisfaction that he was certain he'd detected a flaw in her comment about seeing Alice on the Athens metro.

This time she only paused from sucking her drink through her straw to reply. She continued to hold her drink in front of her lowered face and look out of the top of her eyes across at him, wanting to see and completely enjoy his reaction as she told him, "But I did see her in Lindos on that night we met in Antika last year. When we met by coincidence, you remember."

She raised her head and smiled slightly at her coincidence comment before continuing. A stunned and incredulous look was spreading right across his face once more.

"After you left me in Antika I went to the Courtyard Bar because your friend the barman in Antika told me you drank in there sometimes late. Then, after I got there Jack Constantino told me you did with a group of some of the bar and restaurant workers from the village, but particularly with a woman called Alice Palmer. I mentioned her to you when you were in my bed, remember, that night just after we'd-"

"Yes, yes, ok, I remember what we'd just done."

He interrupted her. He didn't want to hear her description of it, didn't want to hear the words come out of her mouth.

She let out a sort of small giggle at his obvious embarrassment and then continued.

"Anyway, you know where we had that conversation, and what we'd just done, David. I was sure you enjoyed it. I know I did."

She looked across at him squirming at that.

"And I told you then that Constantino said you'd become very friendly with her. What I didn't tell you that night in my bed though was that when she came into his bar later, after your little waitress had finished work presumably, he pointed her out to me in a group of workers at the other end of the bar. I got a good look at her that night, and that's how I recognised her on the metro last Friday."

She took another sip of her drink while she left him dangling once again, almost drowning in uncertainty, before taking continuing pleasure and trying to enjoy the moment and his uncomfortable predicament as much as possible by adding with a contemptable grin, "So, yes, you're right of course, David. I've never actually met her, your little waitress."

Then she added in a much firmer tone of voice, "But I bloody well know what she looks like, and I'm certain that was her I saw on the metro."

He was dumbstruck once again. He took a good drink of his beer and puffed his cheeks slightly in exasperation as he placed the glass back on the table.

Her game wasn't done, however. What she asked him next initially appeared to be unconnected to all this, but there was a method, a plan, in everything she was doing and saying.

"You ever killed anyone, David? Not in the way the organisation you've worked for, the organisations we've both worked for, prefer to do it, or at least some in those organisations prefer to do it, by spreading lies and disinformation. But physically, actually physically, have you actually ever physically killed someone yourself, by your own hands, your own actions, and not by having someone else do it for you? You ever actually killed someone for the organisation you worked for?"

He hesitated.

"You see, from what I know of you, I don't think you ever have, or even ever could. That's why, even before I saw her on the metro, I was sure you hadn't dealt with her, killed her, as you led MI6 to believe."

He never said anything in response to that. What could he. He knew she was right. He'd never killed anyone, and he certainly could never kill Alice. He'd actually been on a short MI6 self-defence course when he first started doing things for them, and he definitely knew how to kill someone, quickly and efficiently, but he'd never needed to put that into practice.

She was sitting back in her chair looking relaxed again and pleased with herself, knowing that now was the time to go in with the deal. She had him exactly where she wanted him. Now all she had to do was offer him a way out, of benefit to him, but mostly to her.

There was a small smile, almost of pity, on her lips as she told him, "You know, David, there's no reason for it to be dealt with that way at all though. No need at all for it to be resolved the way MI6 want it to be, the situation over Alice Palmer being the witness they've been looking for, and her being killed. I'm sure you and I can work out some way it can be resolved the way you'd like it to be, and for the benefit of Alice Palmer's health should I say, plus of course, not forgetting for my benefit, which I'm sure you'll understand is my primary concern. Perhaps, even in some way for your benefit to, and by that I don't just mean Alice Palmer staying alive.

"How?" he asked with a frown across his forehead.

He wasn't happy or relaxed at all with the situation he now found himself in, or, especially with the person opposite he was having to listen to obviously enjoying his discomfort. But he decided to play along with her, for now at least, to buy some time. He couldn't think of any other way of dealing with this at the moment.

"Ok, I get what you mean about Alice. You won't inform MI6 she's still alive and that I lied, never killed her, and she stays safe, but what do you want from me for that?"

She leaned forward to be much closer to him across the table and lowered her voice even more, although there was still a clear firm edge to it.

"Ok, David, this is the deal. It's your choice, although I think you'll realise you don't have much choice, if any at all. Hopefully, you'll realise what I'm about to tell you is big for me. I'm trusting you with this, but there's obvious danger in it for me."

Now he was wondering just what the hell she was going to tell him that would make her vulnerable. Their whole conversation so far had been completely the opposite of that. She had the upper hand and he was the one in a vulnerable position.

"After you gave me that MI6 contact number at the Moscow conference and I defected I was never really completely 'turned' by them, MI6. I never actually stopped being in touch with some of my Russian contacts. I've played both of them, MI6 and the Russians, whenever it was to my personal advantage. So, I've continued to do occasional work inside MI6 for, let's call them my Russian friends, passing some information on to them in Athens."

His jaw dropped. She was, indeed, putting herself in a vulnerable position. What she was telling him certainly was dangerous for her, but he still wasn't clear what the deal was she was offering him over Alice, and her safety. He didn't have to wait long to find out. His jaw dropped even further. If this was big for her, it was bloody big, and dangerous, for him.

She leaned as far across the table as she could without actually leaving her seat and whispered in his ear. Stavros looking on at them from the doorway to the bar smiled a little to himself. He thought she was whispering nice things into David's ear and that they were obviously getting on really well. He couldn't have been more wrong.

"You and I, David, work with me for them as well."

"The Russians?"

He struggled to keep his voice down as it was clearly full of incredulity. He was stunned once again.

"Both of them, David, together we could work for both of them, the Russians and MI6, for both our benefit. Ok, perhaps not so much directly with the Russians for you. All you'd have to do is pass me any interesting stuff, information you come into contact with from MI6 that I don't necessarily see, things that they want you to do for them on certain operations, and I'd pass it on to my Russian contacts. And as I said just now, I only do occasional work for the Russians, so it wouldn't be that regular and often. They pay well though, the Russians, and we'd both benefit."

He was shaking his head slightly in disbelief. In his mind though he quickly realised that this may have seemed a dangerous thing for her to do, to tell him, but it also put him in a vulnerable position, and she knew that very well. She was a clever woman, and not stupid at all. He knew all this now, what she'd been up to with MI6. He couldn't just forget about it. If he didn't tell them he would be in as much danger as her, but if he did tell MI6 so would Alice be.

"Look, David, we'd make a good team you and me," she continued.

With another smile, this time a very broad one, she added, "As well, of course, we could also conveniently enjoy each other's company, here as well as in Athens in that big bed of mine, couldn't we? I'm sure you'd enjoy that. You did last time, remember. Basically, I can help you forget all about your little waitress again, just like I did before on that night in my bed. Or should I say, just like you did?"

Then finally, still firmly, but trying to sound a little more pleasant, she whispered the last part of the deal, the most important part for him.

"And, of course, if you're prepared to do all that with the Russians and me while we continue to enjoy each other's company then there would be absolutely no need at all for me to tell MI6 back at the River House that your little waitress friend was actually still alive and you, how can I put it politely, misled them."

There was a clear edge of contempt in her voice as she added, "It would be a win-win for all three of us as that would mean she could go on living her oh so simple life waitressing wherever she is now, rather than being hunted down by MI6 and disposed of is the polite way of putting it, killed. Now, you wouldn't want me to tell them I saw her and she's very much alive would you? That actually wouldn't be very good for you either would it? They'd be very angry with you and who knows what they might do, to you as well as to her."

Her voice lifted a little as she sat back once again in her chair and almost pleasantly told him, "It will be good, David. We can have a really good time here, as well as in Athens, a good life. That's much the best outcome don't you think, rather than all that alternative mess and the consequences for your waitress friend."

He slumped back in his chair. He wasn't about to immediately give her an answer. He didn't have one. There was no way he was going to do what she wanted, but he needed time to think through the consequences of that. He tried to delay things to give himself time to figure something out, although at that present moment he had no idea at all what it could be, what his options were, if any. All he knew now was they were limited, and none of them were good.

"Ok, I suppose it is, but I need some time to think about the consequences of what you want me to do. It's a big thing you're asking me to do. I know it would be the best thing for Alice, obviously, but ..."

His voice tailed off. For some reason, he had no idea why, what flashed through his mind was something the author E.M. Forster wrote many years ago, "If I had to choose between betraying my country and betraying my friends I hope I should have the guts to betray my country."

He realised why he suddenly remembered that. It was virtually the situation he was in now, only in his head he was replacing "my friends" with "the woman I love."

She could see he was struggling, floundering looking for a solution. She didn't ease off pushing him.

"There actually isn't any 'but', David, is there? Depends on how you feel about her, of course, your little waitress friend, whether you care enough about her to do this with me in order to keep her safe. Not that you'll ever see her or even know that's the case though. You'll just have to take my word on that won't you?"

The contemptable firmness was back in her voice again as she almost lounged back in her chair, determined to demonstrate just how relaxed about the whole thing she was, and in total control.

"So, you know there isn't any 'but' really, and obviously so do I. We have a deal then on our new joint venture my new partner."

She was pushing him hard, and she had one more move to make, one more suggestion, one more thing that surprised him.

"Why don't we seal the deal tonight? Start our new joint venture tonight by me coming back to your flat for the night?"

That threw him completely.

"No, no, no, not tonight ..."

She frowned sternly. She didn't look pleased at all.

He saw the look on her face, but before she could say anything he added quickly, "I can't tonight. I honestly can't."

The frown of displeasure on her face was getting tighter so he told her, "I can't. Really I can't. I promised to meet some friends on holiday here. I was supposed to meet them at ten, but I've already put them off once until twelve after I got your call earlier. They said they'll go to Arches club in the centre so twelve would be ok."

He glanced at his watch and pointed out, "It's already gone twelve so I should really get off. Of course it would have been lovely you coming back to my flat, but it's really not possible tonight. Sorry, but we can have that dinner tomorrow night at Gatto Bianco we spoke about on the phone earlier, and we can talk about the rest of this then. At eight, shall I meet you there at eight? You remember where it is?"

He was rattling all that off nervously, rambling, and she clearly noticed, but simply nodded in silence. It was the first time in their whole conversation that she didn't feel in complete control, even though she could clearly see he wasn't.

He, though, was thinking that at least he'd bought himself some time to try and figure out exactly what to do about her proposal, and her.

"I'll go in and pay Stavros," he told her as he got up out of his chair.

"David," she called as he started to move away from the table. He stopped dead, wondering what she was going to want from him now, just when he thought he was getting away.

He turned around and, raising her voice slightly for others nearby to hear, she simply said with a pleasant condescending smile on her lips, "While you're paying ask him to call me a taxi to my hotel, dear."

His relief was visible, and her smile got broader, this time just to herself as he disappeared inside to pay. She consoled herself over not getting to his flat and into his bed with him with the fact that the way he just reacted when she simply called his name showed that she still had him just where she wanted, nervous and under her control.

Inside the bar he paid and asked Stavros to call her a taxi, then said goodnight to him. When he arrived back to the table he leaned down to kiss her on the cheek as she clearly tried to kiss him on the lips. Then he told her, "Goodnight," followed by, "See you at Gatto Bianco at eight tomorrow," then made his way quickly down the slope and back into the centre of the village.

He wasn't meeting friends though. Instead, knowing he wouldn't be able to sleep straightaway after the evening he'd had, he went straight to the Courtyard Bar and ordered a large vodka and coke. He had a lot to think about, but that became even more after he turned on his phone while he was sitting on a stool at the bar with his drink. He'd deliberately turned it off while meeting Sophia.

He had another missed call from what was showing again as an unknown number, so obviously from a number not in his contacts. He had no idea or way of knowing if it was from the same unknown number as the previous missed call he had on Saturday morning. This time though the caller left a voicemail message. He hit the voicemail icon. As he put the phone to his ear the message started and he got his second surprise of the night, although this one was more pleasant in some ways at least, and certainly more welcome.

"Hi, it's Alice-"

He stopped it playing, quickly got off the stool and went out into the courtyard to find a space with no one nearby to listen to the rest of it. He was standing in a corner at one end of the courtyard as he pressed the voicemail play icon again, desperate to hear what she had to say. He hadn't heard from her at all since she left.

"I think I was spotted on Athens metro on Friday, David. I'm sure a woman followed me. I don't know if it was the Irish woman. I never let her get close enough for me to check, not that I'm sure I would have recognised her anyway. It was too dark to really see her face when I saw what I did in ... well, you know when. I'm just certain a woman was following me, but I managed to lose her in the metro station. It's bloody annoying because I was only crossing the city from the ferry port to the airport. Anyway, I thought I should let you know in case anyone comes looking for you in Lindos asking about me. I presumed you're still there. But there's no point trying to call me on this number after you get this message as I'm going to ditch this phone after this call, as I did with the other phone I used trying to call you early Saturday morning to let you know about this. Sorry, I wasn't sure about leaving a voicemail message then just in case of ... well, I don't know what really.

I'm just confused with it all, David, and very tired of all of it, the whole bloody business, the Irish woman stuff, as well as the probation people asking about me at the restaurant back in Sheffield, if that's who it was."

He could actually hear her let out a big sigh at that point in the message before she added, "Anyway, that's it really. I hope you're ok. I just wanted to let you know about this, just in case anyone turns up in Lindos asking about me, if you're still there of course."

She was rambling and repeating herself, obviously worried and scared. There was a bit more as she continued; the best and most pleasant bit for him.

"And I ... err."

There was another couple of seconds silence before she told him, "I ... err ... I ... oh sod it, I love you, David. I miss you. There I've said it now."

There was another audible sigh from her in the message before she said, "Take care. Don't worry, I'm ok. I'll be ok. I'm in your safe place now."

"Phew, quite a Lindos night" he muttered to himself as the voicemail finished. At least he knew what she meant, where she meant, with her last comment. If he didn't before, he really knew he had some serious thinking to do now, and he only had until eight that night to do it and his dinner with Sophia and her deal. He didn't even bother to go back inside the bar to finish his drink or say goodnight to Jack and the bar staff. He headed straight to his flat for what he knew would no doubt be a long sleepless night going over and over in his head what he could do about Sophia and her threats, not just to him but also Alice's safety.

26

Monday 7th September 2020

David was right. He did have a very restless night. When he got into his bed on that Sunday night after meeting Sophia, as well as getting Alice's voicemail message, his brain couldn't shut down, particularly over what Sophia wanted him to do. Also though, much more pleasantly, over what Alice said at the end of her voicemail message, how she really felt about him. In all the time he'd known her over those two summers she'd never been as open as that about her feelings. What she said made him feel good, very good. It was also how he felt, and what he wanted. However, it wouldn't resolve his dilemma at all over what Sophia wanted him to do. That's what his brain wouldn't shut down over most of all as he tussled with trying to get some sleep.

Because of his restless night it was almost noon by the time he managed to get out of his bed. He still hadn't resolved his dilemma over Sophia though, and what she wanted, what he was going to do about it. He decided another refreshing swim on Pallas Beach might help clear his head and his thinking, followed by another few afternoon hours on a sunbed there. He knew what he wanted, to be with Alice. How to get that was the problem.

He dozed off a couple of times between swims, trying to catch up on his sleep before what he knew would be a difficult dinner that night with Sophia. In between his short sunbed naps his mind started to wander across all manner of things, all sorts of options, in trying to determine what he should do to get what he wanted. He came to the conclusion that the main thing was to focus on that, what he actually wanted, no matter what it took to get it; whatever he had to do to get it. For some reason unknown to him that conclusion led him to think about what was known as 'The Sunk Cost Fallacy', an argument he'd read about as being used quite a bit in relation to investments in the finance sector. Basically, it described and defined a situation where a person is reluctant to abandon a strategy or course of action as they have invested so heavily in it, even when it is clear abandonment would be more beneficial.

His present situation was about a choice between trying to revive his relationship with Alice for the longer term or accept it was useless to do so, because of what Sophia wanted him to do and Alice's safety. So, his 'Sunk Cost Fallacy' was that he was certain he couldn't now abandon his course of action of pursuing a relationship with Alice, even if it was clear that abandonment would be beneficial to them both in one way, in terms of their safety. He had, indeed, heavily invested so much, time and emotion in that, pursuing her, over the past two summers. Consequently, now, after what she said in the voicemail, he knew he definitely wanted to abandon his 'lightness of being' life and embrace the 'weight' of a meaningful relationship with her. But first there was the problem of Sophia and what she was wanting, demanding from him. In thinking through the 'Sunk Cost Fallacy' stuff though, he finally understood and realised what he had to do to deal with that problem, deal with Sophia. He spent the rest of his afternoon planning that in his head, as well as checking some timetables on his phone.

He got to Gatto Bianco at ten to eight. It was only around the corner from his flat and he wanted to already be there when Sophia arrived, as well as get a table downstairs in the courtyard of the restaurant that was not too close to any table nearby, again because of the conversation he expected them to have and he didn't want anyone overhearing.

Gatto Bianco had an open courtyard at ground level with eight tables of various sizes, as well as, up a flight of wrought iron stairs, a roof terrace looking out over the square with the ancient remains of an Amphitheatre on one side. There were a further dozen tables on the roof terrace, also of varying sizes. The restaurant was busy, but the owner, another Valasi, who he knew well, greeted him with a hug and showed him to just the sort of table in the courtyard David wanted, asking as he did so if it was for just him. David told him, "No," he was expecting a friend to join him.

A few minutes later Sophia arrived. This time she had abandoned her flat leather sandals for some expensive brand red high heels, which perfectly matched the colour of her knee length similarly expensive looking dress, finished off with a thin silver chain around her waist and a small matching red shoulder strap handbag.

He got up as she saw him across the restaurant courtyard and approached the table. This time, after she said, "Hello," she did manage to manoeuvre to kiss him lightly on the lips. They ordered a bottle of Italian white wine, some still water, and some very good fresh fish from the menu with salad. The general small talk between them about Lindos and the fine weather ended after the waiter took their order and left.

"I presume you've had enough time to think about my suggestion," she immediately started to say in a very serious tone of voice, taking for granted he'd agreed to it, and thinking in reality he had no choice. She reached across the table to take his hand briefly before staring into his eyes and saying, "So, I think we have to talk now about some of the details on how it's all going to work between us two, and the Russian Security Services and MI6."

She'd managed to put him off guard again. He didn't expect her to go straight into it, and he certainly didn't expect her to presume he was simply going to do exactly what she wanted. Reaching to take his hand across the table suggested she clearly did. Before he could say anything though, she went on.

"I have some ideas about that. I could say proposals, but that would imply they depended on your agreement, wouldn't it?"

A small smile of some contempt crept across her lips, signifying that she wouldn't contemplate at all any thought that he wouldn't agree, couldn't afford not to.

"Obviously I should deal with the Russian end of things, deal with the Russian Security Services, and of course we are both in a position to deal with MI6, as I'm sure you are well aware of now with regard to me. Anything you get from them, any information you come across or can find, anything they ask you to do, which you think might be useful for the Russians you'll have to pass through me. Also, of course, there will be certain specific things the Russians will want to know about, want us to find out information on, and that'll be your job, my dear, where you can. Find it and pass it on to me, and I'll let the Russians have it. They'll pay handsomely for some things, some information, and of course, we will have to work out how that is divided between us. Although I suggest, prefer, I should say insist, on seventy percent to thirty, in my favour, naturally."

She smiled across at him once more.

At that point the waiter arrived with their water and bottle of wine. They sat in silence while he opened and poured some of the wine into their glasses.

She appeared to have it all worked out, and was definitely taking for granted that he'd agree, not just to their deal, but also for it to operate precisely the way she wanted. He decided the best thing for now was to play along.

"What about MI6 and anything they want about the Russians though," he asked, implying he was simply agreeing to what she'd outlined. "Would you be able to get any of that?"

She knew she most probably wouldn't be able to, but she told him, "Yes, yes, that's how it will work, almost in reverse. Anything I come across, information on the Russians, that I think will be of use to MI6 I can pass on to you to pass on to them, rather than it coming direct from me to them. Similarly, if you know there is anything specific MI6 wants information on about the Russians you can ask me and I'll try to get it for you to pass on to them."

Implying his agreement to that, he nodded just as their food arrived and said, "This looks delicious."

In between taking mouthfuls from her plate she told him, "I'm glad you see things my way, and we have an agreement, a new partnership, you and me, and as I suggested in our conversation last night there can be other benefits for us both, side benefits enjoying each other's company. As I reminded you as well last night, it was good before in Athens last October wasn't it? We were good together. You know we were. You enjoyed it, David. I know you did."

She put down her knife and fork and reached across to grasp one of his wrists whilst fixing a stare into his face once more with her steel grey eyes.

"Do this, work with me, and your precious Alice will be safe. They need never know she's still alive, MI6, and that you didn't actually do what you led them to believe you had."

Now he was feeling really uncomfortable over all this; sick to his stomach. She really was a nasty person, who was clearly only interested in herself. Every comment she made was loaded with veiled threats in order to get what she wanted. He couldn't stop himself now diverting a little from his planned fake acquiescence to what she wanted.

He took another mouthful from his plate, put down his knife and fork, and after he swallowed he surprised her by saying, "Ok, I can see that would probably be the sensible thing for me to do, and Alice would be safe. But what if I were to tell MI6 what you've just told me about you still working for the Russians. Sophia"

She glared across at him in silence for five seconds or more. Her face was coated in real anger now. She clearly didn't like being challenged.

In a low, but firm voice she almost spat out the words at him across the table as she replied, "And how are you going to prove that, David? How do you propose to go about that?"

In her mounting anger she wasn't about to stop there. She leaned towards him across the table, almost menacingly.

"Who do you think they'll believe? Me, a prized asset for them, or you an unreliable sleeper part-timer, especially when I tell them you've been lying to them about disposing of your precious Alice."

She picked up her glass of wine and sat back in her chair to take a drink, confident that she'd firmly and logically dispelled and quashed any thought in his mind of rebellion against what she wanted.

In fact, through her answer she'd actually simply clarified in his mind what he needed to do, and it was far from what she wanted.

It was clear to him that sleeping with Sophia now to protect Alice would amount to a total clash between his love and infidelity. That was something he might well have done in his past, and indeed, regrettably had done that once in Athens with Sophia whilst he struggled with his feelings over those two things; his love and infidelity. He wasn't willing to do that now though in relation to his love for Alice and hers for him, which she'd finally expressed so clearly emotionally in her voicemail message.

He decided he had only one option.

27

The Acropolis and the beauty of a Lindos Harvest Corn full moon

Towards the end of their meal in Gatto Bianco, convinced she had persuaded him to agree to their deal, she raised her wine glass in his direction across the table and told him, "Let's have a toast. To us, David, and our new partnership."

Again, he went along with it and raised his glass to clink it with hers. He was actually thinking now was the time to get the bill. They'd finished the wine and it was approaching midnight. They'd spent a long time talking, although it had mostly been her doing the talking, or at times, it seemed to him like demanding.

He called over the waiter to ask for the bill. As he went off to get it she reached over to take his hand again, squeezed it slightly, and this time fixing a stare straight into his eyes which was clearly intended to be more inviting, said, "You said you couldn't last night, but now we have actually agreed why don't we seal our new partnership in your flat?"

She paused for a second, raised her eyebrows slightly and her eyes widened as she added, "Seal it in your bed, David."

He was desperately searching his brain quickly for an answer that wouldn't be, "No," not a straight, "No," at least, but wouldn't be a straight agreement, an immediate, "Ok."

He found one, thanks to the time of year and the solar system. He'd actually thought it all through earlier on Pallas Beach. He was pretty certain she would suggest going back to his flat for them to have sex. So he'd spent a fair bit of time on his sunbed that afternoon thinking of a diversion; a way to avoid that in order instead to be able to do what he'd come to the conclusion he now he had to do. The full moon and the Lindos Acropolis came to his rescue and offered him the perfect opportunity to do that.

"Sure, of course we can, but there is a Harvest Corn full moon tonight. I'm guessing that you've never seen a full moon here over the Acropolis have you? It's beautiful, very dramatic, and ..."

Now it was his turn to hesitate for effect and look straight across into her once again widening steel grey eyes as he added, "Very romantic."

Luckily for him she had no idea where he was going with this or that it was a delaying tactic, at least in part, although there was more to it than that.

However, she began to look sceptical, so he quickly told her, "Then we can go to my flat after, of course. It'll put us in an even more romantic mood."

Her sceptical look disappeared to be replaced with a broad positive smile. She started to raise herself out of her seat to lean across the table and kiss him, but thankfully for David the waiter returned with the bill.

While he paid it she went off to the toilet. When she returned five minutes later she had clearly made a point of re-applying her lipstick and brushing her hair. He had to admit she looked even more stunning, but at least it reassured him that she appeared convinced by his full moon and the Acropolis suggestion.

"How do we get the best view of it, the moon and the Acropolis together?" she asked as they left the restaurant. She looked up into the Lindos starlit sky above and pointed, "Obviously we can see the moon up there in the sky from here, or anywhere in Lindos, I guess, but where with the Acropolis as well, with it bigger and over the Acropolis?"

"The best views are from some of the places on the path up to the Acropolis. It's amazing, and somewhat strange. The full moon seems to get even bigger, more beautiful and corn coloured, the further you go up towards the Acropolis," he replied.

He was about to suggest they did that, but he didn't have to, she did, and then tucked her arm into his.

"Ok, well let's go up to some of those places towards the Acropolis for an even better view, David. Perhaps, then it won't just be the full moon that seems to get even bigger, but our romantic moment."

He gave her arm a slight squeeze of approval with his as they made their way across the square from Gatto Bianco towards the alleyway on the far side that came out opposite Giorgos Bar. As they reached there the bar was still busy, but luckily as he glimpsed across there was no one outside he recognised, or would recognise him. It was obviously tourists. He quickened his step anyway and hurried them past, her arm still tucked into his. He thought she might ask why he'd speeded up, but she didn't. Clearly she thought he just wanted to get her up towards the Acropolis as soon as possible so they could see the moon over the Acropolis, kiss passionately and then get to his bed. They turned right opposite Giorgos, then down another alleyway to the left, up a few steps, and past the small white Greek Orthodox chapel. Eventually, after walking down three more small steps and turning right they arrived at the fork in the alleyways by the Broccolino Restaurant, one leading down to Pallas Beach and the other fork leading up to the Acropolis. As they'd made their way to that point he had been wondering if Broccolinos would still be open, with customers still sat outside eating. But it was now gone half-past midnight and he was relieved when it came into view that the restaurant had closed for the night. There wasn't even any sign of any staff clearing and cleaning up.

He pointed to the slight slope to the right with its low well-spaced steps, only a few of which were in view in the darkness as the slope went off to the right about thirty metres further up. But she stopped and asked, "Are there many steps. I do have these high heels on, David. They are not very practical really for climbing a lot of steps."

At that moment he thought his plan might fail if she wouldn't go any further up the steps. So, he turned to face her, put his arms around her waist and kissed her quite passionately, Her slight smile returned as after that he told her, "No, it's ok, there's a really great place to see the moon over the Acropolis quite close up just around that bend to the right up there." He pointed, telling her, "It's just a few of these low steps, and they are very far apart."

She placed her right hand behind his neck and pulled him into her to kiss him, just as passionately. As their lips parted he added a reassuring comment to convince her to just go a little further up the path.

"Then we can go back to my bed together."

She smiled again and took his hand as they walked towards the bend, partly to steady her in her heels on the path and the steps, but also because she wanted to anyway. As they reached the bend a clear view of the large Harvest Corn moon looming over the Acropolis confronted them. It wasn't actually the best view, or even probably the most dramatic, but it was as far as he wanted them to go up the slope, and, given her comment a minute or so earlier about her high heels, he thought it was as far up as she was likely to go.

They took a long, lingering look up at the full striking bright moon shining down on them as they both stood in silence with his arm around her shoulders. She looked away from the moon and up at him for a moment, placed her hand on the back of his neck again and kissed him, then said, "Thank you for bringing me here."

That was a very difficult moment for him. It made what he was about to do even harder. He tried to simply focus on all the nasty and vicious things he knew she'd probably done in the past, as well as the threat she posed now to Alice.

He had no choice. He knew what he had to do, even though he'd never actually done it before, only practiced it in a course in his MI6 training. He had to get it right, perfectly so, as he knew he'd only get one chance. In her Russian Security Service training she would no doubt have been trained in self-defence, and how to take out an attacker.

During the next half a minute or so he scanned quickly behind them and further up to make sure there was no one in view nearby, no possible witness, ensuring as he did so that she never noticed. Then he asked, "Have you ever heard the Greek myth of the Labyrinth, Sophia?"

She shook her head slightly, replying, "No, is it related to this Acropolis?"

"No, it's a Greek myth about danger and possible death at the centre of a maze at the hands of a half-man, half beast monster, a Minotaur, lurking there at the centre of the puzzle."

"And?" she asked as he stopped for a moment, turned and placed his hands tenderly on either side of her cheeks shimmering in the moonlight.

As he looked straight into her eyes she assumed he was going to kiss her again. That is certainly what she wanted, what she hoped for. He wasn't.

With anger in his voice he told her, "Yes, a Labyrinth, that's the puzzle, the maze you've been constructing, a sort of game involving the lives of real people, not a Greek myth. A game you've been playing with my life and Alice Palmer's, but not anymore."

A confused look just slightly began to spread across her face, mixed with concern as she realised he wasn't going to kiss her at all.

He never gave her any chance whatsoever to respond to his comments or his actions.

As he finished what he said he immediately tightened his grip on her cheeks a little and then applied a firm, rapid, severe sharp twist of her head and neck. There was an instant accompanying sound of a snapping crack. He knew it wasn't about being a strong person physically, but was all about the correct angle and the sudden sharp twist of the head and neck. It worked perfectly, precisely in the way he'd practiced it a few times before on that MI6 training course. It was instantaneous. She never even had a chance to scream. There was just an audible crack and she was dead. He removed his hands from either side of her face and allowed her limp body to slump to the path. There were no marks, not even from his grip on either of her cheeks.

He quickly scanned around to check again if there was anyone now nearby at all. There wasn't. He reached down and removed her handbag from her limp shoulder, and then checked inside that her phone and Acquagrand Hotel room card was in it. However, her passport wasn't. He assumed it must be in her hotel room, probably in the safe in the room. He knew it would be much too dangerous to go there. He wanted her passport in order to delay the police in trying to identify her. That would give him time to get away off the island first thing in the morning, as he'd planned. He decided he had to forget about her passport, but at least taking her phone would prevent MI6 trying to contact her, as well as avoid any chance the Greek police would find it and be able to read messages and check calls on it as well as her contacts. His number would obviously be in those. Also, her calls to him and any messages from the past between them would be in her phone. Her handbag was only small and not bulky, so he was able to stuff it partially into the waistband at the back of his shorts under his polo shirt as he made his way down the back alleys to his flat, deliberately avoiding passing any of the bars he knew would still be open and busy.

In a matter of minutes he was at the entrance doors to the courtyard that led to his flat. As he entered he knew his neighbours wouldn't be around to notice him come in as they would still be working in the Antika Bar.

He'd meticulously planned his next moves in his head whilst enjoying the last rays of the Lindos afternoon sun on Pallas Beach, including checking the timetable for the first bus from Lindos to Rhodes the next day, as well as for any early morning ferries from Rhodes Port. He wanted to avoid taking a taxi, just in case the Police started looking for him for any reason and checked with the taxi drivers. He knew the owner, Valasi, would remember him having dinner with Sophia in Gatto Bianco that evening if they managed to identify her at some point. He couldn't do anything about that now, however, and in any case he told himself, it would probably take the police sometime to discover that and by then he'd be long gone from Lindos. The bus would take longer to get to Rhodes Town, but he would be much more anonymous. It was much more unlikely anyone would remember him, such as the bus driver. Before meeting Sophia he'd packed some clothes into a medium size holdall bag, as well as his passport, some cash and credit cards. He removed his MI6 'Burner' phone taped to the bottom of one of the bedside draws in his flat and placed it in a side pocket of his holdall, along with Sophia's small handbag containing her phone and hotel room key card.

Once he'd focused his thoughts that afternoon on Pallas Beach, and realised exactly what he had to do about Sophia, he'd planned everything, including his escape, his disappearance. So, everything was prepared for him to leave first thing in the morning.

By the time he'd got back to his flat it was just gone one o'clock. He knew it would be difficult to get some sleep, just as it had been on the previous night. His brain was still experiencing the adrenalin rush from what he'd done, and now there was less than five hours until he had to go through the village and up the hill to Krana to take the early bus to Rhodes Town.

He took a shower and tried to at least get some sleep.

28

Tuesday 8th September 2020: the safe place

He left his flat, he thought quietly, at just before six the next morning to go up to the bus stop at Krana for the six-thirty bus to Rhodes Town. However, after he closed his flat door one of his two neighbours, Ledi, who he knew well from him working behind the bar in Antika, appeared bleary eyed in a vest and boxer shorts in the doorway of his flat. David apologised for if he'd disturbed him, telling him he had to go away for a few days and had an early start. Ledi, was still half-asleep, but replied that it wasn't a problem as he had to get up early as well anyway because he had to be at the restaurant at St. Paul's Bay, where he also worked, for a delivery at seven.

The bright red sun never came up at that time of year in Lindos until around quarter to seven or just after. Consequently, except for a few small lights, and ironically he thought, the lingering effect of the large full Corn Harvest moon above, the village was mostly still shrouded in darkness as David made his way through the narrow alleys towards the Main Square and up the hill to the Krana bus stop.

His bus wasn't due until six-thirty for the one hour forty minute journey to the centre of Rhodes Town. There were three other men waiting at the stop when he got there, all of whom looked like Greeks. He assumed they were either waiting for the bus to go home to one of the nearby villages after work in the Lindos bars and clubs, or waiting for the early bus to go to work in one of the villages or Rhodes Town. He wanted to avoid as much as possible anyone remembering at all the English looking man getting the early bus to Rhodes with a bag, or at least a man who didn't look Greek. So, he made his way to one of the darker areas, slightly away from the bus stop and the pale lights of the closed ticket kiosk. That wasn't staffed at that time of the morning so he'd have to pay the driver for his ticket. He made sure he had exactly the correct amount, as again, he didn't want to linger waiting for change in case the driver remembered him.

There were only six others on the bus when it arrived from its departure point from further south of the island. He made his way towards the back and a seat a few away from any of the other passengers, placing his holdall on the empty seat next to him. There were quite a few stops on the way, but less than a dozen further passengers got on, while a couple of the existing ones got off

The bus pulled into the road of what is loosely designated as the Rhodes Town bus station at just after ten past eight. He'd been a little concerned that if there was any delay on the journey it wouldn't leave him much time to make his way from there to the ferry port, a fifteen minute walk away. He'd decided it would be best to take a ferry, rather than a flight. With a flight from Rhodes Airport his name would be recorded on the airline passenger manifest, even if it was an internal one in Greece. He knew that with a ferry though he could just buy a ticket from the booth at the Rhodes ferry port. When he'd checked early ferry times and destination options from Rhodes on his phone on Pallas Beach the previous afternoon, as well as for flights from any destination he chose to where he eventually wanted to end up, the best and earliest ferry was to Heraklion on Crete. He could then get a flight from there to where he was aiming for. He reckoned that although that would also be a flight from a Greek airport, and his name would be on the flight passenger manifest, as it wasn't from Rhodes Airport the police in Lindos wouldn't necessarily check that, plus even if they eventually did check other Greek airports and flight manifests it would take them some time, giving him more time to get away.

After his fifteen minute walk to the port he bought a ticket to Heraklion for the nine o'clock ferry, paying cash, as he didn't want any of his credit cards and transactions being traced. Once the ferry had cleared the port he took Sophia's small handbag containing her phone and hotel room key card, as well as his

MI6 'Burner' phone, out of one of the side pockets of his holdall and discreetly dropped them over the side into the sea. Then he found and settled down on a comfortable seat on the inside deck to try and catch up on some of his sleep during the nine and a quarter hour journey.

He managed to catch up on his sleep a little on his ferry journey, but it was only spasmodic bouts of short naps. His brain wouldn't shut down completely, preventing him getting any deep sleep.

The ferry pulled into Heraklion at quarter past six on that Tuesday evening. His flight to Milan wasn't until ten thirty-five the next morning, so he'd booked an overnight stay in a hotel quite near the airport. He jumped in a taxi at the ferry port for the ten minute trip to the hotel, checked in and then crashed out on the bed in his room shattered, from his journey as well as the trauma of what he'd done to Sophia. He slept for three hours and then ordered some food from Room Service.

His flight to Milan was on time the next morning and actually landed twenty minutes early, at twelve-fifteen, which was just as well as he'd only initially had two hours till his final flight to Reggio Calabria, but had to change Milan airports. His flight from Heraklion landed at Malpensa, but his flight to Reggio was from Linate. When he'd checked the estimated time for the journey between the two airports online it said forty-five minutes by taxi, but that clearly hadn't allowed for the driving of Italian taxi drivers, especially after he explained to his on his journey between the two airports that he had a tight schedule. He obviously thought he was a Formula One Grand Prix driver, but from David's previous experiences of them all Italian taxi drivers did. The journey took just under thirty minutes, and he had plenty of time for his two-thirty flight, which was also on time. This one was an hour and forty minutes, landing at Reggio Calabria at almost four-fifteen on the Wednesday afternoon.

As he sat in his taxi during the twenty-minute journey from Reggio Airport to the Centrale train station he was thinking that Sophia's body would probably have been discovered early on the morning of the previous day, Tuesday, and the police would no doubt already be investigating her death. In his mind he went through everything he could think of from the night he'd killed her, as well as his leaving Lindos early the next morning and every element of his journey so far. Because of what he'd done in taking Sophia's handbag, he was sure it would take the police some time to actually even find out where she was staying and who she was, at least a couple of days, which would have bought him some time to cover his tracks and get away. The only people he could think of who had even seen him with her in Lindos was Stavros, the owner of the Atmosphere Bar, when they had their drink there on Sunday evening, and Valasi, the owner of the Gatto Bianco restaurant, where they had their meal on Monday evening, before he killed her. He was certain it would also take the police some time to discover those instances, however, as it would take them a while to check with all the bar and restaurant owners in the village. He knew that his neighbour, Ledi, had seen him leaving early on Tuesday morning, but he'd only told him he had to go away for a few days, but obviously not where.

Everything he'd planned on his escape had so far worked perfectly. He could begin to relax. There was just one more part of it, one that was in no way stressful. It was what he'd wanted for two summers.

The taxi pulled up outside Reggio Centrale Station and he paid the driver, then went inside and bought a ticket for his short train journey. The train he wanted was in twenty minutes, just time for him to relax a little more and enjoy a real Italian cappuccino.

He always loved the stunning views out over the Straits of Messina on that twenty-five minute train journey he'd done many times before. This time though it was the best one, and not only because of the coastal views of the shimmering sea and across to Sicily.

He left the train at his final destination, Scilla, and walked quickly down the two flights of steps and across the road into the Hotel U'Bais. It was just approaching six o'clock on that Wednesday evening as he opened the door and made his way up the three steps into the reception lobby. Alfredo appeared from the small office room behind the reception desk and greeted him with a smile, and "Buongiorno, welcome again, Senor David. Your friend is in your usual room."

"Grazie," David told him, only very briefly stopping to add, "Could you please call to reserve a table for two for eight-thirty tonight at Il Pirata?"

"Of course, no problem," Alfredo replied as David headed towards the stairs to climb up to the third floor. He was in too much of a hurry to wait for the lift.

Il Pirata was a restaurant owned by the same owner of the hotel. It was in the older part of Scilla, Chianalea, with its narrow lane and restaurants and accommodation looking out over the port and the sea. The restaurant was in a beautiful romantic setting on a platform out over the sea.

David reached the door of his usual room, 305, stopped for a very brief couple of seconds and took a deep breath before tapping gently on the door. A woman opened it with the broadest smile he'd ever seen across her lips. She almost leapt into his arms before kissing him long and passionately.

As their lips eventually parted she told him, "I hoped you'd come. I knew you would. I knew you'd understand my message. That I was here, for a better life, us together in your 'safe place'."

She took hold of a handful of his polo shirt and pulled him into the room before kissing him again, just as passionately. This time as they finished kissing he stared straight into her teary, happy eyes and told her, "A better life for us to enjoy together now. Life's not a rehearsal, Alice. We only get one, and now we've a chance to enjoy it together. You're safe now. I've seen to that," he promised her.

Now the 'weight' of responsibility and fidelity could really begin in their life. They were both certain this time they wanted that, and were finally done with the 'unbearable lightness' in their lives.